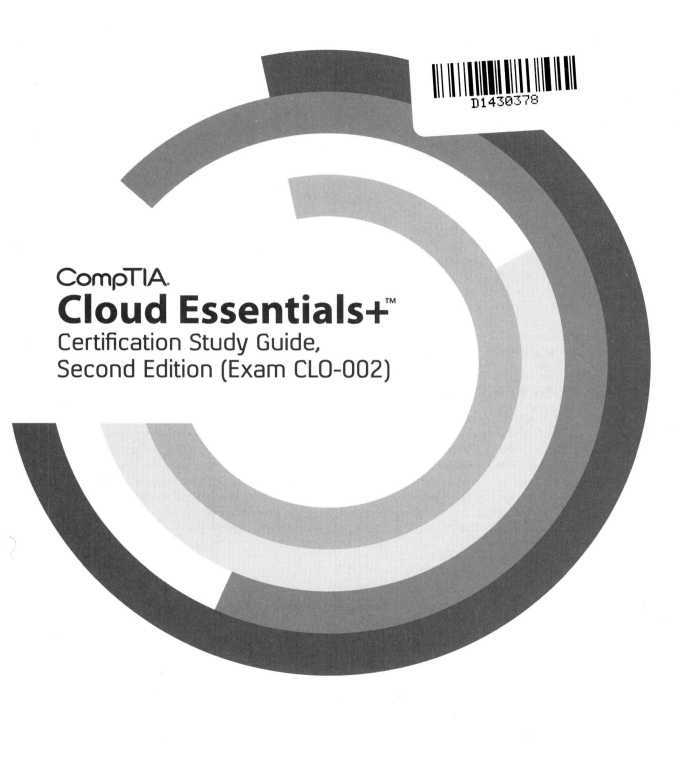

CompTIA.
Cloud Essentials+™
Certification Study Guide,
Second Edition (Exam CLO-002)

ABOUT THE AUTHOR

Daniel Lachance, CompTIA Cloud Essentials+, CompTIA Cloud+, CompTIA Server+, CompTIA A+, CompTIA Network+, CompTIA Security+, MCT, MCSA, MCITP, MCTS, is the owner of Lachance IT Consulting, Inc., based in Halifax, Nova Scotia. Dan has delivered technical IT training for a wide variety of products for more than 20 years. He has recorded IT support videos related to security and various cloud-computing platforms. Dan has developed custom applications and planned, implemented, troubleshot, and documented various network configurations and conducted network security audits. Dan has worked as a technical editor on a number of certification titles and has authored titles including *CompTIA Server+ Certification All-in-One Exam Guide (Exam SK0-004)* and *CompTIA Security+ Certification Practice Exams, Third Edition (Exam SY0-501)*.

Dan is an avid reader of nonfiction, loves family gatherings, and enjoys tinkering around with guitars.

About the Technical Editor

Eric Vanderburg is Vice President of Cybersecurity at TCDI and is a well-known blogger, speaker, and thought leader. He is best known for his insights on cybersecurity, privacy, cloud, and storage. Eric is also a licensed private investigator with an MBA and several undergraduate degrees. He is a continual learner and has earned over 40 technology certifications from Microsoft, Cisco, CompTIA, (ISC)[2], Rapid7, EMC, CWNP, and Hitachi Data Systems. Eric is passionate about sharing cybersecurity and technology news, insights, and best practices. He regularly presents on security topics and publishes insightful articles. You can find him throughout the day posting valuable and informative content on his social media channels:

Twitter: @evanderburg
LinkedIn: https://www.linkedin.com/in/evanderburg
Facebook: https://www.facebook.com/VanderburgE

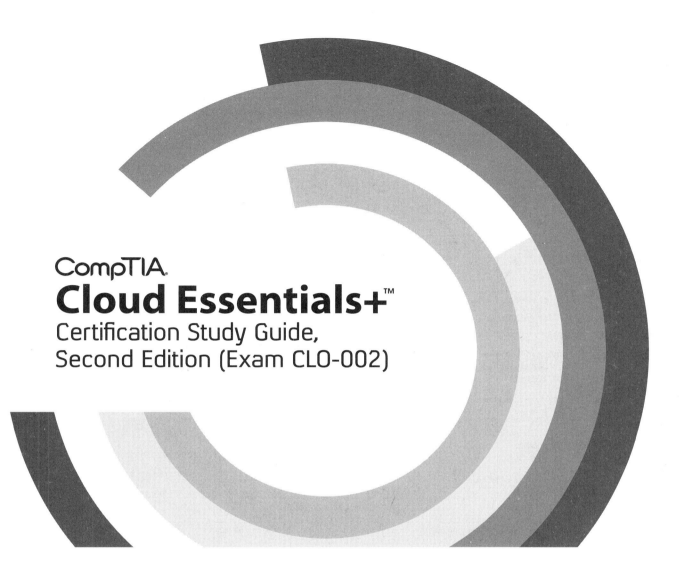

CompTIA.
Cloud Essentials+™
Certification Study Guide,
Second Edition (Exam CLO-002)

Daniel Lachance

New York   Chicago   San Francisco
Athens   London   Madrid   Mexico City
Milan   New Delhi   Singapore   Sydney   Toronto

1 2 3 4 5 6 7 8 9 LCR 24 23 22 21 20

Library of Congress Control Number: 2019954758

ISBN   978-1-260-46178-7
MHID   1-260-46178-5

Sponsoring Editors	**Technical Editor**	**Production Supervisor**
Amy Stonebraker Gray and Wendy Rinaldi	*Eric Vanderburg*	*James Kussow*
Editorial Supervisor	**Copy Editor**	**Composition**
Janet Walden	*William McManus*	*Cenveo Publisher Services*
Project Manager	**Proofreader**	**Illustration**
Sarika Gupta, Cenveo® Publisher Services	*Lisa McCoy*	*Cenveo Publisher Services*
Acquisitions Coordinator	**Indexer**	**Art Director, Cover**
Emily Walters	*Karin Arrigoni*	*Jeff Weeks*

This book is dedicated to my fiancé Tammy, for all her love and patience. Long live our scholarly discussions on taxation, IT security, and politics!

CONTENTS AT A GLANCE

CONTENTS

ix

The objective of this study guide is to prepare you for the CompTIA Cloud Essentials+ exam by familiarizing you with the alignment of cloud IT solutions to business needs, which serves as the basis of the exam. Because the primary focus of the book is to help you pass the exam, it doesn't always cover every aspect of the related technology. Some aspects of the technology are only covered to the extent necessary to help you understand what you need to know to pass the exam, but I hope this book will serve you as a valuable professional resource after your exam.

In This Book

This book is organized in such a way as to serve as an in-depth review for the CompTIA Cloud Essentials+ exam for new and experienced cloud computing professionals. Even small business owners that plan on using consultants to manage their cloud usage will benefit from this book. Each chapter covers a major aspect of the exam, with an emphasis on the "why" as well as the "how to" of working with and supporting cloud computing solutions.

Each chapter includes a set of components that call your attention to important items, reinforce important points, and provide helpful exam-taking hints:

- Every chapter begins with **Certification Objectives**—what you need to know in order to pass the section on the exam dealing with the chapter topic. The Certification Objective headings identify the objectives within the chapter, so you'll always know an objective when you see it!

- **Exam Watch** notes call attention to information about, and potential pitfalls in, the exam. These helpful hints are written by the author, who has taken the exam and received certification—who better to tell you what to worry about?

- **Step-by-Step Exercises** are interspersed throughout the chapters. These are typically designed as hands-on exercises that allow you to get a feel for the real-world experience you need in order to pass the exam. They help you master skills that are likely to be an area of focus on the exam. Don't just read through the exercises; they are hands-on practice that you should be comfortable completing. Learning by doing is an effective way to increase your competency with a product.

- **On the Job** notes describe the issues that come up most often in real-world settings. They provide a valuable perspective on certification- and product-related topics. They point out common mistakes and address questions that have arisen from on-the-job discussions and experience.

- **Inside the Exam** sidebars highlight some of the most common and confusing problems that students encounter when taking a live exam. Designed to anticipate what the exam will emphasize, getting inside the exam will help ensure you know what you need to know to pass the exam. You can get a leg up on how to respond to those difficult-to-understand questions by focusing extra attention on these sidebars.

- The **Certification Summary** is a succinct review of the chapter and a restatement of salient points regarding the exam.

- The **Two-Minute Drill** at the end of every chapter is a checklist of the main points of the chapter. It can be used for last-minute review.

Q&A

- The **Self Test** offers questions similar to those found on the exam. The answers to these questions, as well as explanations of the answers, can be found at the end of each chapter. By taking the Self Test after completing each chapter, you'll reinforce what you've learned from that chapter while becoming familiar with the structure of the exam questions.

Online Content

For more information on the practice exams and other online content included with the book, please see the About the Online Content appendix at the back of the book.

Exam Readiness Checklist

At the end of the Introduction you will find an Exam Readiness Checklist. This table lists the exact CompTIA domains and objectives for the CLO-002 exam, and each objective has a cross-reference to the chapter or chapters in which it is covered in this book.

Some Pointers

Once you've finished reading this book, set aside some time to do a thorough review. You might want to return to the book several times and make use of all the methods it offers for reviewing the material:

1. *Reread all the Two-Minute Drills*, or have someone quiz you. You also can use the drills as a way to do a quick cram before the exam. You may want to make flashcards out of 3 × 5 index cards with the Two-Minute Drill material.

2. *Reread all the Exam Watch notes and Inside the Exam elements.* Remember that these notes are written by the author who has taken the exam and passed. They know what you should expect—and what you should be on the lookout for.

3. *Retake the Self Tests.* Taking the tests right after you've read the chapter is a good idea, because the questions help reinforce what you've just learned. However, it's an even better idea to go back later and answer all the questions in the book in a single sitting. Pretend that you're taking the live exam. When you go through the questions the first time, you should mark your answers on a separate piece of paper. That way, you can run through the questions as many times as you need to until you feel comfortable with the material.

4. *Complete the Exercises.* Did you do the exercises when you read through each chapter? If not, do them! These exercises are designed to cover exam topics, and there's no better way to get to know this material than by practicing. Be sure you understand why you are performing each step in each exercise. If there is something that you do not understand clearly, reread that section in the chapter.

ACKNOWLEDGMENTS

Amy Stonebraker, acquisitions editor, along with Wendy Rinaldi, editorial director, and Emily Walters, editorial coordinator, were the driving forces that brought this product together. Thank you for making this project a joy to work on!

The intelligent and always insightful input from Eric Vanderburg, technical editor on this project, inspired me to make this the best possible study guide for the CompTIA Cloud Essentials+ CLO-002 certification exam. His watchful eye ensured the accuracy of the content.

The copyediting provided by Bill McManus kept the logic and flow in sync with the purpose of the book—thank you for truly making a difference!

This section discusses the nature and specific details of what you can expect to encounter when preparing for and taking the actual CompTIA Cloud Essentials+ CLO-002 certification exam. It gives you a few pointers for preparing for the exam, including how to study and register, what exam format to expect, and what to do on exam day. This section also contains a description of this book, what it is, and how to use it to make sure that you are ready for the CLO-002 exam on the day that you take it.

CompTIA Cloud Essentials+ Relevance

So why should you spend your valuable time preparing to take the CLO-002 exam? Because most organizations are either considering the use of cloud computing components, migrating existing IT systems to the cloud, or managing their existing cloud computing environment. Even small business owners who may not be tech-savvy will benefit from the Cloud Essentials+ certification.

Acquiring the CompTIA Cloud Essentials+ certification validates your knowledge of how cloud computing can serve business needs cost-effectively while adhering to laws and regulations. This will serve you well whether you already work in IT and are seeking a promotion or if you are looking for work as a cloud computing consultant.

Test Structure

CompTIA Cloud Essentials+ CLO-002 is a multiple-choice exam consisting of a maximum of 75 questions selected from the four exam domains listed in the following table. You will have 60 minutes to complete the exam. There is no published passing score.

Domain	Exam Percentage
1.0 Cloud Concepts	24%
2.0 Business Principles of Cloud Environments	28%
3.0 Management and Technical Operations	26%
4.0 Governance, Risk, Compliance, and Security for the Cloud	22%

Remember that the exam will focus on the business impact of implemented cloud solutions. You can expect many questions that use wording such as:

- "What is the most likely…"
- "What is the first step…"
- "What is the last step…"
- "Which solution best addresses the requirements…"

Exam Preparation

Aside from going through this entire book twice in an environment where you can focus, make sure you go through all of the test questions at the end of each chapter, as well as the practice exams. Take the time to truly understand why the correct answers are correct and why the incorrect answers are incorrect. A fun way to prepare for the exam is to imagine that your own company is planning to adopt cloud computing and the success of the entire project is up to you.

Nothing beats actually performing a task repetitively to truly embed the associated concepts in your brain. Bear in mind, however, that this exam is focused on the marriage of cloud computing solutions and their business impact as opposed to being strictly technical, so while it serves as an in-depth review for cloud professionals, it's also geared toward non-IT folks and businesspeople. You'll still need to know some technical details, but most exam questions will have a business twist to them.

Registering for the Exam

Registering for the CompTIA Cloud Essentials+ CLO-002 exam is an easy process. Essentially, you book the exam online and then show up at the Pearson VUE testing center you have chosen at the specified date and time. You can register for the exam online at https://www.vue.com/comptia or https://home.pearsonvue.com/test-taker.aspx; both URLs take you to the same site where you will need to create a free Pearson VUE web account or sign in if you already have an account.

If you are creating a new account, make sure to use the exact spelling of your name as it appears on the two forms of identification (such as driver's license and passport) that you must present at the testing center. Be sure to use the e-mail address that you would like exam reminders sent to. You will then be prompted to "Find an Exam." The CompTIA Cloud Essentials+ exam code is CLO-002. Select a date and time at a testing center near you. The exam cost is $119 USD, and you can pay using a credit card or, if you have one, an exam voucher number.

Taking the Exam

The best method of preparing for the exam is to create a study schedule and stick to it. Although teachers have probably told you time and time again not to cram for tests, some information just doesn't quite stick in your memory. It's this type of information you want to look at right before you take the exam so it remains fresh in your mind. The following are some things to remember when preparing for and taking the exam:

- Get a good night's sleep. Don't stay up all night cramming. If you don't know the material by the time you go to sleep, your head won't be clear enough to remember it in the morning.

- The Pearson VUE testing center requires you to present two forms of identification, one of which must have your picture on it (for example, your driver's license or your passport). Social Security cards and credit cards are also acceptable forms of identification.

- Arrive at the test center at least 15 minutes early.

- Don't spend too much time on one question. If you think you're spending too much time on it, just mark it and return to it later if you have time.

- If you don't know the answer to a question, think about it logically. Look at the answers and eliminate the ones that you know can't possibly be the answer. This may leave you with only two possible answers. Give it your best guess if you have to, but you can resolve most of the answers to the questions by process of elimination. Remember, unanswered questions count as incorrect whether you know the answer to them or not.

- No books, calculators, laptop computers, or any other reference materials are allowed inside the testing center. The tests are computer based and do not require pens, pencils, or paper, although the test center will provide scratch paper or a laminate page and marker to aid you while taking the exam.

- You will receive your exam score (pass or fail) immediately after you complete the test.

EXAM READINESS CHECKLIST

Official Domain and Objective (Exam CLO-002)	Ch #	Study Guide Coverage	✓
1.0 Cloud Concepts			
1.1 Explain cloud principles.	1	The Principles of Cloud Computing	☐
1.2 Identify cloud networking concepts.	6	Cloud Network Infrastructure	☐
	7	Cloud Compute Infrastructure	
1.3 Identify cloud storage technologies.	5	Cloud Storage Infrastructure	☐
1.4 Summarize important aspects of cloud design.	3	Cloud Planning	☐
	10	Security and the Cloud	
2.0 Business Principles of Cloud Environments			
2.1 Given a scenario, use appropriate cloud assessments.	3	Cloud Planning	☐
2.2 Summarize the financial aspects of engaging a cloud provider.	2	The Business Side of Cloud Computing	☐
2.3 Identify the important business aspects of vendor relations in cloud adoptions.	2	The Business Side of Cloud Computing	☐
2.4 Identify the benefits or solutions of utilizing cloud services.	1	The Principles of Cloud Computing	☐
	2	The Business Side of Cloud Computing	
	8	Applications and Big Data in the Cloud	
2.5 Compare and contrast cloud migration approaches.	3	Cloud Planning	☐
3.0 Management and Technical Operations			
3.1 Explain aspects of operating within the cloud.	2	The Business Side of Cloud Computing	☐
	3	Cloud Planning	
	10	Security and the Cloud	
3.2 Explain DevOps in cloud environments.	9	Cloud DevOps	☐
3.3 Given a scenario, review and report on the financial expenditures related to cloud resources.	2	The Business Side of Cloud Computing	☐

Official Domain and Objective (Exam CLO-002)	Ch #	Study Guide Coverage	✓
4.0 Governance, Risk, Compliance, and Security for the Cloud			
4.1 Recognize risk management concepts related to cloud services.	11	Managing Cloud Risk	☐
4.2 Explain policies or procedures.	11	Managing Cloud Risk	☐
4.3 Identify the importance and impacts of compliance in the cloud.	4	Compliance and the Cloud	☐
4.4 Explain security concerns, measures, or concepts of cloud operations.	10	Security and the Cloud	☐

Part I

Cloud Computing Introduction

Chapter 1

The Principles of Cloud Computing

The CompTIA Cloud Essentials+ exam is designed to test whether a candidate has knowledge of how cloud computing solutions address business problems. This chapter introduces you to cloud computing concepts. It defines the characteristics of cloud computing and identifies cloud service models and cloud deployment models. This chapter also helps you to recognize where responsibility lies when deploying different types of cloud services. You finish this chapter by learning about the essential role of hypervisors and virtualization in cloud computing.

CERTIFICATION OBJECTIVE 1.01

Identifying Cloud Computing Characteristics

Cloud computing, from a simplistic view, allows you to run IT solutions on somebody else's equipment. Technology that has been around for a long time is simply being used in a different way over a network. But is it really that simple? Of course not! If it were, you wouldn't need to study hard to obtain the CompTIA Cloud Essentials+ certification. As the old saying goes, "The devil is in the details."

On the Internet, cloud service providers (CSPs) are also application service providers (ASPs) that provide the IT infrastructure and services that allow the use of IT systems over a network. While ASPs are focused on applications, CSPs offer the provisioning of apps and the underlying infrastructure. Cloud customers are also called *cloud tenants*. The cloud is described as a *multitenant* environment, much like an apartment building hosts multiple tenants that use the same infrastructure. A CSP keeps the data and configuration settings for each cloud tenant isolated from those of other cloud tenants. But what exactly is "the cloud"? To define this concept, we will examine the common characteristics shared by cloud computing implementations.

Elasticity and Scalability

To conceptualize elasticity as a cloud characteristic, think of an elastic rubber band. When you pull it, the rubber band stretches to accommodate the change, and when you release the tension, it shrinks back to its normal size. In the cloud, *elasticity* is the dynamic provisioning and deprovisioning of resources to meet demand. Examples of this include

- Increasing or decreasing the amount of cloud storage
- Adding or removing virtual machines (VMs) to support an e-commerce web application

FIGURE 1-1 Microsoft Azure virtual machine scale set autoscaling

Create virtual machine scale set

Use managed disks ⓘ   ○ No   ● Yes

+ Show advanced settings

AUTOSCALE

Autoscale ⓘ   ○ Disabled   ● Enabled

* Minimum number of VMs ⓘ | 2   ✓ |

* Maximum number of VMs ⓘ | 6   ✓ |

Scale out

* CPU threshold (%) ⓘ | 80   ✓ |

* Number of VMs to increase by ⓘ | 1 |

Scale in

* CPU threshold (%) ⓘ | 25 |

* Number of VMs to decrease by ⓘ | 1 |

Adding virtual machines to support a busy application is also called *scaling out*, a form of *horizontal scaling*. When application requests return to a normal level, the removal of VMs is called *scaling in*.

In the cloud, an autoscaling configuration for an application could be configured to keep a minimum of two virtual machines running but can grow to six virtual machines if the virtual machines' central processing unit (CPU) percentage thresholds are violated. You can see an example of this configuration in Figure 1-1.

Besides scaling in and out, or horizontal scaling, *vertical scaling* is another option to increase or decrease performance (and costs). With vertical scaling, *scaling up* refers to increasing existing virtual machine virtual CPU and RAM settings to improve application performance. *Scaling down* reduces the number of virtual CPUs and RAM (and cost!). Figure 1-2 shows virtual machine sizing for an existing Microsoft Azure virtual machine.

on the **job**

Resizing cloud-based virtual machines to increase the number of CPUs and the amount of RAM can increase application performance, but it can also increase the cost of running the VMs. Scale up only when necessary.

FIGURE 1-2   Microsoft Azure virtual machine sizing

VM SIZE	OFFERING	FAMILY	VCPUS	RAM (GI...	DATA DISKS	MAX IOPS	TEMPORARY ST...	PREMIUM DISK ...
B1ls	Standard	General purpose	1	0.5	2	200	4 GB	Yes
B1ms	Standard	General purpose	1	2	2	800	4 GB	Yes
B1s	Standard	General purpose	1	1	2	400	4 GB	Yes
B2ms	Standard	General purpose	2	8	4	2400	16 GB	Yes
B2s	Standard	General purpose	2	4	4	1600	8 GB	Yes
B4ms	Standard	General purpose	4	16	8	3600	32 GB	Yes
D2s_v3	Standard	General purpose	2	8	4	3200	16 GB	Yes
D4s_v3	Standard	General purpose	4	16	8	6400	32 GB	Yes
DS1_v2	Standard	General purpose	1	3.5	4	3200	7 GB	Yes

Self-service

Without cloud computing, if you need to deploy a new virtual machine or database, you probably need to submit a request to the IT department to make it happen. Cloud computing puts deployment and full or limited management control into the hands of the cloud computing user.

Cloud users can deploy and manage cloud services on demand through a graphical user interface (GUI), which normally comes in the form of a web application or a mobile device app, an example of which is shown in Figure 1-3.

Cloud resources can also be deployed and managed using command-line interface (CLI) tools. Major public CSPs, such as AWS and Microsoft Azure, offer cloud management using Microsoft PowerShell cmdlets, as well as a CLI that can run on Linux and macOS. Developers can also access cloud resources programmatically through application programming interface (API) calls.

API calls made over the Hypertext Transfer Protocol (HTTP) are done using what is called the Representational State Transfer (REST) API. CLI and API access to cloud resources lends itself to automation and repeatability.

Broad Network Access

In the business world, smartphones, tablets, laptops, and desktop computers all can be used to access cloud resources, making broad network access a key characteristic of cloud computing. Additionally, specialty devices in manufacturing, medicine, and other fields and

FIGURE 1-3   Amazon Web Services (AWS) Console app installation screen

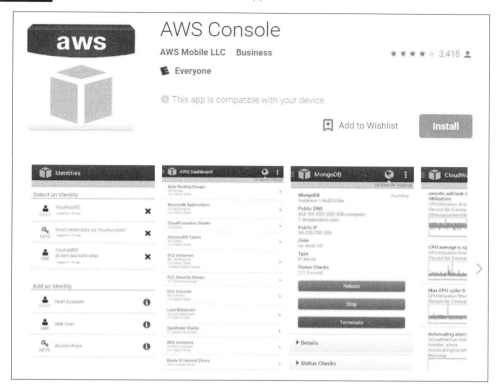

Internet of Things (IoT) devices such as smart cars and baby monitors send data over the Internet. All of these devices can be configured to access cloud services.

Using any type of device to access IT solutions over a network is what *broad network access* refers to. Depending on the cloud service, a web browser or a specific app might be required on the device. For example, users can access Dropbox cloud storage using a web browser or an app. Security is ensured by using generic apps such as the Microsoft VPN client to establish an encrypted virtual private network (VPN) tunnel between the client device and a cloud-based virtual network.

Pay-as-You-Go

Some cloud subscriptions charge a small monthly fee in addition to charges for cloud resources used during the month. Other subscriptions might only charge for usage and nothing else. For organizations, using cloud computing means what was formally an on-premises capital expense (CAPEX) for equipment, software, licensing, and support is now a monthly operating expense (OPEX).

Think of how you pay for water or electricity—it's based on your consumption; you only pay for what you use—this is what *pay-as-you-go* is all about. You might also hear this referred to as *metered usage*.

You can quickly and easily spin up a dozen virtual machines in the cloud. Once you shut down the VMs, you are no longer charged, although there might still be small charges for storing the VM hard disks or public IP addresses you might have assigned to VM network interfaces. Compare this to having to acquire and pay for the hardware and software to accomplish the same task—cloud computing, at least in the short term, is usually less expensive than provisioning the same services yourself on your network.

Availability

CSPs publish service level agreements (SLAs) for each cloud service offering, such as cloud storage, virtual machines, and databases. One provision contained within the standard SLA is a designated level of guaranteed uptime (such as 99.9 percent), which relates to service and data availability. Often, the SLA provides details on cloud computing credits allocated to customers who experience outages that fall within the scope of the SLA.

Another aspect of availability falls on the shoulders of the cloud customer. If you depend on public cloud computing services and your Internet link goes down, you have a problem. Organizations should consider implementing redundant Internet links through different Internet service providers (ISPs) to maximize cloud service and data availability.

Individuals and organizations can also synchronize or back up data to the cloud—this is commonly done by smartphone users. If a user replaces her smartphone, she can simply sign in to her cloud account on the new phone to gain access to pictures, music, contact

FIGURE 1-4   Google account sync settings

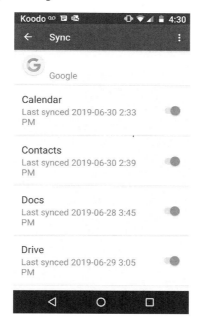

lists, and so on. A smartphone app might need to be installed to allow the user to first sign in to her cloud account. Figure 1-4 shows synced Google account items on an Android smartphone.

CERTIFICATION OBJECTIVE 1.02

Identifying Cloud Service Models

Humans like to categorize, well, pretty much everything. Cloud service offerings are no exception. Some cloud service models appeal to end users, others to developers, others to server administrators, security professionals, and so on. As a CompTIA Cloud Essentials+ exam candidate, you need to understand these cloud service models. Cloud services model names normally begin with the type of service followed by "as a service," as you will see in the following text.

Software as a Service (SaaS)

Years ago, before you could run an application such as e-mail, you would first need to install and configure the software on your computer. If you didn't have a mail server to connect to, you'd also have to acquire the hardware to run the server, then install and configure the e-mail server software—an especially long task if you were installing from floppy disks back in the day.

With cloud computing, accessing hosted software over a network is referred to as *Software as a Service (SaaS)*. Users typically access a SaaS solution through a web browser or through an installed app. With SaaS, users are essentially renting the use of software over a network, although some services are free. SaaS examples include

- Gmail
- Dropbox
- Netflix
- Uber
- Microsoft Office 365

Infrastructure as a Service (IaaS)

You wouldn't refer to a donut shop as infrastructure. But the existence of that donut shop is possible because of the surrounding infrastructure: water, electricity, roads, bridges, railway tracks, and so on. With cloud computing, *Infrastructure as a Service (IaaS)* refers to the underlying components that allow software solutions to run. Examples of IaaS include the following components that can be provisioned to cloud customers:

- Dedicated physical servers
- Virtual machines
- Virtual networks
- Virtual firewall appliances
- Virtual VPN configurations
- Virtual firewall access control lists (ACLs)
- Cloud storage

Platform as a Service (PaaS)

A *platform* refers to a conceptual workbench from which IT technicians can solve business problems with IT solutions—all without having to manage the underlying infrastructure.

You can deploy IaaS cloud resources individually, but when deploying more complex cloud services such as a web application, database, or big data analytics clustered solutions, with *Platform as a Service (PaaS)*, the underlying infrastructure is configured for you; you only need to specify relevant details for what you are deploying. This is sometimes referred to as *serverless* computing; PaaS customers know that, in fact, there are underlying servers providing the solution, but they do not have to install, configure, or directly manage those servers. Another term for this is *managed service*. Examples of PaaS include

- Microsoft Azure SQL Database
- Amazon Web Services Relational Database Service (RDS)
- Microsoft Azure Functions
- Google App Engine

Other Cloud Service Models

Any type of cloud-based IT service packaged up into a manageable bundle is referred to as *Anything as a Service (XaaS)*. Table 1-1 summarizes other common cloud service models.

TABLE 1-1   Other Common Cloud Service Models

Cloud Service Model	Examples
Business Process as a Service (BPaaS)	Payroll; payment systems for e-commerce
Communications as a Service (CaaS)	Voice over IP (VoIP); instant messaging
Database as a Service (DBaaS)	Microsoft Azure SQL Database, the underlying virtual machines and database software are installed automatically
Information Technology as a Service (ITaaS)	Can include hardware, software, and IT technical services
Monitoring as a Service (MaaS)	Monitoring of a wide variety of IT systems, including security monitoring
Metal as a Service (MaaS)	Provisioning of real physical servers running operating systems of the user's choice

Identifying Cloud Deployment Models

Whereas cloud service models are categorized based on the service that each model offers, *cloud deployment models* are categorized based on where the cloud computing infrastructure physically exists, who owns and controls it, and who uses it. The following are the four common cloud deployment models:

- **Public cloud**   Cloud services available to anybody over the Internet, owned and managed by a CSP (any type of entity offering cloud computing services), such as Amazon Web Services, Microsoft Azure, Google Cloud, IBM Cloud, or a even a government agency offering online citizen services such as driver's license renewals.
- **Private cloud**   Cloud computing infrastructure owned, managed, and used by a single organization, even if it is provisioned by a third party on-premises or off-premises.
- **Hybrid cloud**   The extension of an on-premises network into the cloud either during migration to the cloud or for the long term. Hybrid clouds can also combine private clouds (sensitive IT systems used only by one organization) and public cloud resources.
- **Community cloud**   Cloud services for a user base with the same computing needs, often driven by industry regulations. Examples would include government agency clouds that provide cloud-based software and security mechanisms required by government departments.

Understanding Cloud Shared Responsibility

Cloud computing means using IT services running on infrastructure managed by somebody else. This is true even with a private cloud, which is usually controlled by a central IT department within an organization. Departmental use of private cloud services is tracked and charged back to individual organizational departments (departmental chargeback). But where should the line of responsibility for these IT services be drawn? The answer is, it depends on the specific cloud service, and even then, sometimes it is a shared responsibility.

Shared Responsibility Examples

The underlying networking, storage, and servers (IaaS) for a SaaS solution like web-based e-mail are under the control of the CSP, and as such, the responsibility for managing those items falls upon the CSP. Management means

- Hardware acquisition and configuration
- Firmware updates
- Software installation, configuration, and updates
- Maintaining service and data availability in alignment with SLAs

But what about the e-mail messages themselves? Contact information? Calendar entries? Who is responsible for the e-mail settings and archiving? Encryption? It boils down to this: cloud customers are responsible for managing any data they create. As always, there are exceptions, such as cloud providers encrypting data at rest in accordance with applicable SLAs.

Deploying an IaaS virtual machine means that the VM is under the control of the cloud customer, and as such, the management responsibility of the VM falls upon the cloud customer.

Deploying a managed database hides the infrastructure details from the cloud customer. The underlying infrastructure is the responsibility of the CSP, but the configuration of that solution and the management of the data stored in the database are responsibilities of the cloud customer.

EXERCISE 1-1

Sign up for a Free Microsoft Azure Cloud Subscription

In this exercise, you will sign up for a free trial of a Microsoft Azure account. To create a public cloud account, do the following:

1. Use your web browser to navigate to https://azure.microsoft.com.
2. Click the Free Account button, and then click the Start Free button twice.
3. Sign in with a Microsoft or GitHub account. If you don't have one, you'll need to create one to proceed.
4. On the About You page, fill in the required information, as depicted in Figure 1-5. Click Next.

FIGURE 1-5   Signing up for an Azure cloud account

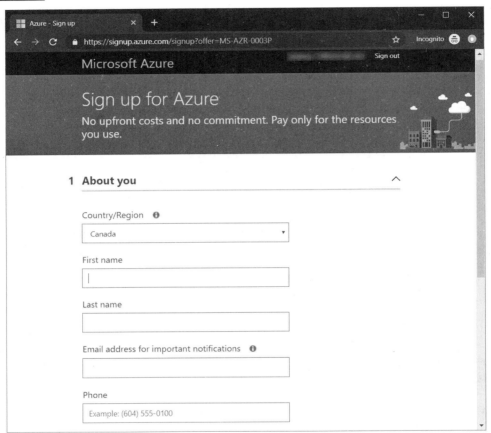

5. On the Identify Verification by Card page, specify credit card information, which is used only to prove your identity; you won't be charged. Then click Next.

6. On the Agreement page, check the box for the "I agree to the subscription agreement, offer details, and privacy statement" option, then click Sign Up.

7. After a moment you will be taken to the Microsoft Azure portal (the management GUI), as shown in Figure 1-6.

FIGURE 1-6   The Welcome to Microsoft Azure screen that appears after signing up

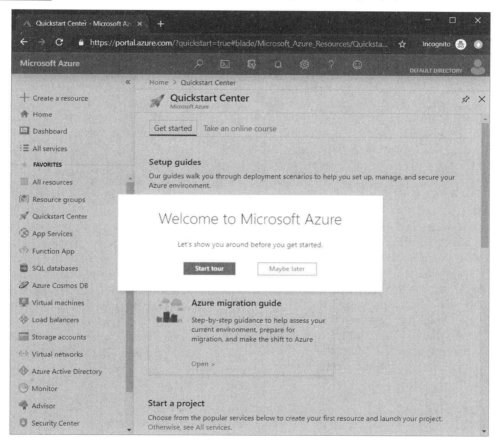

INSIDE THE EXAM

Hypervisors and Virtualization

Although not listed in the official exam objectives, the CompTIA Cloud Essentials+ CLO-002 exam expects you to be familiar with hypervisors and virtualization as they relate to cloud computing.

A *hypervisor* is a computer that can host multiple running virtual machines (this is one type of virtualization), also called *guests.* It does so by running virtualization software. The purpose of a hypervisor is to manage physical hardware resource access among running guests.

Cloud computing depends on virtualization, but virtualization does not depend on cloud computing. Just because you are using virtualization, this does not mean you have a "cloud." Remember that cloud computing exists only when the six characteristics discussed at the beginning of this chapter (elasticity, scalability, etc.) are in place.

While a hypervisor itself can be run within a VM, this is done for testing purposes only and is not suitable for a production environment. There are two common types of hypervisors:

- **Type 1 hypervisors** Also called *bare metal* hypervisors, this software is designed to run directly on physical server hardware. The hypervisor is the operating system, so an existing operating system is not needed. Type 1 hypervisors are used to run VMs in a production environment. Examples of type 1 hypervisors include Microsoft Hyper-V, VMware ESXi, and the open-source XEN hypervisor.

- **Type 2 hypervisors** This virtualization software runs as an application within an existing operating system, so there is an additional layer between the hypervisor and the physical hardware. Type 2 hypervisors are commonly used by developers and IT technicians for testing purposes. Examples of type 2 hypervisors include VMware Workstation for Windows machines, VMware Fusion for macOS machines, and Oracle VM VirtualBox, which can run on Windows, Linux, Unix, and macOS (see Figure 1-7).

FIGURE 1-7   VMware Workstation, a type 2 hypervisor

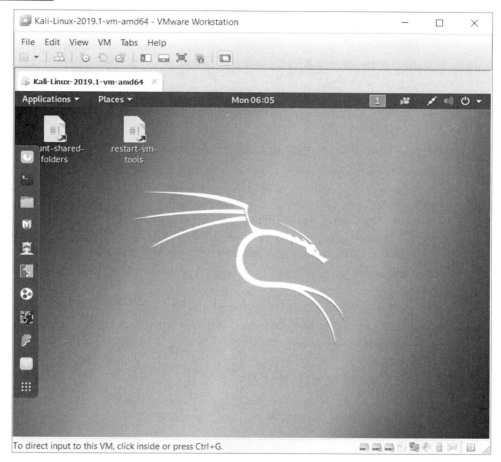

CERTIFICATION SUMMARY

This chapter serves as an introduction to cloud computing. You have been introduced to the characteristics that define cloud computing: elasticity, self-service, scalability, broad network access, pay-as-you-go, and availability.

In addition, you have been exposed to cloud service models, such as Software as a Service (SaaS), Infrastructure as a Service (IaaS), and Platform as a Service (PaaS), that are used to provision resources via various cloud deployment models such as public, private, and hybrid clouds.

You also learned how the responsibility for managing different types of cloud resources sometimes falls upon the CSP and other times upon the cloud tenant. Finally, you learned about type 1 and type 2 hypervisors and how cloud computing relies on virtualization.

TWO-MINUTE DRILL

Identifying Cloud Computing Characteristics

❑ Elasticity allows for the rapid provisioning and deprovisioning of cloud resources.

❑ Scalability is the designing of cloud services to be able to increase or decrease virtual machine CPU and RAM amounts (vertical scaling) or to add or remove virtual machines (horizontal scaling) to support an IT workload.

❑ Self-service means cloud users can provision and deprovision cloud resources using a GUI, command-line tools, or programmatically through API calls.

❑ Broad network access allows a multitude of device types to access cloud services over a network.

❑ Pay-as-you-go means cloud consumers pay only for the cloud resources they use.

❑ Availability ensures that cloud-based IT systems and data are always available. The cloud SLA provides uptime guarantees.

Identifying Cloud Service Models

❑ Software as a Service (SaaS) refers to software solution rentals where the software is accessed and used over a network.

❑ Infrastructure as a Service (IaaS) refers to the underlying items such as storage, networking, and virtual machines that support cloud-based software solutions.

❑ Platform as a Service (PaaS) refers to managed database and developer cloud services that do not require cloud users to configure the underlying supporting infrastructure.

Identifying Cloud Deployment Models

❑ Public clouds are owned and managed by CSPs. The cloud services are available to anybody with Internet access.

❑ Private clouds are owned, managed, and used by a single organization.

❑ Hybrid clouds are composed of an on-premises network linked to a cloud virtual network.

❑ Community clouds address organizations with the same computing needs, often within the same industry.

Understanding Cloud Shared Responsibility

❑ With SaaS, the management of settings and data is the responsibility of the cloud customer. The CSP is responsible for managing the underlying infrastructure that supports the software solution.

❑ With IaaS, the cloud customer is responsible for all management aspects of storage, network configuration, and virtual machines. The CSP is responsible for the underlying hardware, including routers, switches, storage arrays, and physical servers.

❑ With PaaS, the cloud customer is responsible for the details regarding the PaaS solution, such as database settings and data. The CSP is responsible for the underlying infrastructure, such as storage and virtual machines that support the PaaS solution.

SELF TEST

The following questions will help you measure your understanding of the material presented in this chapter. As indicated, some questions may have more than one correct answer, so be sure to read all the answer choices carefully.

Identifying Cloud Computing Characteristics

1. Which cloud computing characteristic is most closely related to OPEX?

A. Broad network access

B. Elasticity

C. Pay-as-you-go

D. Self-service

2. Your manager has asked you to review the storage SLA for a public cloud provider to determine the potential amount of annual downtime. Which of the following cloud characteristics is most closely related to this scenario?
   A. Broad network access
   B. Pay-as-you-go
   C. Scalability
   D. Availability

3. Your cloud-hosted public website experiences more traffic during the holiday season. You need to design a configuration that responds to application requests to add or remove back-end virtual machines as required. The maximum number of VMs should never exceed four. Which cloud characteristic does this most closely relate to?
   A. Metered use
   B. Scalability
   C. Broad network access
   D. Availability

4. Users in your company use their work-issued laptops and personal smartphones to access web apps hosted on a company's private cloud infrastructure. Which term best describes this scenario?
   A. Broad network access
   B. Scalability
   C. Elasticity
   D. Availability

Identifying Cloud Service Models

5. Which of the following cloud resource deployments is an example of IaaS?
   A. Web e-mail
   B. Instant messaging
   C. Managed database
   D. Virtual machines

6. You have decided to deploy your own cloud-based virtual machines hosting a Microsoft SQL Server database. Which type of cloud service model is this?
   A. CaaS
   B. PaaS
   C. IaaS
   D. SaaS

7. What type of cloud computing service model does cloud-based storage apply to?
   A. SaaS
   B. IaaS

C. PaaS

D. CaaS

Identifying Cloud Deployment Models

8. What makes private clouds different from public clouds? (Choose two.)

A. Service availability

B. Limited user base

C. Security of data at rest

D. Responsibility for infrastructure

9. Your on-premises network is linked to a cloud-based virtual network through a VPN tunnel. What type of cloud deployment model is this?

A. Hybrid

B. Private

C. Public

D. Extended

10. Which of the following is a true statement?

A. Anybody with Internet access can potentially access public cloud services.

B. Anybody with Internet access can potentially access private cloud services.

C. Private clouds are available to any user with a paid subscription.

D. Public clouds are used by a single organization.

Understanding Cloud Shared Responsibility

11. Which term best describes deploying a cloud-based database without having to configure the underlying virtual machine?

A. Horizontal scaling

B. Managed service

C. Vertical scaling

D. Infrastructure as a Service

12. You have manually deployed an Ubuntu Linux virtual machine in the public cloud. Who is responsible for applying Linux operating system updates to the VM?

A. Cloud service provider

B. Cloud tenant

C. Ubuntu

D. Cloud service provider and cloud tenant

13. Which type of hypervisor requires an existing operating system?
   A. Type 1
   B. Type 2
   C. Type 3
   D. Type 4

14. Which statements regarding cloud computing are correct? (Choose two.)
   A. Virtualization relies on cloud computing.
   B. Cloud-hosted virtual machines normally run on type 2 hypervisors.
   C. Cloud computing relies on virtualization.
   D. Cloud-hosted virtual machines normally run on type 1 hypervisors.

15. Which of the following is considered a "bare metal" type of hypervisor?
   A. Type 1
   B. Type 2
   C. Type 3
   D. Type 4

SELF TEST ANSWERS

Identifying Cloud Computing Characteristics

1. ☑ **C.** Operating expenses (OPEX) relate to paying for cloud resource usage, such as on a monthly basis, as opposed to hosting the same IT services on premises, which requires a capital investment in hardware, software, licensing, and technician fees.
☒ **A, B,** and **D** are incorrect. They are not as closely related to OPEX as the pay-as-you-go cloud computing characteristic.

2. ☑ **D.** One of the details in a service level agreement (SLA) is the expected uptime (availability) for the cloud service.
☒ **A, B,** and **C** are incorrect. They are cloud characteristics that do not relate to downtime.

3. ☑ **B.** Scalability refers to achieving elasticity through scalability configurations, such as the maximum number of virtual machines.

   ☒ **A, C,** and **D** are incorrect. Metered use, also referred to as "pay as you go," charges cloud customers based on their use of cloud resources. Broad network access does not involve adding or removing resources to improve resource performance. Availability ensures that cloud-based IT systems and data are available when needed and is normally addressed through backups and IT system and data redundancy.

4. ☑ **A.** Broad network access relates to the use of different types of devices to access cloud-based IT services over a network.

   ☒ **B, C,** and **D** are incorrect. Scalability refers to the long-term design of constraints, such as the maximum number of virtual machines. Elasticity is the dynamic response to resource requirements. Availability ensures that cloud-based IT systems and data are available when needed and is normally addressed through backups and IT system and data redundancy.

Identifying Cloud Service Models

5. ☑ **D.** Virtual machines are considered Infrastructure as a Service (IaaS).

   ☒ **A, B,** and **C** are incorrect. **A** and **B** are incorrect because they are considered Software as a Service (SaaS). **C** is incorrect because managed databases are considered Platform as a Service (PaaS).

6. ☑ **C.** If virtual machines are manually configured with software such as Microsoft SQL Server, this is considered Infrastructure as a Service (IaaS).

   ☒ **A, B,** and **D** are incorrect. Communications as a Service (CaaS) relates to cloud-based services such as instant messaging. Platform as a Service (PaaS) provides services such as developer tools and databases without having to manually configure the underlying infrastructure. Software as a Service (SaaS) refers to a software solution available over a network, such as web e-mail provided over the Internet by a cloud service provider.

7. ☑ **B.** In the cloud, storage is considered Infrastructure as a Service (IaaS).

   ☒ **A, C,** and **D** are incorrect. None of these cloud service models is considered IaaS.

Identifying Cloud Deployment Models

8. ☑ **B and D.** Private clouds are the responsibility of and used by a single organization, but still adhere to cloud computing characteristics such as self-service and elasticity.

   ☒ **A** and **C** are incorrect. Service availability and security of data at rest are items that apply to private and public clouds.

9. ☑ **A.** Hybrid cloud solutions combine on-premises and cloud solutions, such as linking an on-premises network to a cloud network via a VPN tunnel.

   ☒ **B, C,** and **D** are incorrect. Private clouds are the responsibility of and used by a single organization, whereas public clouds are potentially available to anybody over the Internet. "Extended" is not a valid cloud deployment model.

10. ☑ **A.** Private clouds are the responsibility of and used by a single organization, whereas public clouds are potentially available to anybody over the Internet.
    ☒ **B, C,** and **D** are incorrect. Private clouds are owned and used by a single organization. Public clouds are available to all Internet users.

Understanding Cloud Shared Responsibility

11. ☑ **B.** In the cloud, a *managed service* provides a solution, such as deploying a database, without having to deal with the underlying virtual machine, network, and storage configuration details.
    ☒ **A, C,** and **D** are incorrect. Horizontal scaling adds or removes virtual machines to support an application. Vertical scaling increases or decreases virtual machine power through items such as the number of virtual CPUs and the amount of RAM. Infrastructure as a Service (IaaS) requires the detailed configuration of resources such as virtual machines, storage, and networking.

12. ☑ **B.** Cloud tenants are cloud customers, and as such are responsible for applying updates to manually deployed virtual machines.
    ☒ **A, C,** and **D** are incorrect. These entities are not responsible for applying updates to a manually deployed virtual machine.

13. ☑ **B.** Type 2 hypervisors require an existing operating system since they run as an app in the operating system.
    ☒ **A, C,** and **D** are incorrect. A type 1 hypervisor installs directly on hardware; it *is* the operating system. Type 3 and type 4 are invalid hypervisor categories.

14. ☑ **C** and **D.** Virtualization in the form of virtual machines makes cloud computing possible.
    ☒ **A** and **B** are incorrect. Virtualization can be used outside of a cloud environment. Cloud-hosted virtual machines run on type 1 hypervisors (bare metal) in the cloud.

15. ☑ **A.** Type 1 hypervisors run directly on hardware (bare metal) and do not need an existing operating system. They are often referred to as a *bare metal* hypervisor.
    ☒ **B, C,** and **D** are incorrect. Type 2 hypervisors run as an app and require an existing operating system. Type 3 and type 4 hypervisors do not exist.

Chapter 2

The Business Side of Cloud Computing

Despite its many benefits, cloud computing isn't for everyone, whether an individual or an organization. In some cases data privacy laws and regulations limit the use of cloud computing. This chapter introduces you to cost factors to consider when adopting or managing existing cloud resources.

We'll start by identifying the benefits of cloud computing compared to provisioning the same computing resources on premises. This will lead into a discussion of the business side of cloud computing in terms of ensuring cloud solutions address business needs while minimizing costs.

Next, we'll dive into cloud service–specific service level agreements (SLAs) and how they relate to IT system and data availability. Finally, we'll talk about managing cloud costs using a variety of strategies.

CERTIFICATION OBJECTIVE 2.01

The Business Case for Cloud Computing

Cloud computing has become wildly popular. Individuals and organizations benefit from using computing services running on somebody else's equipment for a small usage fee—small, at least, in comparison to running those same services on your own equipment in your own facility that you must also manage. But the cost really is about more than just the direct fees. For example, are IT services deployed more efficiently? Is customer service improved? Answering such questions is described as *proof of value (PoV)*.

Cloud adoption begins with mapping available cloud services to computing needs and conducting proof of concept (PoC) pilots to ensure chosen cloud services work as expected. This can include software developers using automated testing for quality assurance (QA) purposes in the cloud or using cloud-based file share folders to address file access needs. Instead of manually provisioning cloud resources, such as virtual machines and databases, cloud users can also use templates (essentially blueprints) to quickly create or even manage cloud resources over and over again.

Cloud computing is a collection of IT solutions that is of interest not only to the organization's chief technology officer (CTO) but also to the chief financial officer (CFO) since there is a potential reduction in up-front, large IT investments.

Ongoing Operating Expenses (OPEX)

As discussed in Chapter 1, the pay-as-you-go cloud computing characteristic represents the fact that most cloud computing pricing models charge customers only for the cloud resources that they use. This ongoing variable monthly expense is called an *operating expense (OPEX)*.

on the job

You might hear other IT technicians refer to *metered usage* when it comes to paying only for cloud resources that are used. In the context of cloud computing characteristics, this is synonymous with *pay-as-you-go*.

An organization that deploys IT services on premises using its own hardware, software, and licenses incurs a much larger up-front, fixed cost, which is called a *capital expense (CAPEX)*. This doesn't mean that cloud computing costs are always cheaper than on-premises computing costs; many factors feed into a return on investment (ROI) analysis, such as a reduced time to market, which can save money in other areas and provide organizations with a competitive advantage. To illustrate this, consider the following example:

Your company requires a back-end database server to process customer transactions for a public-facing website. Following is a comparison of the steps for provisioning the server on premises and the steps for provisioning the server via the cloud:

On Premises	Cloud
1. Acquire server/hypervisor hardware. 2. Acquire storage. 3. Acquire operating system and database software and licenses. 4. Install, configure, and patch operating system and database software. 5. Troubleshoot future infrastructure issues. 6. Connect the website to the database.	1. Deploy a managed cloud database. 2. Connect the website to the database.

exam

watch   **You can expect to be tested on OPEX and CAPEX. Remember that OPEX does not always mean IT costs are less expensive than CAPEX; it depends on the specific IT solution and the time over which that solution will be used.**

Clearly, the cloud deployment option requires less work and allows technicians to focus on the business problem instead of the underlying technology. Using this type of comparison when presenting to management makes a great business case for cloud computing and, over time, can reduce the total cost of ownership (TCO) of the IT solution.

Information Technology Infrastructure Library (ITIL) and the Cloud

ITIL originally was an acronym for Information Technology Infrastructure Library—and it is still identified as such in the Cloud Essentials+ Acronyms list—but the official name of the framework was changed to ITIL by its owner, AXELOS, more than five years ago.

In a nutshell, ITIL is an IT service framework with the goal of providing IT services as efficiently and cost-effectively as possible. This framework relates to cloud computing characteristics such as self-service provisioning, as well as to promoting professional development through providing proper training for technicians (human capital) who will manage cloud services. From cloud technicians to cloud end users, the framework is all about IT service management continuous improvement.

Let's say your organization wants to run important IT services in the cloud such as

- Customer relationship management (CRM)
- Enterprise resource planning (ERP)
- Digital marketing campaigns, including e-mail campaigns
- Social media feed analytics

Part of ITIL relates to supplier management. The cloud service provider (CSP) is the supplier in this case, and your organization must take care to ensure these listed items are available from the CSP at a reasonable cost over time. Using these cloud services provides customers with the benefit of quick and easy deployment. For example, executing e-mail marketing campaigns in the cloud doesn't even require the installation of or permission to use an SMTP e-mail server, where this might be required on-premises.

Careful planning and ongoing monitoring are the key to the efficient and effective use of cloud computing services, given that the success criteria have been defined. This could include smaller website deployment times for testing purposes in the cloud. Cloud computing allows for a faster pace and larger scale of data generation and consumption than was previously possible, and this must be managed carefully for organizations to derive as much business value for as little cost as possible.

CERTIFICATION OBJECTIVE 2.02

Service Level Agreements

A *service level agreement (SLA)* is a contract between a CSP and a cloud customer. An SLA is specific to a cloud service. For example, Figure 2-1 shows an excerpt from an SLA for a cloud storage solution. These terms will differ from the terms in an SLA for virtual machines, websites, and so on.

FIGURE 2-1   Excerpt from Amazon Web Services (AWS) S3 cloud storage SLA

Monthly Uptime Percentage	Service Credit Percentage
Less than 99.9% but greater than or equal to 99.0%	10%
Less than 99.0% but greater than or equal to 95.0%	25%
Less than 95.0%	100%

SLAs focus on cloud service performance, availability, and technical support. A statement of work (SOW) provides details about deliverables that result from a contract, such as an SLA. If the SLA does not mention these items, you can submit a *request for information (RFI)* to the CSP to receive further details.

To determine acceptable performance and availability values, you must first establish a baseline of normal acceptable performance and availability for the use of IT services. Let's say an SLA specifies monthly cloud storage uptime of 99.9 percent, which represents the industry standard benchmark for cloud storage availability. How much downtime is possible given this value? Potentially, cloud storage could be unavailable for 43 minutes and 12 seconds per month, as shown in Figure 2-2 (using the SLA Uptime Calculator at www.slatools.com/sla-uptime-calculator). If the CSP fails to meet the SLA obligations, cloud service credits are applied to the customer's cloud computing charges.

FIGURE 2-2   Determining cloud service uptime from the SLA monthly uptime percentage

FIGURE 2-3 Tag names and values for a Microsoft Azure virtual machine

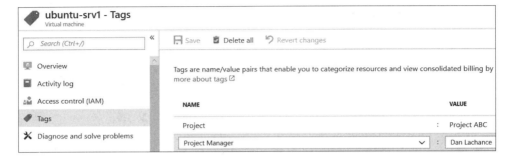

In some cases the details in the SLA can be modified or negotiated. This is especially true with larger organizations or government agencies.

Chargeback

SLAs define not only cloud service availability but also the related pricing structure. In some organizations, this even applies to a private cloud. The IT department provides the private cloud services, and each department within the organization is charged for its use of private cloud resources (departmental chargeback).

Tracking cloud resources based on details such as department or project is easily accomplished with *resource tagging*, which means adding metadata to further define that resource. For example, deploying storage, virtual machines, and websites in the cloud means deploying numerous cloud resources, each of which might be tagged with a "Project" tag with a value of "Project ABC," as shown in Figure 2-3. This way, all cloud resources related to "Project ABC" can be listed together to facilitate management and billing allocation.

CERTIFICATION OBJECTIVE 2.03

Managing Cloud Costs

Even though cloud computing costs are monthly recurring operating costs, it doesn't mean it is less important to plan and track cloud computing charges. For example, leaving a cloud database or virtual machine deployment running for months when it is only needed for a

FIGURE 2-4   Microsoft Azure virtual machine auto-shutdown options

single day could result in large cloud computing bills that could have been easily avoided. Cloud-based policies and permissions can be used to limit which cloud users can deploy specific cloud services. There are options to automate actions, such as virtual machine auto-shutdown, as shown in Figure 2-4.

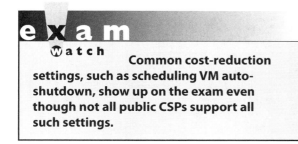

Reserved and Spot Instances

Most CSPs allow you to reserve compute capacity (virtual machine usage) ahead of time for an extended period of time, such as up to three years. This is referred to as a *reserved instance*. If you know you will need compute capacity in the cloud for that period of time, you can cut cloud costs by doing this because the CSP offers discounts for reserved instance configurations.

Another cost-saving measure is to use *spot instances*. This refers to virtual machine compute capacity that is currently unused and can be used at a minimal cost, but there is no guarantee it will always be available to you. If you want to use cloud-based VMs for testing or noncritical IT workloads at a minimal cost, using spot instances fits this need.

Cloud Subscription Types

Cloud subscriptions define a billing and management boundary. You could have a single public CSP account with multiple subscriptions.

The subscription is where payment information, such as credit card details, is specified along with billing e-mail and physical addresses. You can beef up subscriptions with additional cloud features, enhanced technical support, and so on, at an increased cost. Some CSPs such as Microsoft Azure provide different types of subscriptions; for example:

- Free Trial (30 days or use of $260 credit)
- Pay-As-You-Go
- Pay-As-You-Go Dev/Test (for developers)

Licensing

Most open-source software does not require users to pay for licenses. *Open source* means the source code is freely available to anyone on the Internet, and any modifications to the source code must be made freely available to all users on the Internet. Examples of popular open-source software include the Ubuntu Linux operating system and the LibreOffice productivity suite.

The opposite of open-source software is *proprietary* software. An example is Microsoft Windows; Microsoft owns the Windows OS source code and does not make it freely available for modifications. Also, most proprietary software requires a fee for licensing the software.

Most CSPs offer a *bring your own license (BYOL)* option when deploying resources such as virtual machines or databases, as shown in Figure 2-5. If your organization has already

FIGURE 2-5   Microsoft Azure virtual machine BYOL option

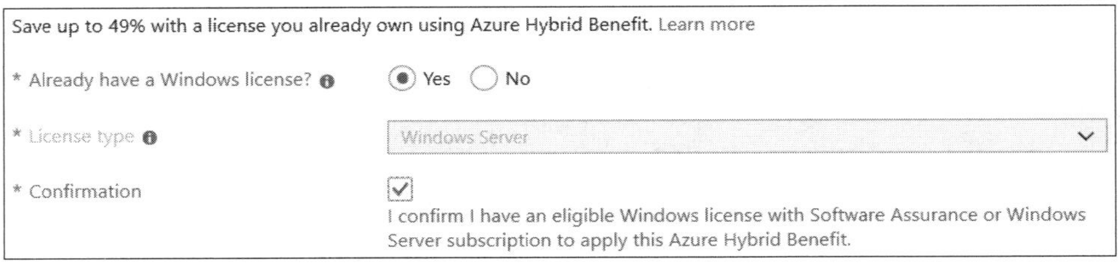

Save up to 49% with a license you already own using Azure Hybrid Benefit. Learn more

* Already have a Windows license? ⓘ   ● Yes   ○ No

* License type ⓘ   Windows Server ⌄

* Confirmation   ☑
          I confirm I have an eligible Windows license with Software Assurance or Windows
          Server subscription to apply this Azure Hybrid Benefit.

paid licensing fees, you can continue to use them in the cloud to reduce costs. When configuring an OS and supplying license information, you'll normally have to accept the End User Licensing Agreement (EULA) before continuing.

EXERCISE 2-1

Microsoft Azure Pricing Calculator

In this exercise, you will determine the approximate monthly cost of deploying IT services in the Microsoft Azure public cloud using the Microsoft Azure Pricing Calculator. The following instructions depend on having completed Exercise 1-1 in Chapter 1.

1. Use your web browser to navigate to https://azure.microsoft.com/en-ca/pricing/calculator.
2. Click the Virtual Machines tile, and then scroll down to the Virtual Machines section of the web page.
3. From the Instance drop-down list, choose the D4 instance type.
4. Scroll down and enter **40** in the Hours field.
5. Scroll back up to the very top of the web page and click the Storage Accounts tile. Scroll down to the Storage Accounts section and review the default settings, but do not change any of the Storage Account settings.
6. Scroll back up to the very top of the web page and click the Azure SQL Database tile.
7. Scroll down the web page to the Azure SQL Database section.
8. From the Backup Storage Tier drop-down list, choose RA-GRS.
9. Scroll down to the very bottom of the web page to view the estimated monthly cost for all the selected cloud products.

EXERCISE 2-2

Microsoft Azure Budgets and Alerts

In this exercise, you will configure an Azure budget and alert. The following instructions depend on having completed Exercise 1-1 in Chapter 1.

1. Sign in to https://portal.azure.com.

2. From the search field at the top center of the Azure portal, type **Subscriptions** and click the search result of the same name.

   a. Click your subscription name.

   b. In the left-hand navigator, click Budgets.

3. Click the Add button:

   a. Name the budget **Budget1**.

   b. Type **300** in the Amount field.

   c. Enable the check box for the Alert Recipients (Email) section, then type in a fictitious group e-mail address such as **admins@fakeco.com**.

   d. Click Create.

INSIDE THE EXAM

Match Requirements to Cloud Service Configurations

In some cases the CompTIA Cloud Essentials+ CLO-002 exam might ask what the best cloud solution is given a business requirement. An example might look like this:

- Your organization needs a software sandbox testing environment for website development. The environment needs the ability to spin up rapidly at a minimal cost.

One possible solution is

- Create resource deployment templates for the required testing resources and ensure spot-instance virtual machines are used.

CERTIFICATION SUMMARY

This chapter discussed how to bridge the gap between the business side of computing and the details related to cloud computing service delivery.

You have been exposed to the difference between CAPEX and OPEX and how cloud managed services allow cloud technicians to focus on the business problem instead of the underlying IT complexities.

You also learned how ITIL relates to the cloud and how SLAs define expected cloud service levels and pricing structures. This chapter covered how cloud resource tagging facilitates organizing cloud resources for billing purposes.

Saving money is always important; strategies such as virtual machine auto-shutdown and the use of spot instances can help achieve this. Finally, you learned about cloud subscriptions and licensing options.

TWO-MINUTE DRILL

The Business Case for Cloud Computing

❑ Operating expenses (OPEX) map to monthly recurring cloud computing charges.

❑ Capital expenditures (CAPEX) map to purchasing, configuring, and managing IT infrastructure onsite.

❑ ITIL is an IT service framework that strives to increase the quality and efficiencies related to IT service delivery while reducing costs.

Service Level Agreements

❑ A service level agreement (SLA) is a contract between a cloud provider and cloud customer specifying uptime and cloud usage charges.

❑ Chargeback is used to track cloud service usage by a specific group or user for billing purposes.

❑ Tagging cloud resources means adding metadata to further describe the resource, normally to facilitate management and billing.

Managing Cloud Costs

❑ Reserved instances offer preplanned compute capacity over time at a discount.

❑ Spot instances offer the use of available cloud compute resources at a discount, but the availability can change at any time.

❑ Cloud subscriptions determine which cloud features are available.

❑ Bring your own license (BYOL) allows the use of existing software licenses in a cloud computing environment.

SELF TEST

The following questions will help you measure your understanding of the material presented in this chapter. As indicated, some questions may have more than one correct answer, so be sure to read all the answer choices carefully.

The Business Case for Cloud Computing

1. Which term is most closely related to ensuring that cloud solutions improve the customer experience and increase efficiencies?
   A. Proof of concept (PoC)
   B. Return on investment (ROI)
   C. Proof of value (PoV)
   D. Total cost of ownership (TCO)

2. Which term is synonymous with metered usage?
   A. Elasticity
   B. Pay-as-you-go
   C. CAPEX
   D. Managed service

3. Which two terms are the most closely related to ITIL?
   A. Service delivery
   B. Supplier management
   C. Service level agreement
   D. Managed service

4. From the cloud customer's perspective, to which business role does the CSP apply?
   A. Cloud tenant
   B. Regulator
   C. Supplier
   D. Enforcer

Service Level Agreements

5. Which of the following two items are commonly found in a cloud SLA?
   A. Data retention options
   B. Expected uptime
   C. Subscription limits
   D. Service credits

6. You are evaluating cloud service SLAs. What is required to determine if the SLA performance guarantees are suitable for a specific IT workload?
   A. Template
   B. Baseline
   C. Pricing calculator
   D. Migration toolkit

7. Your organization runs a private cloud. Cloud usage is tracked by department for monthly billing purposes. Which term best describes this model?
   A. Service level agreement
   B. Chargeback
   C. IaaS
   D. SaaS

Managing Cloud Costs

8. You need to minimize cost when periodically testing new OS updates in cloud-based Windows virtual machines. What should you do?
   A. Use spot instances
   B. Use reserved instances
   C. View the virtual machine SLA
   D. Deploy the virtual machine using a template

9. Your on-premises, mission-critical Windows server is already licensed. You plan to migrate the server to a cloud-based virtual machine. What should you do to reduce costs?
   A. Use the BYOL option when creating the cloud virtual machine
   B. Deploy the server as a spot instance
   C. Increase the virtual machine compute power
   D. Switch to an open-source OS

10.   Which term is associated with agreeing to licensing terms?
   A.   BYOL
   B.   EULA
   C.   SLA
   D.   TCO

11.   Developers in your company have been leaving cloud-based virtual machines running long after they are needed. What should you configure to reduce costs?
   A.   Auto-shutdown
   B.   Spot instances
   C.   Reserved instances
   D.   Virtual machine templates

12.   You want to be made aware of cloud computing charges when a certain dollar amount is reached. What should you configure?
   A.   Reserved instances
   B.   Cloud pricing calculator
   C.   Cloud templates
   D.   Billing alerts

13.   What should you configure to control which types of virtual machines can be deployed in the cloud?
   A.   Cloud policies
   B.   Cloud template
   C.   Cloud SLA
   D.   Cloud subscription

14.   Your company has a three-year military contract that will require the use of many virtual machines that must be left running all the time. You need to minimize cloud computing costs. Which cloud virtual machine option should you consider?
   A.   Spot instances
   B.   Reserved instances
   C.   Auto-shutdown
   D.   Template deployment

15.   Which type of software does not normally charge users for licensing?
   A.   CAPEX
   B.   Open source
   C.   Proprietary
   D.   BYOL

SELF TEST ANSWERS

The Business Case for Cloud Computing

1. ☑ **C.** In a cloud computing context, proof of value (PoV) identifies the business value of cloud computing.
    ☒ **A, B,** and **D** are incorrect. Proof of concept (PoC) provides assurances that a plan will function correctly. Return on investment (ROI) is used to determine if an expenditure has increased or decreased in value over time. Total cost of ownership (TCO) identifies costs associated with using a product or service, including ongoing management and maintenance costs, over time.

2. ☑ **B.** Metered usage is synonymous with pay-as-you-go; cloud usage is tracked and billed accordingly.
    ☒ **A, C,** and **D** are incorrect. Elasticity refers to the ability to quickly provision or deprovision cloud resources on demand. Capital expenditures (CAPEX) refer to large investments in equipment. Managed services in the cloud take care of the underlying infrastructure configurations required to support a higher-level service such as a database.

3. ☑ **A** and **B.** The ITIL framework strives to provide efficient IT services with a minimum of cost. Part of this framework relates to service delivery and supplier management.
    ☒ **C** and **D** are incorrect. Service level agreements (SLAs) are contracts between cloud providers and cloud customers. Managed services in the cloud take care of the underlying infrastructure configurations required to support a higher-level service such as a database.

4. ☑ **C.** Cloud service providers (CSPs) are suppliers from the cloud customer's perspective.
    ☒ **A, B,** and **D** are incorrect. Cloud tenants are cloud customers. Regulators set policy to control industry through regulations. Enforcer is not a common cloud role.

Service Level Agreements

5. ☑ **B** and **D.** Service level agreements (SLAs) include details about cloud service uptime and service credits for cloud customers if SLA metrics are not honored.
    ☒ **A** and **C** are incorrect. SLAs do not reference data retention policies or cloud subscription limits.

6. ☑ **B.** Baselines set a standard for performance under normal load conditions. Without baselines, determining if details such as network bandwidth or monthly uptime percentages fulfill business requirements is difficult.

   ☒ **A, C,** and **D** are incorrect. Templates define cloud resources to be created or managed in some way. Pricing calculators and migration toolkits are not related to SLAs.

7. ☑ **B.** Chargeback refers to tracking usage for a group or department and then billing it accordingly.

   ☒ **A, C,** and **D** are incorrect. Service level agreements (SLAs) include details about cloud service uptime and service credits for cloud customers if SLA metrics are not honored. Infrastructure as a Service (IaaS) and Software as a Service (SaaS) are cloud service models.

Managing Cloud Costs

8. ☑ **A.** Spot instances are extra compute capacity that can be "rented" when needed, but uptime is not guaranteed, so for testing OS updates, this would be acceptable.

   ☒ **B, C,** and **D** are incorrect. Reserved instances require a long-term commitment for compute services at a discount. SLAs for VMs do not provide a method for minimizing costs, nor does deploying a VM using a template.

9. ☑ **A.** Bring your own license (BYOL) allows cloud customers to use their existing software licenses with cloud deployments such as virtual machines.

   ☒ **B, C,** and **D** are incorrect. Mission-critical servers should not be deployed as spot instances because uptime is not guaranteed. Increasing VM compute power increases costs. Switching to an open-source OS does not reduce costs from the perspective that a Windows server license has already been acquired.

10. ☑ **B.** The End User License Agreement (EULA) is normally accompanied by a check box that users must check after having read a software licensing agreement.

    ☒ **A, C,** and **D** are incorrect. Bring your own license (BYOL) allows cloud customers to use their existing software licenses with cloud deployments such as VMs. Service level agreements (SLAs) include details about cloud service uptime and service credits for cloud customers if SLA metrics are not honored. Total cost of ownership (TCO) specifies the direct cost of an item or service plus the management costs over time.

11. ☑ **A.** Enabling auto-shutdown allows you to schedule when virtual machines are automatically turned off.

    ☒ **B, C,** and **D** are incorrect. Spot instances are extra compute capacity that can be "rented" when needed, but uptime is not guaranteed. Reserved instances require a long-term commitment for compute services at a discount. Virtual machine templates contain instructions on deploying VMs and can accept parameters for unique values such as the VM name or OS image.

12.   ☑   **D.** Billing alerts are configured to notify administrators when monthly cloud charges reach a specified amount.
☒   **A, B,** and **C** are incorrect. Reserved instances require a long-term commitment for compute services at a discount. Cloud pricing calculators allow users to add the anticipated usage of specific cloud services to get a sense of how much cloud services might cost. Cloud templates are used to facilitate the deployment and management of cloud resources.

13.   ☑   **A.** Cloud policies not only control which administrators can deploy and manage virtual machines but also control granular resource details such as which type of VMs can be deployed.
☒   **B, C,** and **D** are incorrect. Cloud templates are used to facilitate the deployment and management of cloud resources. Service level agreements (SLAs) include details about cloud service uptime and service credits for cloud customers if SLA metrics are not honored. Cloud subscriptions serve as a billing and features boundary for cloud computing. A single cloud account can contain multiple subscriptions.

14.   ☑   **B.** Reserved instances require a long-term commitment for compute services at a discount.
☒   **A, C,** and **D** are incorrect. Spot instances are extra compute capacity that can be "rented" when needed, but uptime is not guaranteed. Enabling auto-shutdown allows you to schedule when VMs are automatically turned off. Cloud templates are used to facilitate the deployment and management of cloud resources.

15.   ☑   **B.** Open-source software means the source code is freely available to everybody over the Internet, and normally license fees do not apply to use the software.
☒   **A, C,** and **D** are incorrect. Capital expenditures (CAPEX) refer to large investments in equipment. Proprietary software does not make source code freely available over the Internet, and normally license fees are required to use the software. Bring your own license (BYOL) allows cloud customers to use their existing software licenses with cloud deployments such as VMs.

Part II

Cloud Design Requirements

CHAPTERS

Chapter 3

Cloud Planning

T his chapter emphasizes the importance of planning the use of cloud computing services. New companies can adopt cloud computing with relative ease, while organizations already using on-premises solutions have more to consider.

In this chapter, we explore how to determine whether or not cloud services address business needs, how to choose the correct cloud services, and how to plan a cloud migration strategy.

Cloud Feasibility

Like all business endeavors, the adoption of cloud computing requires careful analysis, planning, and testing. Formulating a solid business plan and identifying how business needs are addressed by technology play important roles in a successful cloud adoption strategy. When assessing the feasibility of extending IT services beyond existing on-premises solutions, an organization needs to identify the potential benefits that cloud computing offers. Some of these benefits might include

- Less up-front capital costs
- Quicker deployment of IT services
- More time to focus on using IT to solve business problems, instead of focusing on configuring the technology
- Quicker time to market for products and services

The current and future needs of the organization must be factored in, such as the capability to add users to e-mail systems, the capability to deploy more virtual machines, the capacity to increase cloud storage—this cloud scalability fits in well with capacity planning. A technical *gap analysis* is used to identify whether current IT solutions properly address business needs, such as determining that cloud-stored data must reside in data centers within national boundaries. If not, the analysis results can identify what needs to be changed, such as moving cloud storage within national boundaries or switching to a cloud service provider (CSP) that supports this option. In this example, a business gap analysis is also applicable since the IT cloud solutions map to business process requirements.

A point of contact needs to be established when reporting to stakeholders as cloud adoption progresses. Affected stakeholders can included end users of cloud services, IT teams supporting cloud services, and management.

As an example, let's say current on-premises file server data will be migrated to a cloud-based file sharing system. Affected users must be notified of this change to ensure their continued file access, and a method of reporting on the status of the migration must be established. CSPs provide audit and log functionality for all aspects of cloud resource management, including the migration of data to the cloud.

Feasibility Study

A feasibility study factors in items such as technical constraints, regulatory compliance, and cost to determine whether a proposed solution has a realistic chance at succeeding.

Documentation can aid in determining how realistic and practical (feasible) a proposed cloud computing solution will be in addressing business needs. As discussed in Chapter 1, CSP service level agreements (SLAs) define expected uptime for specific cloud services. CSP compliance web pages show which security and data privacy standards the CSP supports.

Network and data flow diagrams are important in showing how IT systems and data will interact with one another, such as using a site-to-site VPN tunnel to link on-premises IT services to a public CSP service. Other relevant documentation types include

- Change management
- Resource management
- Configuration management
- Standard operating procedures

For instance, automating the management of storage resources in the cloud might now be done using command-line tools such as Microsoft PowerShell using scripts or templates, where previously this task was handled using on-premises proprietary storage solution tools. The various types of documentation and diagrams are useful not only during a feasibility study but also during solution implementation and future troubleshooting.

Cloud Pilot Program

Whereas a cloud feasibility study addresses general questions such as "Can our organization use cloud computing to more efficiently use technology to serve business needs," a pilot program actually implements a cloud service on a small scale for purposes of evaluating the service.

Think of pilot programs as being more specific to *how* feasibility can be measured. For example, a pilot program could consist of five users (a control group) from a department using cloud services to do their jobs for a period of time while others continue to use on-premises IT services. The results of conducting pilot programs are then reported to relevant stakeholders to determine the feasibility of implementing the cloud services on a larger scale.

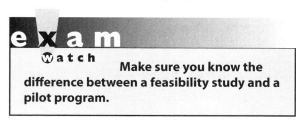

exam

ⓦatch   **Make sure you know the difference between a feasibility study and a pilot program.**

Pilot programs can be used as a "proof of concept" tool to test the migration of on-premises IT systems and data to the cloud and then the use of those systems and data in the cloud.

CERTIFICATION OBJECTIVE 3.02

Solving Business Problems with the Cloud

Organizations don't use technology because the gadgets are cool. They use technology to solve business problems and to save money. Money can be saved with *right*-sizing, which strives to use IT infrastructure efficiently, such as reducing the number of virtual machines supporting an application when requests slow down, otherwise known as *scaling in* (see Chapter 1).

Map Computing Requirements to Cloud Services

Planning for the use of cloud computing means looking at the organization's current and future anticipated IT needs and then finding services in the cloud that fulfill those needs. For example, if your organization needs to quickly test custom software application changes, deploying application containers in the cloud might be faster and cheaper than deploying virtual machines. This is true because an application container, unlike a VM, does not contain an entire operating system; instead, it simply uses an underlying operating system that is already running.

Table 3-1 shows a sample of common IT needs and corresponding cloud solutions.

Using cloud services is one thing, but logging and monitoring usage is also crucial for continuous improvement over time. You can configure alerts so that you are notified, for example, if the average CPU utilization of a virtual machine exceeds a given percentage value within a specific time frame, as shown in Figure 3-1.

Data Sovereignty and Privacy

Cloud computing services run on physical hardware that exists somewhere in a data center. The location of that data center can play a crucial role in determining if a specific CSP or cloud service should be used.

TABLE 3-1   Common Computing Needs and Cloud Solutions

IT Need	Cloud Solution
Secure data storage with the ability to grow rapidly	Amazon Simple Storage Service (S3) Microsoft Azure Storage Microsoft OneDrive Dropbox Google Drive
Software testing for software developers and IT technicians	Virtual machine template for quick VM deployment into an isolated cloud virtual network Virtual machine horizontal autoscaling to add or remove VM nodes depending on application workload requirements Deployment of application containers for software testing
Analysis of large datasets, machine learning (ML), artificial intelligence (AI)	AWS big data analytics Microsoft Azure big data analytics
Office productivity and collaboration without installing software locally	Google Docs Microsoft Office 365
Dedicated private network integrating on-premises IT services to the CSP without using the Internet	AWS Direct Connect Microsoft Azure ExpressRoute
Ability to export cloud-generated data and use in other CSP environments	Analyze CSP file and storage formats to avoid vendor lock-in

Upon creation, cloud services generally let the creator specify a location (or region) into which a cloud resource will be deployed, as shown in Figure 3-2. Organizations may need to ensure sensitive data resides in data centers within national boundaries for legal or regulatory compliance. Data sovereignty refers to keeping sensitive data within national boundaries to control jurisdictional rule of law related to data.

Data privacy has become a global issue due to the global nature of the Internet. Personally identifiable information (PII) refers to any piece of information or combination of pieces of information that can uniquely identify an individual. Examples of PII include

- Social Security number
- E-mail address
- IP address
- Street address
- Mother's maiden name

FIGURE 3-1   Configuring a Microsoft Azure alert rule

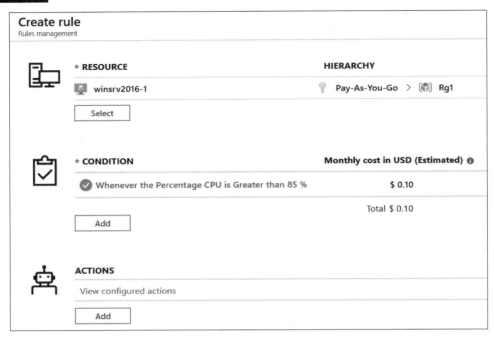

Protected health information (PHI) refers to any piece of medically related information about an individual. Protection of PII and PHI normally requires encryption to provide data confidentiality. Examples of PHI include

- Blood type
- Prescribed medications

FIGURE 3-2   Deploying a Microsoft Azure storage account in the Canada East region

Instance details

The default deployment model is Resource Manager, which supports the latest Azure features. You may choose to deploy using the classic deployment model instead. Choose classic deployment model

* Storage account name ❶	storageaccount888	✓
* Location	(Canada) Canada East	∨

- Past medical procedures
- Health insurance coverage
- Medical procedure payment history

PII and PHI, as well as payment card information, must be protected both on premises and in the cloud. The following discussion provides further details on a few data privacy standards that might affect an organization's decision regarding whether it should engage the services of a particular CSP.

General Data Protection Regulation (GDPR)

Because data privacy is such a common theme, lawmakers around the world have been scrambling to create a framework of rules to protect the collection, retention, use, and sharing of private data. The GDPR is a legislative act of the European Union (EU) that is intended to put control of PII into the data owner's hands.

The GDPR states that individuals are entitled to clear communication and consent regarding how their personal data will be collected and used. Individuals also have the right to access their collected data and to ensure its accuracy.

The GDPR applies to organizations within the EU that collect and process personal data, and it applies to any entity located outside the EU that processes personal data of EU citizens.

Health Insurance Portability and Accountability Act (HIPAA)

In the United States, HIPAA is designed to keep individuals' health information protected from unauthorized access and use. American healthcare providers and health plans must comply with HIPAA regulations using methods such as

- Strong user and device authentication
- Data encryption
- Data integrity checking to detect tampering
- Ongoing monitoring to detect potential security breaches

Like all rules, there are exceptions. Consider the example of people participating in a medical study in which each person consents to having activity-monitoring devices attached to their body. If the collected data from multiple users is analyzed and summarized, then HIPAA may not apply. Any medically related information that can be traced back to an American citizen could be subject to HIPAA.

TABLE 3-2	PCI DSS Requirements and Suggested Security Controls

PCI DSS Requirement	Security Control
Build and maintain a secure network	Network intrusion detection system (NIDS) Firewall
Maintain a vulnerability management program	Periodic device inventory Centralized method of applying software updates
Implement strong access control	Grant only those permissions required to perform a task Multifactor authentication (MFA)
Protect cardholder data	Encryption of data in transit Encryption of data at rest

Payment Card Industry Data Security Standard (PCI DSS)

Merchants dealing with payment cards such as debit and credit cards must adhere to the PCI DSS framework. Unlike some other data privacy standards, such as GDPR and HIPAA, PCI DSS is not limited to a country or group of countries; it is international.

Protecting cardholder data could require securing the transmission and storage of that information, if it is being stored at all. Much of PCI DSS consists of general recommendations; it's up to IT security experts to determine the best security control to mitigate risks. The other thing to consider is that compliance details vary from one card type to the next (Visa, MasterCard, American Express). Table 3-2 provides a subset of PCI DSS security requirements and solutions.

From a security analyst standpoint, auditing IT environments for PCI DSS can include

- Identifying cardholder data
- Assessing existing security controls
- Remediation through reconfiguration or the use of new security controls
- Reporting on Compliance (RoC) for PCI DSS audits

CERTIFICATION OBJECTIVE 3.03

Cloud Migration Strategies

After an organization has completed a feasibility study, followed by pilot programs to test specific cloud solution viability, and has determined that, yes, moving IT services from on premises to the cloud *does* make sense, it can focus on cloud migration strategies.

An important consideration when choosing a migration strategy is that it can also help fulfill disaster recovery and business continuity planning by replicating data to the cloud in various regions so that a disaster does not destroy all copies of the data.

Remember, with cloud computing, depending on the services you deploy, there is a shared responsibility between you, the cloud customer, and the CSP. For instance, if you deploy virtual machines in the cloud, it's up to you to manage them, including patching the OS, but the underlying physical hypervisor hardware, storage, and network infrastructure on which the virtual machines run is the responsibility of the CSP, who, in this context, can also be referred to as a managed service provider (MSP).

Most cloud migrations use a *phased* approach. In simple terms, it could consist of the following phases:

1. Evaluate on-premises candidates for cloud migration.
2. Place IT systems and data in the cloud.
3. Synchronize data between on premises and the cloud.
4. After a period of time during which cloud adoption is successful, decommission the on-premises IT systems and data.

Of course, you might never decommission the on-premises components, which results in running a *hybrid* cloud solution.

Lift and Shift

While some customized IT solutions may need to be redesigned to work in the cloud, other solutions can be moved from the on-premises IT configurations into the cloud with little to no modification. Commercial off-the-shelf (COTS) software often lends itself to a lift and shift migration strategy from on premises to the cloud, whereas customized, resource-intensive solutions typically do not. Lift and shift migrations are often referred to as *rehosting* migrations. Rebuilding IT systems to work in the cloud is referred to as *refactoring*, which is central to the rip and replace migration strategy discussed in the next section.

e x a m

ⓦatch Be prepared to answer exam questions that test your knowledge of the difference between lift and shift migrations versus refactoring.

Large Datasets

If you have large on-premises datasets, your cloud migration strategy might include employing CSP large data transfer services such as AWS Snowball. With AWS Snowball, a secured storage device is sent to your location, your data is copied (with 256-bit encryption) to the device, and the device is shipped back to AWS, where the data is then copied into the AWS cloud. Transferring very large amounts of data (think petabytes) over the Internet sometimes is not feasible, even with the fastest Internet connections, because it would take too long. It might also be too expensive or not sufficiently secure.

Physical to Virtual (P2V)

Physical on-premises servers can be migrated into the cloud as virtual machines. This process is referred to as physical to virtual (P2V) migration and normally occurs through an agent installed on the physical server that communicates with a management console. The agent analyzes the hardware and OS configuration so that the virtualized environment is configured accordingly. The opposite, meaning migrating a virtual machine to a physical host, is referred to as virtual to physical (V2P).

You might also consider a P2V migration if you want to run a private cloud on your own equipment by virtualizing existing physical servers. The free VMware Converter tool can be used to perform P2V migrations for physical Windows and Linux hosts.

Virtual to Virtual (V2V)

This one is interesting; most folks assume that V2V means migrating on-premises VMs to the cloud, which is correct. This can be much quicker than deploying a brand-new VM in the cloud and configuring it to meet your needs.

But V2V can also mean migrating cloud-based VMs back to the premises when required. For example, Microsoft Azure VMs use virtual hard disks (VHDs). You can download VHDs from Azure, as shown in Figure 3-3, and then create on-premises VMs using the downloaded VHDs.

FIGURE 3-3   Downloading a Microsoft Azure VM VHD file

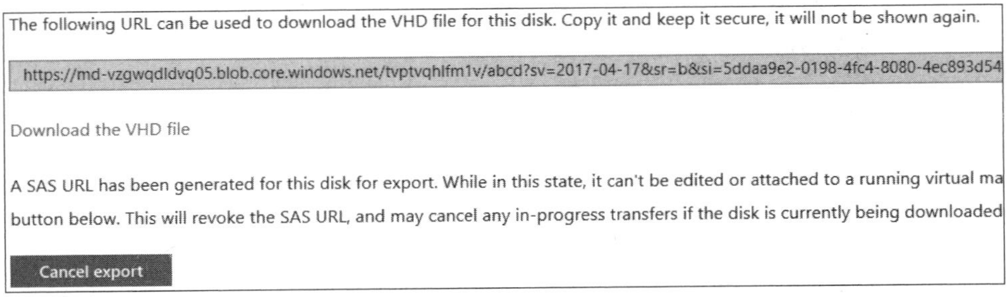

The following URL can be used to download the VHD file for this disk. Copy it and keep it secure, it will not be shown again.

https://md-vzgwqdldvq05.blob.core.windows.net/tvptvqhlfm1v/abcd?sv=2017-04-17&sr=b&si=5ddaa9e2-0198-4fc4-8080-4ec893d54

Download the VHD file

A SAS URL has been generated for this disk for export. While in this state, it can't be edited or attached to a running virtual ma button below. This will revoke the SAS URL, and may cancel any in-progress transfers if the disk is currently being downloaded

Cancel export

Rip and Replace

The previous section discussed the notion of refactoring IT solutions—essentially, rebuilding an IT solution to suit a cloud environment. That's precisely what the *rip and replace* migration strategy entails, and it's often used to migrate customized, complex IT solutions for which there is no functional equivalent service available in the cloud.

CSPs offer a wide variety of infrastructure and development solutions to facilitate rip and replace migrations, including

- Cloud-based server-less programmatic functions that don't require setting up the underlying infrastructure
- Web application deployment slots to swap out testing and production versions of a web application
- Message queues to allow software components to communicate even if they are not running at the same time
- Integration with software developer tools such as Microsoft Visual Studio
- Templates to quickly deploy load-balanced app-testing environments

EXERCISE 3-1

Run an On-Premises Cloud Migration Assessment for Microsoft SQL Server

In this exercise, you will download, install, and run the Microsoft Data Migration Assistant. This exercise relies on having an on-premises Microsoft SQL Server reachable over the network.

1. Download the free Microsoft Data Migration Assistant tool from https://www .microsoft.com/en-us/download/details.aspx?id=53595.
2. Run the MSI installer and accept all installation defaults. On the last installation screen, shown in Figure 3-4, check the Launch Microsoft Data Migration Assistant check box and click Finish.
3. In the left-hand navigation pane of the Data Migration Assistant, click the + sign to create a new migration assessment (see Figure 3-5).
4. With the Assessment radio button selected (the default), name the project **HfxProj1**.

FIGURE 3-4   Launch the Microsoft Data Migration Assistant after installation

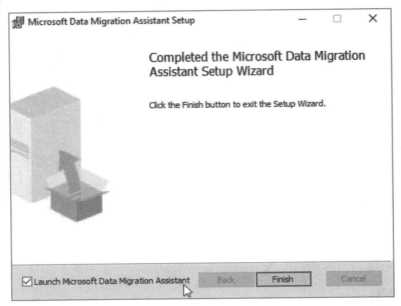

FIGURE 3-5   Create a new assessment or migration

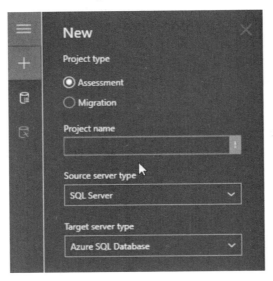

5. Ensure that the Source Server Type field is set to SQL Server and the Target Server Type field is set to Azure SQL Database, and then click Create and click Next. (Note that after the assessment indicates success, you could come back here and choose the Migration radio button to actually perform a SQL Server data migration.)

6. Specify the name of your on-premises SQL Server and the appropriate authentication type. If somebody else set up the SQL Server, get this information from that person.

7. Click Connect and select one or more databases to run the assessment against. Click Add.

8. Click the Start Assessment button in the bottom right of the screen.

9. After the assessment concludes, review the results to determine if the on-premises SQL database can be easily migrated to Azure.

INSIDE THE EXAM

Databases

Although not listed in the official exam objectives, the CompTIA Cloud Essentials+ CLO-002 exam expects you to be familiar with basic database terminology.

Most CSPs support the managed deployment of SQL databases such as MySQL, Oracle SQL Database, and Microsoft SQL Server. Remember, managed services take care of the underlying virtual machines and storage for you. This is often referred to as Database as a Service (DBaaS).

Most CSPs also support a variety of NoSQL database types. Unlike SQL, NoSQL does not use a rigid database schema, or blueprint, of exactly what type of data can be stored.

CERTIFICATION SUMMARY

This chapter discussed factors to consider when planning the adoption of cloud computing services.

You have been exposed to the importance of ensuring that CSP service offerings address business needs. A business gap analysis assesses the current state of a business process and the desired state. A technical gap analysis identifies the current technical configuration of a current solution compared to the desired configuration to efficiently support business processes. If a feasibility study determines that a proposed cloud solution can realistically succeed in meeting business needs, then further detailed testing is done on a small scale via pilot programs, which test exactly how feasibile proposed cloud solutions are.

You learned how planning the use of cloud services includes determining how deployed cloud solutions will be monitored to ensure the best performance and security possible. Alerts can be configured so that notifications of detected anomalies are sent to cloud administrators.

You also learned about sensitive individual data and data privacy in the cloud and how related laws and regulations can influence the use and configuration of cloud services. You learned that personally identifiable information (PII) refers to any individual or combination of details that can uniquely identify an individual, such as street address or Social Security number. Protected health information (PHI) is similar to PII but differs in that the details are medically related.

You have been exposed to data privacy standards such as the European Union's General Data Protection Regulation (GDPR), the American Health Insurance Portability and Accountability Act (HIPAA), and the international Payment Card Industry Data Security Standard (PCI DSS).

Finally, you learned about cloud migration strategies, including lift and shift versus rip and replace. You also learned about migrating virtual machines to physical nodes (V2P) and migrating physical nodes to virtual machines (P2V).

TWO-MINUTE DRILL

Cloud Feasibility

❏ A cloud feasibility study determines whether or not cloud computing can address business needs.

❏ Cloud pilot programs implement proposed cloud solutions on a small scale; results must be analyzed to determine success or failure before deploying on a larger scale.

Solving Business Problems with the Cloud

❏ Current and future computing needs must be accounted for in the cloud.

❏ Right-sizing uses cloud resources efficiently while reducing costs.

❏ Scaling in refers to the removal of virtual machines supporting an application, normally due to reduced application requests.

❏ Mapping computing needs to cloud services requires a thorough understanding of CSP service offerings.

❏ Organizations in certain industries and some government agencies might be bound by data privacy standards, laws, and regulations such as GDPR, HIPAA, or PCI DSS.

❏ Data sovereignty refers to keeping sensitive data within national boundaries to control jurisdictional rule of law related to data.

❏ Personally identifiable information (PII) is any combination of sensitive data that can be traced back to an individual.

❏ Protected health information (PHI) is any combination of medically related data that can be traced back to an individual.

Cloud Migration Strategies

❏ Lift and shift cloud migrations involve moving IT systems and data from on premises to the cloud with little or no changes.

❏ Commercial off-the-shelf (COTS) solutions lend themselves to the lift and shift strategy.

❏ Rip and replace cloud migrations involve refactoring or redesigning IT solutions to suit the cloud environment.

❏ You can migrate physical nodes to virtual machines using a physical to virtual (P2V) migration.

❏ You can migrate virtual machines to physical nodes using a virtual to physical (V2P) migration.

SELF TEST

The following questions will help you measure your understanding of the material presented in this chapter. As indicated, some questions may have more than one correct answer, so be sure to read all the answer choices carefully.

Cloud Feasibility

1. You need to perform a general analysis to determine if cloud computing will address business needs. What should you perform?
   A. Pilot program
   B. Feasibility study
   C. Phased cloud migration
   D. Disaster recovery planning

2. Which term best relates to analyzing test results to identify shortfalls where cloud solutions might not address specific computing requirements?
   A. Pilot program
   B. Feasibility study
   C. Disaster recovery planning
   D. Gap analysis

3. You would like to automate the deployment of a cloud-based software testing environment. What should you use? (Choose two.)
   A. Command-line scripting
   B. Gap analysis
   C. GUI deployment tools
   D. Templates

4. Which activity determines whether an implemented cloud solution will address business requirements?
   A. Pilot program
   B. Feasibility study
   C. Gap analysis
   D. Cloud migration

Solving Business Problems with the Cloud

5. What makes the use of application containers more desirable to developers than virtual machines?
   A. Quicker startup time
   B. Better security
   C. More network options
   D. Support for MFA

6. When scaling in for a cloud-based web application, what are you doing?
   A. Decreasing the compute power
   B. Increasing the compute power
   C. Removing virtual machine instances
   D. Adding virtual machine instances

7. You need a dedicated network circuit to link your on-premises network to the cloud. Which of the following options provide this capability? (Choose two.)
   A. Microsoft Azure ExpressRoute
   B. AWS DirectConnect
   C. Microsoft Azure Virtual Network Gateway
   D. AWS Snowball

8. Which of the following is most closely related to sensitive medical information?
   A. PHI
   B. PII
   C. COTS
   D. SLA

9. Which data privacy standard is a legislative act of the European Union?
   A. HIPAA
   B. PCI DSS
   C. GDPR
   D. COTS

10. Your manager instructs you to deploy cloud-stored data only within Canada. Which term best describes this scenario?
    A. Disaster recovery planning
    B. Load balancing
    C. Service level agreement
    D. Data sovereignty

Cloud Migration Strategies

11. What is the first phase of a cloud migration?
    A. Migrate data to the cloud
    B. Perform an on-premises cloud readiness assessment
    C. Synchronize on-premises and cloud data
    D. Decommission on-premises IT systems

12. Which cloud migration strategy is best suited for commercial off-the-shelf software?
    A. Rip and replace
    B. On-premises assessment
    C. Lift and shift
    D. Rip and shift

13. What is another term commonly used to describe the rip and replace migration strategy?
    A. Refactoring
    B. Migrating
    C. Replication
    D. Reproducing

14. Which AWS service is designed to allow physical storage appliances to transfer large volumes of on-premises data to the cloud?
    A. AWS Direct Connect
    B. AWS Snowball
    C. Amazon S3
    D. Amazon EC2

15. Which type of migration converts a physical server to a virtual machine?
    A. V2V
    B. V2P
    C. P2P
    D. P2V

SELF TEST ANSWERS

Cloud Feasibility

1. ☑ **B.** A feasibility analysis is the first type of analysis to determine, in general terms, whether or not a cloud solution is realistic and practical.
    ☒ **A, C,** and **D** are incorrect. Pilot programs are focused on whether an implemented solution solves business problems on a small scale and can also identify shortcomings. A phased cloud migration uses a structured approach to assess on-premises cloud readiness before migrating IT systems and data. Disaster recovery planning in the context of cloud computing normally refers to replicating data to various geographical locations.

2. ☑ **D.** A gap analysis identifies shortcomings between a requirement and a proposed solution.
    ☒ **A, B,** and **C** are incorrect. Pilot programs are focused on *how* a solution solves business problems and can also identify shortcomings. A feasibility study is the first type of analysis to determine, in general terms, whether or not a cloud solution is realistic and practical. Disaster recovery in the cloud normally refers to running additional systems and replicating storage to alternative geographical locations.

3. ☑ **A** and **D.** Command-line scripting using tools such as Microsoft PowerShell can be used to automate cloud resource deployment and management, as can templates. Both options remove the need for cloud technicians to manually deploy cloud resources.

    ☒ **B** and **C** are incorrect. A gap analysis identifies shortcomings between a requirement and a proposed solution. GUI deployment tools do not lend themselves to automation since they require user interaction.

4.   ☑ **A.** Pilot programs are focused on whether an implemented solution solves business problems and can also identify shortcomings.

    ☒ **B, C,** and **D** are incorrect. A feasibility study is the first type of analysis to determine, in general terms, whether or not a solution is realistic and practical. A gap analysis identifies shortcomings between a requirement and a proposed solution. Cloud migrations are actions that take place after ensuring cloud solutions will address business requirements.

Solving Business Problems with the Cloud

5.   ☑ **A.** Application containers use the underlying operating system that is already running, whereas a VM contains an entire OS that must be started. Starting a container means starting application software only and not the OS.

    ☒ **B, C,** and **D** are incorrect. Application containers do not provide more security or options than virtual machines do. Multifactor authentication (MFA) is not an application container feature.

6.   ☑ **C.** With horizontal scaling, scaling in means removing virtual machine instances in response to a decline in application requests.

    ☒ **A, B,** and **D** are incorrect. Vertical scaling encompasses increasing and decreasing virtual machine compute power. Adding virtual machines is referred to as *scaling out*.

7.   ☑ **A** and **B.** Microsoft Azure ExpressRoute and AWS Direct Connect are cloud service offerings that allow customers to link their on-premises networks to the cloud using a dedicated private network circuit that does not traverse the Internet.

    ☒ **C** and **D** are incorrect. The Microsoft Azure Virtual Network Gateway can be used to link Microsoft Azure ExpressRoute circuits or standard site-to-site IPSec VPN devices together. AWS Snowball is a large-scale data transfer service that can be used when network transmission is not feasible.

8.   ☑ **A.** Protected health information (PHI) is medically sensitive private information.

    ☒ **B, C,** and **D** are incorrect. Personally identifiable information (PII) is any combination of personal data that can be traced back to an individual. Commercial off-the-shelf (COTS) software refers to standard software solutions available to anybody. Service level agreements (SLAs) are contracts between cloud customers and CSPs that detail items such as expected service uptime.

9.   ☑ **C.** The General Data Protection Regulation (GDPR) is a data privacy legislative act of the European Union.

    ☒ **A, B,** and **D** are incorrect. The Health Insurance Portability and Accountability Act is a U.S. data privacy act related to medical information. Payment Card Industry Data Security Standard (PCI DSS) is a security framework designed to harden the use of cardholder data. Commercial off-the-shelf (COTS) software refers to standard software solutions available to anybody.

10. ☑ **D.** Data sovereignty refers to keeping data within geographical boundaries so that specific laws and regulations are applicable.

    ☒ **A, B,** and **C** are incorrect. Disaster recovery in the cloud normally refers to running additional systems and replicating storage to alternative geographical locations. Load balancing is used to funnel incoming client app requests to the load balancer, which then redirects the request to the least-busy back-end VM that supports the app. Service level agreements (SLAs) are contracts between cloud customers and CSPs detailing items such as expected service uptime.

Cloud Migration Strategies

11. ☑ **B.** When performing a cloud migration, the first task is to conduct an on-premises cloud readiness assessment.

    ☒ **A, C,** and **D** are incorrect. Data migration, synchronization, and the decommissioning of on-premises systems should take place after having a performance and on-premises assessment.

12. ☑ **C.** A lift and shift migration essentially moves IT solutions to the cloud with little to no modification, which makes it the best strategy for migrating COTS software because it doesn't require refactoring.

    ☒ **A, B,** and **D** are incorrect. Rip and replace migrations require refactoring an IT solution so that it will work in the cloud, and COTS software doesn't require refactoring. When performing a cloud migration, the first task is to conduct an on-premises cloud readiness assessment. Rip and shift is not a valid cloud migration strategy.

13. ☑ **A.** Rip and replace migrations require refactoring an IT solution so that it will work in the cloud.

    ☒ **B, C,** and **D** are incorrect. These terms do not describe rip and replace migrations.

14. ☑ **B.** AWS Snowball is a large-scale data transfer service that can be used when network transmission is not feasible.

    ☒ **A, C,** and **D** are incorrect. AWS Direct Connect is a cloud service offering that allows customers to link their on-premises networks to the cloud using a dedicated private network circuit that does not traverse the Internet. Amazon S3 is a cloud storage solution. Amazon EC2 is a cloud-based virtual machine solution.

15. ☑ **D.** Physical to virtual (P2V) refers to the process of using a software agent installed on a physical host to convert it to a virtual machine.

    ☒ **A, B,** and **C** are incorrect. Virtual to virtual (V2V) converts a virtual machine from one virtualization format to another. Virtual to physical (V2P) converts a virtual machine to a physical server. Peer to peer (P2P), in a networking context, refers to a network where each device can act as both a client and a server.

Chapter 4

Compliance and the Cloud

This chapter focuses on why organizations need to evaluate how well potential cloud service providers (CSPs) comply with laws, regulations, and security standards. This factor can have enormous influence on the selection of a CSP and the use of specific cloud services.

We start by discussing how laws and regulations are similar yet different and why CSP and cloud customer compliance with laws, regulations, and security standards is important. Next, we focus on the meaning of common security standards that apply to specific industries and government agencies. Finally, we address how to determine whether offered CSP solutions are compliant with laws and regulations relevant to the cloud customer.

CERTIFICATION OBJECTIVE 4.01

Laws, Regulations, and Security Standards

The adoption of cloud computing is a form of outsourcing; you, the cloud customer, depend on IT services running on cloud service provider equipment in a data center at some undisclosed location. But as an organization, how can you trust that the CSP has done its due diligence in protecting sensitive IT systems and data in the cloud?

That's where proof of CSP adherence to laws and regulations such as HIPAA (protection of sensitive patient health information in the United States) comes in. The physical location of IT systems and data can be crucial—data collected, stored, and used in a foreign country normally falls under acts of legislation of that country (data sovereignty), and that could prove problematic in some cases. Some industry-based security standards, such as the Payment Card Industry Data Security Standard (PCI DSS), apply to cardholder data regardless of local laws and regulations.

Legal and Regulatory Compliance

Laws and regulations are not quite the same thing. Laws are created by government bodies, whereas regulations focus on the implementation details as to how laws are enforced. Several factors determine whether an organization is subject to specific laws and regulations applicable to cloud computing:

- Type of industry
- Physical location of the organization
- Citizenship of clients
- Location of physical compute equipment
- Location of transmitted and stored data

Both the breaking of laws and a lack of regulatory compliance can in some cases result in fines or imprisonment, or both. All of the listed items must be considered to ensure legal and regulatory compliance when using cloud computing. One way to do this is to refer to any compliance details listed on a CSP's website, such as the AWS Compliance Programs web page shown in Figure 4-1.

CSPs do not publicly disclose the specific addresses of their data centers, although maps providing addresses have been made available, such as through WikiLeaks. CSP employees and contractors need to know where to show up for work, but that's about it. The fewer people who know where IT systems and data are physically housed, the more secure those items are.

While CSP compliance with security standards is important, as discussed, bear in mind that the bad guys always use good things in bad ways. For example, providing massive compute power in the cloud at a minimal cost is one way that malicious users can attack cryptographic security measures that were once considered nearly impenetrable. Cloud service providers can monitor the frequent deployment and use of high-powered compute resources in an attempt to detect the criminal use of cloud computing environments, even when not required by laws or regulations.

FIGURE 4-1   Amazon Web Services (AWS) Compliance Programs web page

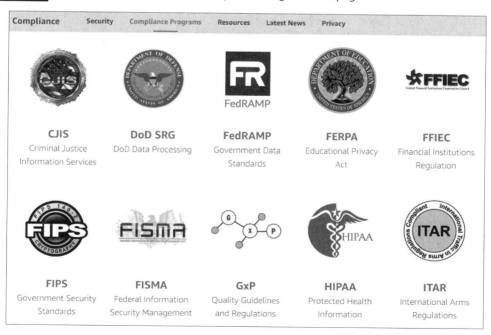

CERTIFICATION OBJECTIVE 4.02

Cloud Service Provider Compliance

For many organizations, the selection of a CSP hinges on two things:

■ The CSP's cloud services meet business computing requirements.
■ The CSP is in compliance with security and auditing standards relevant to the organization.

The following discussion covers only a handful of security standards and regulations that might be applicable during CSP selection.

NIST SP 800-53

In the United States, the National Institute of Standards and Technology (NIST) has published an extensive series of Special Publications (SPs) covering computer security, one of which is SP 800-53, "Security and Privacy Controls for Federal Information Systems and Organizations." Section 2.5 of this document ("External Service Providers") discusses how organizations using cloud computing services share the security responsibility with the CSP. CSPs must be able to demonstrate their compliance with security standards through independent audits and security accreditations. The chain of trust becomes more complex when CSPs themselves depend on other external entities such as IT consultants and hardware and software vendors.

There will always be risks associated with cloud computing. An organization's risk appetite determines if and how cloud computing services are used. A security control mitigates a threat against an asset. An example of this is cloud customers using their own encryption keys and Public Key Infrastructure (PKI) certificates to protect data in transit and data at rest, as opposed to using CSP-generated encryption keys and PKI certificates. Both are valid technical solutions, but laws or regulations might require keys and certificates to remain under the control of the data owner. Figure 4-2 shows an example of the use of customer-managed encryption keys for cloud storage.

ISO/IEC 27017:2015

The International Standards Organization (ISO) and International Electrotechnical Commission (IEC) standard 27017:2015 is titled "Information Technology – Security Techniques – Code of Practice for Information Security Controls Based on ISO/IEC 27002 for Cloud Services." That's a long title, but why is it relevant?

FIGURE 4-2   Microsoft Azure customer-managed key configuration for a storage account

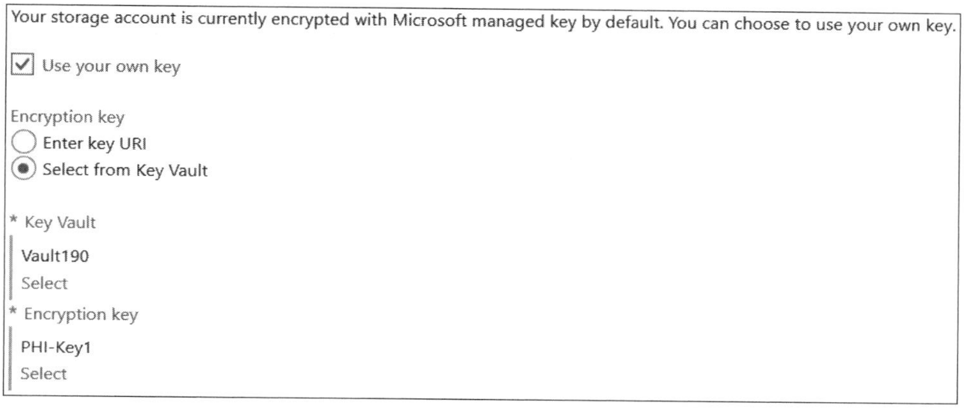

Your storage account is currently encrypted with Microsoft managed key by default. You can choose to use your own key.

☑ Use your own key

Encryption key
◯ Enter key URI
◉ Select from Key Vault

* Key Vault

Vault190
Select

* Encryption key

PHI-Key1
Select

ISO/IEC 27017:2015 is relevant because it focuses on the use of effective security controls to mitigate cloud computing risk. Your chosen CSP should be certified by an ISO certifying agent for the proper use of CSP security controls. But remember the notion of shared responsibility? You, as the cloud customer, also bear some responsibility for security. Just because your organization uses an ISO-certified CSP, it doesn't mean by extension that your organization is ISO certified. Figure 4-3 shows AWS ISO compliance details.

FedRAMP

The Federal Risk and Authorization Management Program (FedRAMP) applies primarily to U.S. federal government agencies that use, or will use, cloud computing services.

Outsourcing IT services to cloud service providers implies a level of trust and it introduces risk. FedRAMP is designed to ensure that CSPs adhere to NIST SP 800-53 security standards. When researching CSPs, government agencies can refer to the FedRAMP MarketPlace, as shown in Figure 4-4, to find FedRAMP-approved CSPs.

on the
j o b

The FedRAMP MarketPlace is not only for U.S. federal government agencies. Any organization can access this reference list to find FedRAMP-compliant CSPs. This provides assurances about the security posture of CSPs and their service offerings.

FIGURE 4-3 AWS ISO Compliance web page

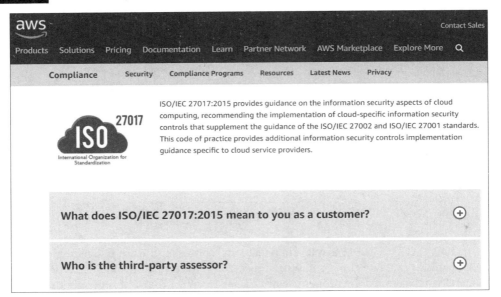

FIGURE 4-4 FedRAMP MarketPlace web page

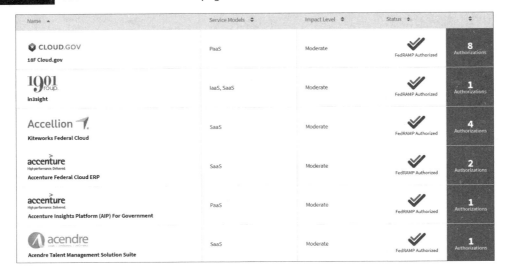

Sarbanes-Oxley Act

Financial scandals related to companies such as WorldCom and Enron received extensive media coverage in the early 2000s. These types of questionable accounting practices and falsification of financial documents led to the creation of the Sarbanes-Oxley (SOX) Act in 2002.

ⓦatch **Regulatory compliance allows for a wide variety of technical solutions. You might see some exam questions that ask for the *best* solution for compliance, where there is not a perfect solution. Read the question text carefully!**

SOX requires public organizations to follow strict rules for accounting and financial document reporting. What does this have to do with the cloud? Organizations affected by SOX who use cloud services must use a CSP that adheres to the Statement on Standards for Attestation Engagements (SSAE) No. 16. SSAE No. 16 is an auditing standard that deals with reporting on security controls within service organizations such as CSPs and their data centers.

CERTIFICATION OBJECTIVE 4.03

Business Requirements and Cloud Solutions

Aside from looking at a CSP's compliance with laws and regulations, other factors such as matching cloud services with IT functional requirements also influence how cloud services will be used. If specific details about a CSP are unavailable on the Web, such as how customer data is permanently deleted, you should contact the CSP to get this information.

Data Artifacts

Deleted data, even from on-premises disks, is often retrievable using freely available tools, especially if the data was deleted using standard operating system functions. For compliance reasons, your organization might need to ensure that sensitive data is permanently removed.

Media sanitization is the process of rendering data so that it is irretrievable using a reasonable amount of effort and time. It's important to think beyond literal storage devices; what about the data or app configuration settings on a smartphone that could allow access to an IT system containing sensitive data? Media sanitization also applies to device storage for devices that connect to the cloud.

FIGURE 4-5 Disk Scrubber tool

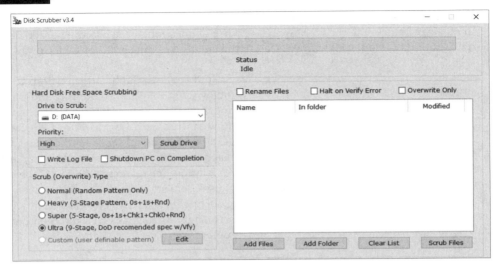

Software Data Removal

Using only an operating system to delete files, format disks, or even repartition disks is not sufficient to ensure that data cannot be recovered. There are plenty of tools that can recover deleted partitions with relative ease, such as EaseUS Partition Master and Acronis Disk Director. If you delete files within a cloud virtual machine using standard operating system methods, malicious users who compromise that virtual machine could potentially retrieve that deleted data.

Sanitizing storage media essentially means overwriting data with random new data. Multiple passes of random data writes reduces the likelihood of data retrieval. Figure 4-5 shows an example of scrub (overwrite) types.

Storage Media Destruction

One way to make sure sensitive data cannot be retrieved is to physically destroy the media or data, whether it is a hard disk or backup tapes. There are a few ways in which this can be done:

- Drill holes into storage media such as hard disk platters
- Physically shred storage media
- Degaussing
  - Data is removed when the storage media is near a strong magnetic field
  - Not applicable to optical storage media or solid state drives (SSDs)

FIGURE 4-6   NSA-approved electromagnetic degausser equipment list

Product Listings
Electromagnetic Degausser Equipment

Manufacturer / Distributor	Model	Tape (Oe)	Disk (Oe)
Secure IT Engineered Solutions 5 Walkup Drive, Westboro, MA 01581 800.225.9293 *www.secure-it.us* ATTN: Michael Paciello	MMD-1000HS	3000	L-5000, P-5000
Security Engineered Machinery, Inc. 5 Walkup Drive, Westboro, MA 01581 800.225.9293 *www.semshred.com* ATTN: Terry Creek, VP Federal Sales	EMP 1000-HS	3000	L-5000, P-5000
VS and Associates 3160 Texas Hill Rd, Placerville, CA 95667 530.626.6924 ATTN: Linda Schiro *Linda.schiro@vssecurityproducts.com*	SDD Master	2800	L-5000, P-5000
Whitaker Brothers Business Machines, Inc. 3 Taft Court, Rockville, MD 20850 800.243.9226 / 301.354.3000 *www.whitakerbrothers.com* ATTN: Lauren Rossi *lrossi@whitakerbrothers.com*	Datastroyer 105 Hard Drive Degausser	2800	L-5000, P-5000

Depending on your organization, the method of storage media destruction might need to comply with specific rules. CSPs can also provide details as to how they dispose of their physical storage media. The U.S. National Security Agency (NSA) has published a list of approved storage media degaussing tools, "Degausser Evaluated Products List," an excerpt of which is shown in Figure 4-6.

Cloud Service Provider Security Control Implementation

Evaluating which CSP is the best fit for an organization or government agency can be facilitated by creating a questionnaire that can be used for internal evaluation purposes or, in some cases, when negotiating with a CSP.

In the case of Amazon Web Services, the AWS Artifact tool provides AWS compliance information, including access to security reports. These reports can provide valuable details that help with creating a CSP security compliance document, shown in in Table 4-1.

TABLE 4-1   Sample CSP Security Compliance Document

Control Group	Control Detail	CSP Implementation
Application Development	Code analysis	Software development life cycle (SDLC)
		Testing types such as regression testing
	Isolated test environment	Cloud virtual network segregation
Regulatory Compliance	Supply chain security	Ensure hardware and software providers adhere to strict security standards
		Thorough data center employee background checks
Physical Security	Data center security	Lighting
		Fencing
		Security guards
		Video surveillance
		Facility access logs
		Man-trap doors
		Locked equipment racks
Network and data security	Encryption, strong tenant isolation	HTTPS
		Default encryption of cloud storage using CSP-managed keys
		Optional customer-managed encryption keys
		Customer ability to select geographical locations of cloud resources
Auditing	Periodic third-party security compliance audits	PCI DSS
		HIPAA
		GDPR
		Vulnerability assessments (considered passive since only identifies vulnerabilities)
		Penetration testing (considered intrusive since discovered weaknesses can be exploited)

EXERCISE 4-1

Review Amazon Web Services Regulatory Compliance

In this exercise, you will use the AWS Compliance Center to get details regarding the use of AWS cloud computing services for financial institutions.

1. Using a web browser, navigate to https://www.atlas.aws.
2. Click the Get Started button.
3. Select your country or region from the drop-down list or make a selection on the map.
4. Click the Download PDF button and save the file to your device.
5. Open the downloaded PDF to read about AWS compliance in your region for financial institutions, as shown in Figure 4-7.

FIGURE 4-7 AWS Canadian country profile for financial institution cloud usage

COUNTRY PROFILE

Canada

⬛ Download PDF

▪ Cloud Use Permitted

This page provides AWS financial institution customers with information about the legal and regulatory requirements in Canada that may apply to their use of AWS services.

Regulations	Resources	Compliance Programs
Can financial institutions use AWS?		⌄
Who is the financial regulator?		⌄
What regulations apply to financial institutions using AWS?		⌄
Key considerations for financial institutions using AWS		⌄
Key data privacy and protection considerations for financial institutions using AWS		⌄

INSIDE THE EXAM

Security Standards

While CompTIA does not expect you to be a legal expert or a regulatory analyst for the CLO-002 exam, you should be aware of a few common standards such as PCI DSS, HIPAA, GDPR, SOX, FedRAMP, and ISO/IEC 27017:2015. You don't need to memorize the details of each of these standards, but you should have the ability to determine if specific CSP accreditations meet organizational requirements for legal and regulatory compliance.

CERTIFICATION SUMMARY

This chapter focused on ensuring that your organization remains compliant with related laws and regulations when using cloud services. When depending on a CSP, an organization should perform due diligence to ensure that the CSP adheres to relevant laws, regulations, and security standards.

The discussion began with a review of how laws and regulations such as HIPAA and PCI DSS can apply to CSPs and cloud customers. An example is where sensitive data is collected, stored, and used. Next, we discussed how laws define general rules, but regulations focus on the details, including how the law is implemented and enforced.

Next, security standards frameworks such as NIST SP 800-53 and FedRAMP were discussed in the context of cloud computing, both from the CSP and cloud customer perspectives.

Finally, you learned about using questionnaires to determine if a CSP adequately meets business needs, including legal and regulatory compliance.

 TWO-MINUTE DRILL

Laws, Regulations, and Security Standards

❏ Laws are general guidelines for controlling behavior.
❏ In the business world, regulations provide the implementation and enforcement details for laws.

❑ The physical location of servers and data can determine which laws are applicable.

❑ HIPAA is an American law protecting sensitive patient medical information.

❑ PCI DSS is not a law, but rather an industry-based security standard designed to protect cardholder data.

Cloud Service Provider Compliance

❑ NIST SP 800-53 details how CSPs must demonstrate security standards compliance through independent assessments.

❑ ISO/IEC 27017:2015 focuses on how security controls reduce the risks associated with cloud computing.

❑ FedRAMP provides security guidelines for U.S. government agency use of cloud computing.

❑ The Sarbanes-Oxley Act imposes accounting and financial reporting requirements for publicly traded U.S. companies, the purpose of which is to mitigate financial reporting falsehoods to protect the public, including investors.

Business Requirements and Cloud Solutions

❑ Media sanitization techniques are designed to prevent the retrieval of sensitive data from storage media.

❑ Storage media physical destruction techniques include drilling, shredding, and magnetic degaussing.

❑ Questionnaires are useful in determining whether CSPs meet specific security and regulatory standards that can factor into CSP selection.

SELF TEST

The following questions will help you measure your understanding of the material presented in this chapter. As indicated, some questions may have more than one correct answer, so be sure to read all the answer choices carefully.

Laws, Regulations, and Security Standards

1. Which of the following statements regarding laws and regulations is accurate?
   A. Regulations provide implementation and enforcement details.
   B. Laws provide implementation and enforcement details.
   C. Breaking laws can result in fines; this is not true for a lack of regulatory compliance.
   D. A lack of regulatory compliance can result in fines, but not imprisonment.

2. Which term refers to the applicable laws based on the location of where data is collected, stored, and used?
   A. Special Publication
   B. Security control
   C. Data sovereignty
   D. PKI

3. You are evaluating CSPs because your organization has decided to adopt cloud computing for some of its IT service needs. What is the quickest way to determine which security standards the CSP is compliant with?
   A. Send an e-mail message to the CSP inquiring about compliance.
   B. Call the CSP to inquire about compliance.
   C. View government legislative bill details.
   D. View the CSP's compliance web page.

4. Which factor has the most influence on which regulations apply to your organization?
   A. Operating system used for cloud virtual machines
   B. Type of industry
   C. Cloud storage encryption strength
   D. Type of cloud media sanitization in use

5. You want to know the specific physical addresses of a CSP's data centers. What should you do?
   A. Run a DNS domain name lookup for the CSP domain suffix.
   B. Send an information request to the CSP.
   C. Review the CSP service level agreement.
   D. Nothing. CSPs do not voluntarily disclose data center physical addresses.

Cloud Service Provider Compliance

6. Which U.S. federal government security standard is most closely related to cloud security?
   A. HIPAA
   B. ISO/IEC 27017:2015
   C. FedRAMP
   D. Sarbanes-Oxley Act

7. Which U.S. regulation is designed to mitigate financial document reporting fraud?
   A. HIPAA
   B. ISO/IEC 27017:2015
   C. FedRAMP
   D. Sarbanes-Oxley Act

8. Why is a CSP's security standards compliance important? (Choose two.)
   A. It provides a level of assurance to cloud customers that the CSP has taken effective steps to mitigate risk.
   B. A CSP's security standards compliance means its cloud customers are also compliant.
   C. It proves that the CSP cannot be hacked.
   D. The CSP security posture is accredited by third parties.

9. Which risk is the most prevalent when adopting cloud computing?
   A. The use of deprecated encryption algorithms
   B. Cloud tenant centralized data storage
   C. Lack of cloud tenant isolation
   D. Trust placed in outsourcing

10. What kind of standard is SSAE No. 16?
    A. Auditing
    B. Encryption
    C. Risk management
    D. Authentication

Business Requirements and Cloud Solutions

11. Which statements regarding a CSP's legal and regulatory compliance are correct? (Choose two.)
    A. All security responsibilities fall upon the CSP.
    B. A CSP's service level agreements list independent third-party auditors.
    C. A CSP provides documentation about its security standards compliance.
    D. Cloud customers also bear some responsibility in securing their use of cloud computing.

12. You are reviewing a CSP's media destruction procedures. Your organization requires that hard disk data is removed magnetically. Which technique does this?
    A. Drilling
    B. Shredding
    C. Hammering
    D. Degaussing

13. Compared to vulnerability assessments, which word is most closely associated with penetration testing?

  A. Documentation
  B. Authentication
  C. Active
  D. Passive

14. To prevent future sensitive data retrieval of cloud-replicated data, you have repartitioned a hard disk within a laptop computer. The computer was running a Windows client operating system at the time of the repartitioning. Which statement regarding this scenario is correct?

  A. A Windows server operating system should have been used.
  B. Deleted partitions are easily recovered.
  C. A Linux server operating system should have been used.
  D. The operating system cannot be running when disk partitions are removed.

15. Which type of security testing identifies weaknesses but does not attempt to exploit them?

  A. Penetration test
  B. Regression test
  C. Load test
  D. Vulnerability test

SELF TEST ANSWERS

Laws, Regulations, and Security Standards

1. ☑ **A.** Regulations are the implementation and enforcement side of laws.
☒ **B, C,** and **D** are incorrect. Laws are statements, or rules, that should not be broken, but do not provide enforcement or implementation details. Since regulations are the implementation and enforcement of laws, breaking laws or failing to comply with regulations can result in fines or imprisonment.

2. ☑ **C.** Data sovereignty is related to where sensitive data is collected, stored, and used and which laws apply to the privacy of that data.

☒ **A, B,** and **D** are incorrect. A Special Publication (SP) is a formal document published by the National Institute of Standards and Technology (NIST). Security controls are implemented to mitigate the risk related to a business asset. Public Key Infrastructure (PKI) is a hierarchy of digital certificates used to secure IT computing environments.

3. ☑ **D.** Most CSPs provide a web page that lists their security standards compliance details.
☒ **A, B,** and **C** are incorrect. Sending the CSP an e-mail or calling the CSP will most likely not be the quickest way to determine CSP compliance. Legislative bills are not specific to a CSP.

4. ☑ **B.** Regulations are normally specific to a type of industry, such as financial or medical.
☒ **A, C,** and **D** are incorrect. Operating system types, encryption strength, and media sanitization methods do not influence which regulations apply to your organization.

5. ☑ **D.** For security reasons, CSPs do not disclose physical data center addresses.
☒ **A, B,** and **C** are incorrect. DNS domain name registrant searches will not show physical data center addresses, nor will CSP information requests or reviewing SLAs.

Cloud Service Provider Compliance

6. ☑ **C.** The Federal Risk and Authorization Management Program (FedRAMP) is a U.S. government standard focused on how government agencies can securely use cloud computing.
☒ **A, B,** and **D** are incorrect. The Health Insurance Portability and Accountability Act (HIPAA) applies to medical and health insurance providers and is designed to protect sensitive medical information. ISO/IEC 27017:2015 is an international standard based on the use of effective security controls to mitigate cloud computing risk. The Sarbanes-Oxley Act is designed to mitigate fraudulent accounting practices and misleading financial document reporting.

7. ☑ **D.** The Sarbanes-Oxley Act is designed to mitigate fraudulent accounting practices and misleading financial document reporting. Organizations regulated by SOX who use cloud services must use only CSPs that adhere to SSAE No. 16.
☒ **A, B,** and **C** are incorrect. HIPAA applies to medical and health insurance providers and is designed to protect sensitive medical information. ISO/IEC 27017:2015 is an international standard based on the use of effective security controls to mitigate cloud computing risk. FedRAMP is a U.S. government standard focused on how government agencies can securely use cloud computing.

8. ☑ **A** and **D.** CSP compliance provides its cloud customers verification from reliable, independent third parties that the CSP has appropriate security controls in place.
☒ **B** and **C** are incorrect. A CSP's compliance with a specific security standard does not automatically extend to cloud customers. While security standards compliance reduces the risk of hacking, it does not completely eliminate the risk.

9. ☑ **D.** Cloud computing adoption means placing trust in the CSP that it is competent in ensuring IT systems and data are available and kept secure.

☒ **A, B,** and **C** are incorrect. CSPs normally keep up with the latest security options for their customers; doing otherwise is bad for business and exposes the CSP to liability. Cloud tenant centralized data storage itself does not present enormous risk. CSPs have strict security guidelines and third-party security audits to ensure this (most private companies cannot afford to implement this kind of security scrutiny). CSPs keep cloud tenant configurations and data isolated from one another.

10. ☑ **A.** SSAE No. 16 is an auditing standard that applies to service organizations such as CSPs. Organizations regulated by SOX who use cloud services must use only CSPs that adhere to SSAE No. 16.

☒ **B, C,** and **D** are incorrect. SSAE No. 16 is not a standard directly related to encryption, risk management, or authentication.

Business Requirements and Cloud Solutions

11. ☑ **C** and **D.** CSPs provide security standard compliance documentation, normally in the form of web pages. Just because a CSP is compliant with a security standard such as PCI DSS, that does not automatically mean its cloud customers are also compliant.

☒ **A** and **B** are incorrect. Security responsibilities fall upon the CSP and the cloud customer. The degree of responsibility depends on the specific cloud service being used. Cloud SLAs do not provide details about third-party auditors.

12. ☑ **D.** Degaussing applies a strong magnetic field to magnetic storage such as hard disks and backup tapes.

☒ **A, B,** and **C** are incorrect. Drilling, shredding, and hammering do not remove data magnetically.

13. ☑ **C.** Penetration tests (pen tests) are considered active since they attempt to exploit discovered vulnerabilities.

☒ **A, B,** and **D** are incorrect. Documentation and authentication are not terms closely associated with penetration testing. Pen tests are active, not passive, as vulnerability tests are.

14. ☑ **B.** Many data recovery tools, including free ones, provide the option of recovering deleted partitions.

☒ **A, C,** and **D** are incorrect. The operating system type does not affect the success or failure of removing disk partitions. As long as the removed partition is not the OS partition, the OS can remain running in most cases.

15. ☑ **D.** Vulnerability tests identify weaknesses but do not attempt to exploit them.

☒ **A, B,** and **C** are incorrect. Regression testing is used to ensure that new changes, such as to software code, have not caused problems in unrelated areas. Load testing is used to identify the performance of a solution under a busy workload. Penetration tests (pen tests) are considered active since they attempt to exploit discovered vulnerabilities.

Part III

Cloud Infrastructure

CHAPTERS

Chapter 5

Cloud Storage Infrastructure

D ata storage continues to be a large part of cloud computing. Cloud service providers support *software-defined storage*, which means cloud customers are spared the complexities of the underlying storage infrastructure when provisioning cloud storage. This chapter introduces you to various types of storage media that can impact cloud storage performance and cost.

We will start with a discussion of cloud storage configurations, such as replication and disk performance settings, that can be enabled to address business needs. Next, we'll identify differences between SQL and NoSQL databases. Finally, we'll examine how data can be copied to geographical regions to place content near users that need it.

CERTIFICATION OBJECTIVE 5.01

Storage Media

Data stored in electronic random access memory (RAM) is referred to as being *volatile*; in other words, its retention depends on the constant flow of electricity to the computer, and it is erased when the computer is turned off. Storage media is referred to as *nonvolatile*; it does not need a constant flow of electricity to retain the data. In the cloud, both RAM and storage media are configurable. Figure 5-1 shows an example of how you can determine the amount of RAM allocated to a virtual machine and the type of storage used.

Cloud service providers are responsible for the physical storage infrastructure upon which cloud storage services are made available to customers. Physical storage comes in a variety of different drive types with varying configuration settings.

Drive Types

Hard disk drive (HDD) storage uses spinning disk platters and stores data magnetically. This type of storage media has moving parts. Solid state drives (SSDs) use flash memory instead of spinning disk platters and are considered quieter and faster than HDDs. As you might expect, choosing SSD in the cloud costs more than choosing HDDs.

FIGURE 5-1   Microsoft Azure virtual machine sizing options

VM SIZE ↑↓	OFFERING ↑↓	FAMILY ↑↓	VCPUS ↑↓	RAM (GIB) ↑↓	DATA DISKS ↑↓	MAX IOPS
B1ls	Standard	General purpose	1	0.5	2	200
B1ms	Standard	General purpose	1	2	2	800
B1s	Standard	General purpose	1	1	2	400
B2ms	Standard	General purpose	2	8	4	2400
B2s	Standard	General purpose	2	4	4	1600

IOPS

Disk throughput is measured in input/output operations per second (IOPS). Figure 5-2 shows virtual machine OS disk options where Premium SSD provides more throughput than Standard HDD. More IOPS means better disk performance, and you should consider whether to increase IOPS depending on the VM workload requirements.

Cloud service providers often arrange their vast storage arrays into dedicated storage area networks (SANs) with Redundant Array of Independent Disk (RAID) configurations to increase performance and resiliency against disk failure. There are many levels of RAID configurations. The following list includes three common RAID levels:

- **RAID 0 (disk striping)**   Uses multiple physical disks working as one (striping) to improve disk I/O, but provides no resilience to disk failure because the failure of a single disk renders the entire disk array unavailable.
- **RAID 1 (disk mirroring)**   Copies data to a secondary disk when it is written to the primary disk and can tolerate the failure of one disk since the second disk has a complete copy of data from the primary disk.
- **RAID 5 (disk striping with distributed parity)**   Improves disk I/O and can tolerate the failure of one disk since data parity information is never stored on the same disk with the data. Parity is error recovery information. This parity information is used to rebuild data that resided on a failed disk in the array.

SAN policies can be set to compress data written to the RAID array using techniques such as *data deduplication*, which reduces duplicate data blocks to single occurrences. Of course, you as the cloud customer can also enable these types of disk options within your cloud-based virtual machines. For example, you can enable compression for files and folders to reduce operating system disk space consumption within a Windows Server 2019 cloud-based virtual machine.

on the
 job

Make sure to monitor VM performance metrics over time. It's common to set VM resources such as virtual CPU and the amount of RAM high initially only to realize over time that less compute power is still sufficient, which reduces cloud computing costs.

FIGURE 5-2   Microsoft Azure virtual machine disk options

Disk options	
* OS disk type ⓘ	Premium SSD ⌃
	Standard HDD
Enable Ultra Disk compatibility (Preview) ⓘ	Standard SSD
	Premium SSD

CERTIFICATION OBJECTIVE 5.02

Cloud Storage Configuration

One great feature of cloud storage is that it offers elasticity along with rapid provisioning, otherwise called *capacity on demand*. A cloud customer can acquire additional storage capacity with the click of a mouse or by issuing a command, which is much faster and often much cheaper than having to physically acquire storage media without cloud computing. Additionally, the cloud customer's data is stored offsite, which provides further backup protection from problems like on-premises theft, floods, and fires.

Some CSPs support the notion of VM *managed disks*. This means the CSP automatically manages the configuration and scaling of the underlying storage of VM virtual hard disks. When you're working with clusters of virtual machines on a large scale, this can make your job much easier.

Depending on your storage needs, you can configure cloud storage settings for frequently versus infrequently accessed data. If availability and security are important, replication and encryption can be enabled. These types of cloud storage settings are detailed in the next sections.

File and Object Storage

File storage uses a file system to organize stored items. File systems are organized into a hierarchy, with a root folder containing subordinate folders and, ultimately, files within the folders.

In the cloud, you can configure file storage using services such as Microsoft Azure Files. Azure Files is essentially a Server Message Block (SMB) shared folder implementation in the cloud. Client devices can connect to the Azure Files shared folder as they would for an on-premises folder using standard drive mapping commands (Windows) or a mount point (Linux), although on-premises firewalls might need to be adjusted to allow SMB traffic, which normally uses TCP port 445. Figure 5-3 shows a Windows machine using the net use

FIGURE 5-3   Mapping a drive letter to a Microsoft Azure file share

```
C:\>cmdkey /add:storvs.file.core.windows.net /user:Azure\storvs /pass:KSTCF
1C+PPdJRikiab0XA==

CMDKEY: Credential added successfully.

C:\>net use P: \\storvs.file.core.windows.net\projects /persistent:Yes
The command completed successfully.
```

command to map drive letter P: to an existing Azure file share. Creating Azure file shares is accomplished using either the Azure portal GUI or command-line tools.

Object storage does not have to adhere to a filing hierarchy as a traditional file system does—in other words, object storage uses a flat storage structure that can be distributed across various platforms. Each object is given a unique identifier that is used to quickly locate the item, whereas file storage uses the directory path to locate the stored item. Accessing object storage is normally done over HTTP using the Representational State Transfer (REST) API instead of older network file access methods such as File Transfer Protocol (FTP) and Secure Shell FTP (SFTP). Block binary large objects (blobs) are used to store common office productivity types of files such as JPGs and PDFs, whereas page blobs are for random reading and writing to files such as VM hard disk files.

Hot and Cold Storage

Cloud storage settings are all about requirements. If your organization requires frequent access to cloud-stored data, you should enable hot storage, which offers higher performance to achieve quicker data access. CSPs will use different terminology for this type of storage, such as the Amazon Web Services (AWS) variations shown in Figure 5-4: *Provisioned IOPS SSD* or *Throughput Optimized HD* for hot storage as opposed to *Cold HDD*.

Using cold storage is cheaper than using hot storage, and thus cold storage should be enabled for data that will be accessed infrequently. Data retrieval is slower with cold storage, which is why cold storage costs less. For longer-term archiving, consider options such as AWS Glacier, which is even less expensive than standard cold storage. AWS Glacier data retrieval time can range from minutes to hours.

FIGURE 5-4   Hot and cold AWS disk volume types

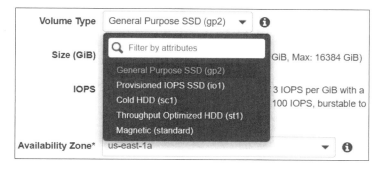

FIGURE 5-5   Microsoft Azure storage account replication options

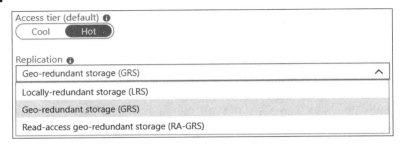

Replication and Encryption

To provide additional resiliency to failure, you can enable cloud storage replication. This is conceptually similar to storing on-premises backup tapes at an alternative location for safety, or replicating data to a different company data center. In disaster recovery terms, storage replication relates to the *recovery point objective (RPO)*, which specifies the maximum amount of tolerable data loss for the organization. Figure 5-5 shows cloud storage replication settings, including geo-redundant storage (GRS). GRS replicates cloud data to an alternative geographical region.

exam

ⓦatch   While backups are related to the RPO, they are also related to the Recovery Time Objective (RTO) which specifies the maximum tolerable amount of downtime for a service or data. The exam could emphasize how quickly data can be restored from backup (RTO), or the emphasis could be on how often backups should occur (RPO).

Legal and regulatory compliance sometimes dictates that data at rest must be protected through encryption, in addition to protection of data in transit using Hypertext Transfer Protocol Secure (HTTPS). Most CSPs support Advanced Encryption Standard (AES) 256-bit encryption, which is required by the U.S. federal government to protect sensitive information.

CSPs can provide encryption keys, but your organization might require full control of custom encryption keys. Figure 5-6 shows how cloud customers can opt to use their own encryption keys in Azure.

FIGURE 5-6   Microsoft Azure storage account customer encryption keys

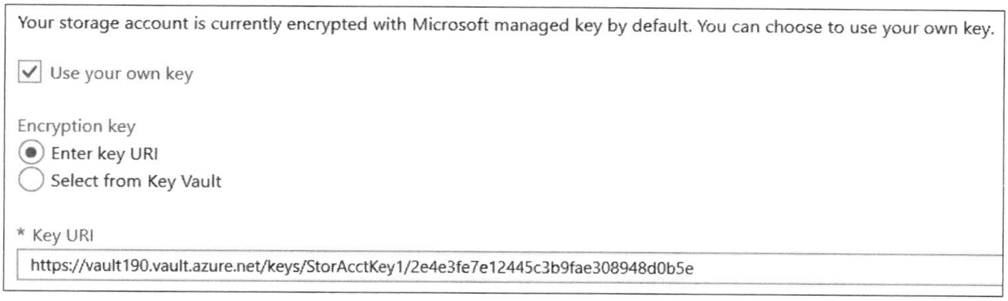

Your storage account is currently encrypted with Microsoft managed key by default. You can choose to use your own key.

☑ Use your own key

Encryption key
◉ Enter key URI
◯ Select from Key Vault

* Key URI
https://vault190.vault.azure.net/keys/StorAcctKey1/2e4e3fe7e12445c3b9fae308948d0b5e

CERTIFICATION OBJECTIVE 5.03

Databases in the Cloud

There are a few methods through which cloud databases can be established:

- Migrated from on premises
- Manually installed and configured within cloud virtual machines
- Deployed as a managed cloud service

Database migration is used to copy on-premises database objects and data into the cloud. Before migrating on-premises databases, you should conduct an on-premises assessment to provide assurances of cloud readiness. One tool for conducting this type of assessment is the Microsoft Data Migration Assistant, shown in Figure 5-7. (Refer to Exercise 3-1 for instructions on downloading, installing, and running the Microsoft Data Migration Assistant.)

The option to manually install and configure a cloud database is in stark contrast to using a managed Database as a Service (DBaaS) solution. A DBaaS solution takes care of all the underlying complexities of managing the database and allows cloud users to focus on using the database itself. Manually installing and configuring a cloud database solution involves provisioning virtual machines and installing database software, as well as updating operating system and database software.

FIGURE 5-7   Microsoft Azure Data Migration Assistant

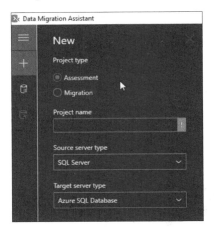

Database Types

One aspect of cloud data planning is determining whether to use a Structured Query Language (SQL) database or a NoSQL type of database; this decision depends on what will be stored in the database and how it will be used, as summarized in Table 5-1.

TABLE 5-1   Comparison of SQL and NoSQL Databases

SQL	NoSQL
Structured schema (blueprint) of how data will be stored.	Semistructured or no schema.
Related data is stored in separate tables and linked via a common field.	Each stored row can contain completely different types of data.
Microsoft SQL Server is commonly accessed over TCP port 1433.	NoSQL databases such as MongoDB are commonly accessed over TCP port 27017.
Not intrinsically designed to be as scalable as NoSQL databases.	Designed for very large datasets and horizontal scaling.
Useful for storing predictable data types such as customer transaction records.	Useful for storing large amounts of unstructured data such as from social media feeds.

FIGURE 5-8   Microsoft Azure SQL Database DTUs

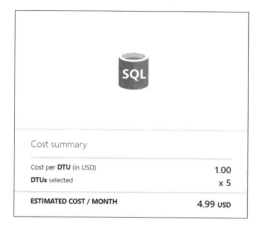

The amount of compute horsepower for underlying virtual machines supporting a database is dependent on the usual suspects:

- Disk IOPS
- Amount of RAM
- Number of vCPUs
- Number of disks

Some cloud service providers such as Microsoft Azure lump these items together into Database Transaction Units (DTUs), as shown in Figure 5-8. Virtual machine disks are referred to as *block storage*. Virtual machine disks can be attached and detached from cloud virtual machines, much like you would physically attach or detach physical disks to and from physical servers.

CERTIFICATION OBJECTIVE 5.04

Content Delivery Networks

Because CSPs have servers placed around the globe, cloud customers should be thinking about how this can serve their interests. Specifically, placing content geographically near the user base that will be accessing that content, such as for large media files stored on a website, could be beneficial to a cloud customer. This is where a content delivery network (CDN) comes in.

CDNs allow data to be copied (*cached*) to various geographical regions to reduce network latency for users accessing that content. You can configure wildcards to cache only specific types of media that tend to have large file sizes, so to cache only .AVI video files, for example, you could specify *.AVI.

But is this copying a one-time thing? What if the source content changes? One CDN configuration item is the Time To Live (TTL) value. This is normally represented in seconds and determines how long before a cached CDN item is checked against the source item to detect changes. User requests for content are satisfied from data in the CDN cache, or if it hasn't yet been cached, the content is fetched from the origin server. Once the TTL for CDN cached content expires, the content is refreshed from the origin server. For data that is rarely modified (static data) such as product lists, the TTL should be set in accordance with how often changes are made to the data. For dynamic data that changes often, a shorter TTL should be configured.

Directing user requests to the nearest CDN endpoint is automatic. References to CDN cached objects, such as for a link to a file on a website, use the CDN Domain Name System (DNS) domain name. If you want to use your own custom DNS domain names, you can create a DNS CNAME, or alias record, that points to the CSP-assigned CDN name.

e x a m
ⓦa t c h   **The exam will often test your ability to apply cloud solutions such as CDNs to business needs. Be prepared for storage solutions that seem similar yet serve different needs. For example, both CDNs and geo-redundant replication copy data to alternative geographical locations.**

Replicated CDN data is only periodically refreshed based on the TTL and is used to improve user access time to content. Geo-redundant storage replication provides data high availability; data is replicated when it is modified and not based on a TTL value.

EXERCISE 5-1

Create a Microsoft Azure Storage Account

In this exercise, you will create a Microsoft Azure cloud storage account. This exercise depends on having successfully completed Exercise 1-1.

1. Using a web browser, sign in to the Azure portal at https://portal.azure.com.
2. At the top of the navigation pane on the left, click the Create a Resource button, as shown in Figure 5-9.

FIGURE 5-9 Creating a resource in the Microsoft Azure portal

3. In the Search field, type **storage account**, select Storage Account from the search results list, then click Create.

4. Configure the storage account with the following settings (accept the default values for all other settings):

   ▪ Resource group: Create a new one named **ResGroup1**

   ▪ Storage account name: **storacct1289**

5. Click Review + Create, then click Create.

6. When the deployment is complete, click the Go to Resource button to view the storage account.

EXERCISE 5-2

Upload Content to a Microsoft Azure Storage Account

In this exercise, you will use the Azure portal to upload sample files to an Azure storage account. This exercise depends on having successfully completed Exercise 5-1.

1. Using a web browser, sign in to the Azure portal at https://portal.azure.com.

2. In the left-hand navigator, click Storage Accounts.

3. On the right, click storacct1289 to open the storage account properties.

4. Scroll down the properties navigation bar and click Blobs.

5. On the right, click the +Container button.

6. Name the container **samplefiles** and click OK.

7. Click the samplefiles container, then click the Upload button, as shown in Figure 5-10.

FIGURE 5-10   Uploading a blob to a storage account

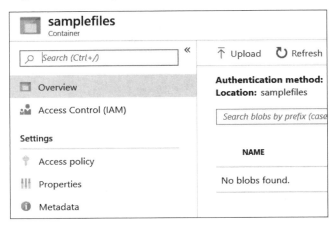

8. Click the folder icon and specify some local sample files to upload, then click the Upload button.
9. After the upload completes, click the name of the uploaded file and verify that server-side encryption is set to a value of true. Microsoft Azure encrypts all storage account blobs by default, as shown in Figure 5-11.

FIGURE 5-11   Storage account blob properties

INSIDE THE EXAM

Cloud Storage and Hands-On

To prepare for answering questions related to cloud storage on the CompTIA Cloud Essentials+ CLO-002 exam, it's helpful to experiment. Create cloud storage accounts, upload sample data, and configure settings such as encryption and replication.

CERTIFICATION SUMMARY

This chapter focused on cloud storage settings that align with business needs. When configuring cloud storage details, how the storage will be used is a major factor in determining whether high performance is important, in which case SSD hot access storage should be enabled. However, as you learned, the SSD option is more expensive than the HDD option because SSDs are faster than HDDs.

When choosing cloud storage options, the disk IOPS measurement represents overall disk I/O performance; opting for more IOPS results in better performance, which in turn means increased cost for the cloud storage service.

Next, hierarchical file storage such as Microsoft Azure Files was compared to flat object storage. Microsoft Azure Files provides cloud-based shared folders. Cloud-based virtual machine virtual disks are referred to as block storage.

We then discussed how replicating cloud storage to multiple regions increases data availability in the event of a regional disaster. Next, we talked about encrypting cloud data using either CSP keys or customer keys.

We next compared SQL databases, which are best suited for related data stored in separate tables, to NoSQL databases, which use a less rigid schema and can store vast amounts of unstructured data. You also learned that managed database solutions spare the cloud customer from the complexities of deploying and managing the underlying database structure.

Finally, you learned about content delivery networks and how they place content near the users that request it, thus improving the user experience by reducing network latency.

TWO-MINUTE DRILL

Storage Media

- ❏ HDD-based cloud storage is slower than SSD-based cloud storage but is less expensive.
- ❏ SSD-based cloud storage is best suited for intensive disk I/O usage.
- ❏ Disk IOPS is a measurement of disk throughput; a higher value means better performance.

Cloud Storage Configuration

- ❏ Managed disks remove the need for cloud customers to provision storage for cloud VM disks.
- ❏ CSP file-based solutions are similar to on-premises shared folders.
- ❏ Accessing Microsoft Azure Files shared folders occurs over TCP port 445.
- ❏ CSP object-based storage is flat compared to file system hierarchies.
- ❏ Network access to cloud-based storage is normally done over HTTP using the REST API.
- ❏ Common file types such as text and media documents are stored as block blobs.
- ❏ Virtual machine disk files are commonly stored as page blobs.
- ❏ Hot storage should be used for data that will be accessed frequently.
- ❏ Cold storage should be used for data that will be accessed infrequently.
- ❏ Cloud storage replication creates additional copies of data for increased resiliency to failure.
- ❏ Cloud customers can use custom encryption keys to secure data at rest.

Databases in the Cloud

- ❏ On-premises databases should be assessed for cloud readiness with a tool such as Microsoft Data Migration Assistant and then be migrated to the cloud.
- ❏ Managed databases remove the underlying infrastructure complexity from the cloud customer; this often referred to as Database as a Service (DBaaS).
- ❏ SQL-compliant databases use a structured data schema and are best suited to store related data stored in separate tables.
- ❏ NoSQL-compliant databases are designed to accommodate vast amounts of unstructured data.

❑ Microsoft SQL Server access occurs over TCP port 1433.

❑ Access by NoSQL databases such as MongoDB occurs over TCP port 27017.

❑ Database Transaction Units (DTUs) are a performance unit consisting of vCPUs, amount of RAM, and disk IOPS.

Content Delivery Networks

❑ CDNs copy (cache) data to different geographical locations near users to improve the user experience.

❑ CDN Time To Live (TTL) values determine how long before the source data is checked for changes.

❑ DNS CNAME (alias) records point to other DNS records.

SELF TEST

The following questions will help you measure your understanding of the material presented in this chapter. As indicated, some questions may have more than one correct answer, so be sure to read all the answer choices carefully.

Storage Media

1. You are planning how cloud storage will address business needs. Choosing which cloud storage option will have the largest positive impact on performance?
   A. Capacity
   B. Storage media brand
   C. Solid state drives
   D. FTP access

2. Which data storage characteristic is the most closely related to minimizing data redundancy?
   A. IOPS
   B. Replication
   C. Deduplication
   D. RAID

3. Which RAID configuration improves disk I/O performance but does not include fault tolerance?
   A. RAID 0
   B. RAID 1
   C. RAID 5
   D. RAID deduplication

4. Which solution protects stored data even if physical storage devices are stolen?
   A. Deduplication
   B. RAID 1
   C. RAID 5
   D. Encryption of data at rest

Cloud Storage Configuration

5. Your organization is configuring cloud backup for on-premises servers. Which cloud backup storage configuration should be used to minimize costs?
   A. Increased IOPS
   B. Cool access tier
   C. Storage replication
   D. Hot access tier

6. Developers are planning to write on-premises code that programmatically accesses cloud storage. You are configuring on-premises firewall rules to allow this storage access. Which type of outbound traffic will you most likely allow in this scenario?
   A. FTPS
   B. SMB
   C. NFS
   D. HTTPS

7. In the event of a regional disaster, you would like cloud-stored data available elsewhere. What should you configure?
   A. RAID 0
   B. Geo-redundant storage
   C. Deduplication
   D. RAID 1

Databases in the Cloud

8. Which type of database solution uses a rigid schema?
   A. NoSQL
   B. SQL

    C. Managed

    D. Replicated

  9. Which TCP port is normally used to connect to Microsoft SQL Server?

    A. 80

    B. 443

    C. 1433

    D. 3389

10. What is another term for DBaaS?

    A. Unmanaged database

    B. NoSQL

    C. Managed database

    D. SQL

Content Delivery Networks

11. What is the primary benefit of using a CDN?

    A. Regulatory compliance

    B. Adherence to standards

    C. Improved performance

    D. Enhanced security

12. Which CDN configuration determines how long before the source of cached data is checked for changes?

    A. TTL

    B. Replication

    C. Path

    D. SSL

13. You need to create a DNS record that redirects a custom domain name for a CDN configuration. What type of record should you create?

    A. MX

    B. A

    C. PTR

    D. CNAME

14. What is the primary benefit of deploying a CDN?

    A. Enhanced security

    B. Improved performance

    C. Reduced costs

    D. Regulatory compliance

15. You are configuring a CDN that will be used to serve media files to users. What should you configure to use the CDN most efficiently?
   A. Increased TTL
   B. Reduced TTL
   C. Wildcard path for media files
   D. Custom encryption keys

SELF TEST ANSWERS

Storage Media

1. ☑ **C.** Solid state drives (SSDs) provide better performance than traditional hard disk drives (HDDs). Naturally, CSPs charge more for the performance improvement, so choosing SSDs over HDDs also increases cloud costs.
☒ **A, B,** and **D** are incorrect. Storage capacity, the brand of storage media, and accessing cloud storage through FTP will not positively impact performance as much as the use of SSDs will.

2. ☑ **C.** Deduplication removes duplicate disk blocks and replaces duplicates with pointers to reduce disk space consumption.
☒ **A, B,** and **D** are incorrect. Disk IOPS is a disk I/O throughput measurement. Replication creates copies of data for increased resiliency to failure at a primary location. Redundant Array of Independent Disks (RAID) organizes multiple disk storage devices together in various ways to improve disk performance and/or to provide fault tolerance.

3. ☑ **A.** RAID 0, disk striping, uses multiple physical disks working as one to improve performance, but the failure of a single disk renders the entire disk array unavailable.
☒ **B, C,** and **D** are incorrect. RAID 1 (disk mirroring) and RAID 5 (disk striping with distributed parity) both provide fault tolerance. RAID deduplication is not a function specifically related to RAID; deduplication is a method of reducing disk space consumption.

4. ☑ **D.** Encrypting data at rest protects stored data. The correct decryption key is required to read information that is encrypted.
☒ **A, B,** and **C** are incorrect. Deduplication is a method of reducing disk space consumption. RAID 1 (disk mirroring) and RAID 5 (disk striping with distributed parity) both provide disk fault tolerance.

Cloud Storage Configuration

5. ☑ **B.** Cool or cold cloud storage is best suited for data that is accessed infrequently, such as backups, and is less expensive than hot cloud storage.
☒ **A, C,** and **D** are incorrect. Increasing disk IOPS and enabling storage replication increase cloud computing charges. Hot access tiers are best suited for data that is frequently accessed, because hot access provides higher performance for quicker data access, but is more expensive than cold access.

6. ☑ **D.** Accessing cloud storage programmatically normally occurs through the REST API, which relies on HTTP and HTTPS.
☒ **A, B,** and **C** are incorrect. These network file access protocols are not used for cloud storage access as often as HTTPS is.

7. ☑ **B.** Geo-redundant storage keeps copies of data in different regions, which is resilient against a regional disaster.
☒ **A, C,** and **D** are incorrect. RAID 0 (disk striping) uses multiple physical disks working as one to increase disk I/O performance. Deduplication is a method of reducing disk space consumption. RAID 1 (mirroring) copies data to a secondary disk when it is written to the primary disk.

Databases in the Cloud

8. ☑ **B.** SQL databases use a structured, or rigid, schema that defines what type of data will be stored.
☒ **A, C,** and **D** are incorrect. NoSQL databases do not use a structured schema; many different types of data can be stored without a definition of how that data will be stored. Managed SQL and NoSQL cloud databases hide the underlying infrastructure complexities related to hosting databases from cloud customers. Database replication is not determined by a structured or unstructured schema.

9. ☑ **C.** By default, Microsoft SQL Server is accessible over TCP port 1433.
☒ **A, B,** and **D** are incorrect. Port 80 is used for HTTP, port 443 is used for HTTPS, and port 3389 is used for Remote Desktop Protocol (RDP; covered in Chapter 6).

10. ☑ **C.** Database as a Service (DBaaS) is a managed database service, which means the CSP takes care of the underlying infrastructure to host the database.
☒ **A, B,** and **D** are incorrect. Unmanaged databases require cloud customers to install and configure the underlying infrastructure to support the database. NoSQL and SQL databases are available as managed and nonmanaged services.

Content Delivery Networks

11. ☑ **C.** A content delivery network (CDN) improves the performance of users' access to content by placing a copy of that content geographically near users, which reduces network latency.
☒ **A, B,** and **D** are incorrect. A CDN does not specifically address regulatory compliance, standards adherence, or improved security.

12. ☑ **A.** The Time To Live (TTL) value determines how long before the CDN cache checks the source data for changes.
☒ **B, C,** and **D** are incorrect. CDN configuration settings for replication, path, and Secure Sockets Layer (SSL) do not determine when cached source data has changed.

13. ☑ **D.** DNS CNAME records are alias records that point to other DNS records.
☒ **A, B,** and **C** are incorrect. MX records are mail exchange records used for e-mail transfer; A records use names to point to IPv4 addresses; and PTR records are reverse lookup records that, given an IP address, return a DNS name.

14. ☑ **B.** A CDN is configured to place data near the users who request it, which improves performance by reducing network latency.
☒ **A, C,** and **D** are incorrect. CDNs do not enhance security, reduce costs, or help with regulatory compliance.

15. ☑ **C.** Wildcard paths are used to specify which files should be included in the CDN.
☒ **A, B,** and **D** are incorrect. Modifying the TTL value or using custom encryption keys for cloud data will not make as big a difference in efficiency than a correctly configured wildcard path to copy only the required files.

Chapter 6

Cloud Network Infrastructure

N etworks provide the foundation that supports cloud services. Careful planning and testing result in a solid cloud-based network infrastructure. This chapter starts by introducing you to a variety of methods through which your on-premises network and cloud networks can be connected.

Next, cloud network components such as virtual subnets and their related IP addressing are discussed. We will then cover common network protocols used with both on-premises and cloud networking. Lastly, we'll examine what to consider when planning and configuring site-to-site VPNs or client-to-site VPNs.

CERTIFICATION OBJECTIVE 6.01

Cloud Network Components

Planning your cloud network environment shares many similarities with planning an on-premises network environment. Let's take a look at some factors that you should consider:

- How many subnets are needed?
- Which IPv4 or IPv6 address ranges will be used?
- Should any IT workloads be isolated from others?
- Should any IT workloads be publicly accessible from the Internet?
- Do remote users need secure VPN access to the company network?
- Are custom routes required to send network traffic to a security appliance?

Fortunately for cloud customers, cloud service providers take advantage of *software-defined networking (SDN)*, which means cloud customers don't have to worry about the detailed complexities of configuring and managing a wide array of network hardware and software. Instead, cloud customers use intuitive graphical user interfaces (GUIs) or command-line tools that then configure the underlying network components.

SDN works well for cloud service providers because it allows their many cloud customers to provision network configurations across many underlying network infrastructure devices such as routers and switches. Without SDN, cloud customers would most likely submit their network configuration requests to cloud data center technicians for implementation. The data center technicians would have to be proficient in configuring a multitude of network devices, potentially from different vendors whose detailed configuration steps differ. Think of SDN as a centralized, easy-to-use software layer that sits on top of network infrastructure hardware.

Connecting to Cloud Environments

Whether you are an individual cloud customer or a member of a corporate enterprise using cloud services, one way or another, you need to connect to a cloud service provider. As you will recall from Chapter 1, an important characteristic of cloud computing is broad access to IT services over a network.

Internet Connectivity

The Internet is the most common way of directly connecting to a public CSP for creating and managing cloud resources, as well as the most common way for users to access those services. When cloud computing services are crucial for the organization's survival, the organization must carefully examine the resiliency of its Internet connectivity. If the organization has a single Internet connection and it fails, then how will public cloud services be accessed? This problem is exacerbated with organizations that funnel all branch office Internet traffic through a single Internet hub location. If the central hub location fails in some way, all branch offices might be unable to contact the public CSP.

What can be done about this single point of failure? The answer is clear—ensure each on-premises location has two Internet connections, ideally through different Internet service providers (ISPs) if possible. If one ISP experiences a network outage, ideally the other ISP will not simultaneously. Addressing single points of failure is not always this simple, of course, but your organization's risk appetite will determine how much importance is attributed to this scenario.

Dedicated Network Circuit

Another option besides the Internet is a dedicated private network link to the public CSP from your on-premises network, essentially a wide area network (WAN) link. Microsoft Azure calls this *ExpressRoute*, and Amazon Web Services (AWS) calls it *Direct Connect*; different names, same end result. Some IT workloads, such as Voice over IP (VoIP) packets, are sensitive to network disruptions and might require a guaranteed quality of service (QoS) to ensure packet loss is minimized. Figure 6-1 shows an example of provisioning an AWS Direct Connect link.

FIGURE 6-1   Creating an AWS Direct Connect link

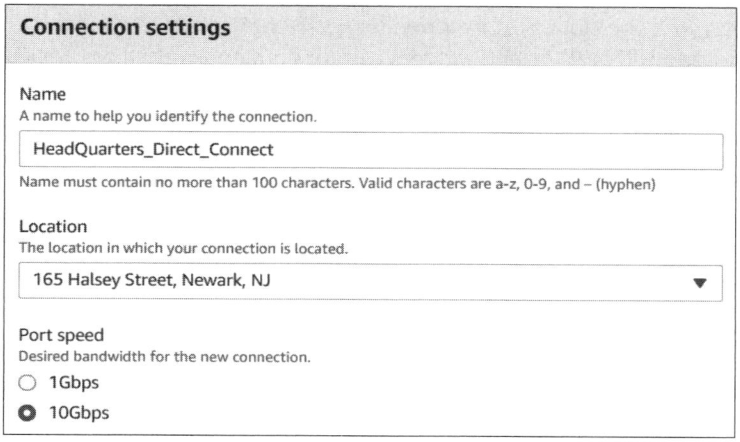

You will need to check your CSP's documentation to determine if it has a local point of presence to which your organization can establish a dedicated private network link.

There are a few potential benefits to using a dedicated network circuit to the public cloud:

- Network traffic does not traverse the Internet.
- Network bandwidth is predictable.
- Network throughput is higher than through the Internet.
- It may be less expensive than a fast Internet connection.

Cloud VPNs

Virtual private networks (VPNs) have been around for a long time. This solution creates an end-to-end encrypted tunnel over an untrusted network such as the Internet. Network traffic sent through the VPN tunnel is protected until it is decrypted at the other end of the VPN connection. This is a great way to connect

- Branch offices over the Internet
- Remote users to a private network over the Internet
- On-premises networks to a cloud-based virtual network

When planning VPNs for connection to a public CSP such as Microsoft Azure, you need to consider the VPN type.

Site-to-Site VPNs

A site-to-site VPN configuration is used to extend your on-premises network into the cloud. VPN configurations require a minimum of two endpoints, and in this case, the endpoints are an on-premises VPN device and a cloud-based VPN device. Your on-premises VPN device could be hardware or software based and must have a public IP address to establish the tunnel with the cloud service provider's VPN appliance.

Site-to-site VPNs allow network devices on both ends of the connection to communicate by sending traffic through the VPN tunnel. In other words, you don't need to install and configure a VPN client on each device. Figure 6-2 shows the configuration of a Microsoft Azure Site-to-Site VPN. The pre-shared key specified in the Shared Key (PSK) field is used to establish the VPN tunnel between the two endpoints.

Multiple branch office locations can be connected to one another using a VPN. If one of those branch offices also has a VPN connection to the cloud, connected branch offices can also be configured to connect to the cloud through that VPN connection.

FIGURE 6-2   Microsoft Azure site-to-site IPsec VPN configuration

Client-to-Site VPNs

Some of today's workforce works remotely—whether from home, from different office locations, or traveling for business. A client-to-site (C2S) VPN, also called a point-to-site (P2S) VPN, connects an individual device to a VPN endpoint to establish an encrypted tunnel. This allows remote users to securely access IT services over an untrusted network. For example, you could allow a user working from home to securely connect to a cloud-deployed database securely through a VPN connection. Figure 6-3 shows a C2S VPN configuration in the Microsoft Azure cloud, which requires client devices to have a security certificate to authenticate to the VPN; that is why the public certificate data is specified. Also note the Download VPN Client button; this downloads a VPN client configuration .zip file for a Windows computer that will be the VPN client.

FIGURE 6-3 Microsoft Azure point-to-site VPN configuration

💾 Save	✕ Discard	↓ Download VPN client

Address pool

10.5.0.0/16

Tunnel type

IKEv2 and SSTP (SSL) ▾

Authentication type
◉ Azure certificate ○ RADIUS authentication

Root certificates

NAME	PUBLIC CERTIFICATE DATA
RootCertPubKey	MIIC4TCCAcmgAwIBAgIQXDbjQ6jyRKhMOPvzbldJoTANBgkqhkiG9w0B ...

e x a m

ⓦ **a t c h** Some exam questions might test your knowledge of solutions that combine cloud network solutions. As an example, for the utmost in security and predictable bandwidth, the scenario might call for a site-to-site VPN configured on a dedicated network circuit.

Cloud Virtual Networks

Because of SDN, creating cloud-based virtual networks is straightforward as long as you plan carefully and research the options offered by various cloud service providers before choosing one. Cloud service providers use their own nomenclature for cloud virtual networks. For example, Microsoft Azure calls them *VNets*, while AWS calls them *Virtual Private Clouds (VPCs)*.

Both VNets and VPCs contain one or more subnets, much like an on-premises physical network switch that can be carved into multiple virtual local area networks (VLANs).

VLANs provide network isolation for security and/or reduced network congestion. You can also control whether or not traffic from one subnet can reach other subnets. Network isolation is commonly maintained between testing and production environments. This is true both on premises and in the cloud.

IP Addressing

Deploying cloud-based virtual networks requires specifying a TCP/IP address range that will be used, normally in what is called Classless Inter-Domain Routing (CIDR) format. CIDR format specifies an IP network address followed by a slash and the number of bits in a subnet mask, such as 10.1.0.0/16, where 10.1.0.0 is the network address with 16 bits in the subnet mask, or 255.255.0.0.

The IP address range used by a cloud-based virtual subnet must fall within the IP range assigned to the cloud-based virtual network, such as the following:

- VNet1: 10.1.0.0/16
- Subnet1: 10.1.1.0/24

The 10.1.1.0/24 network falls within the 10.1.0.0/16 network because, starting from the left, we are adding more binary bits to address networks (24 bits beyond the 16 bits for VNet1). /16 in decimal notation is 255.255.0.0, and /24 in decimal notation is 255.255.255.0. In binary notation, /16 is 11111111.11111111.00000000.00000000, and /24 is 11111111.1111 1111.11111111.00000000.

Preparation is everything—before deploying cloud resources, you need to plan into which network subnets resources will be deployed, as depicted in Figure 6-4.

on the **ⓘ** o b

Because cloud networking is critical (a misconfiguration can render IT services unreachable), be careful when assigning cloud management permissions. Adhere to the principle of least privilege, which states that only the permissions required to do one's job should be granted, and nothing more.

FIGURE 6-4   Deploying an AWS virtual machine into a VPC and subnet

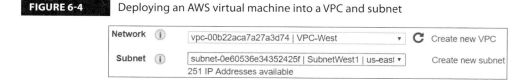

CERTIFICATION OBJECTIVE 6.02

Network Protocols

With cloud computing, everything old is now new. In other words, many old technologies used in on-premises environments work no differently now for cloud computing than they did 25 years ago—the only difference is those services are running on somebody else's equipment that you connect to over a network. Table 6-1 lists common network protocols used both on premises and in the cloud.

Some network protocols such as DNS are integrated with CSP settings. An example is Microsoft Azure–provided DNS. When you deploy a new Azure VNet, by default, virtual machines deployed into subnets within that VNet can resolve names of other resources on the same subnet as well as Internet names. You can see this setting in Figure 6-5. Of course, you can configure custom DNS server IP addresses of your own, if you wish.

TABLE 6-1	Common Network Protocols	
Protocol	**Port Number**	**Description**
Secure Shell (SSH)	TCP 22	Remote management of devices and hosts running an SSH daemon; commonly used to manage network equipment and Unix/Linux hosts.
Remote Desktop Protocol (RDP)	TCP 3389	Remote management of Windows hosts; has also been ported to Linux environments.
Hypertext Transfer Protocol (HTTP)	TCP 80	Client connection to a web server.
HTTP Secure (HTTPS)	TCP 443	Client connection to a web server over a secured connection.
Lightweight Directory Access Protocol (LDAP)	TCP 389	Method of connecting to and querying a network configuration database containing user and computer accounts, groups, and application configurations.
Simple Network Management Protocol (SNMP)	UDP 161	Method of inventorying and monitoring network devices remotely over a network.
Domain Name Service (DNS)	TCP/UDP 53	Name resolution service most commonly used to resolve fully qualified domain names (FQDNs) such as www.mheducation.com to an IP address. UDP 53 is for DNS client requests, while TCP 53 is used for DNS server-to-server communication.

FIGURE 6-5   Microsoft Azure VNet DNS configuration

CERTIFICATION OBJECTIVE 6.03

Cloud Load Balancing

When an application is handling a high volume of client requests, it needs more horsepower to accommodate the increased workload than when demand is lower. Load balancing can be used to solve this problem.

You can configure internal load balancers for line-of-business applications used by employees, or you can configure external load balancers for public-facing applications. Either way, client requests for an app such as www.app1.com are resolved through DNS to the IP address of the load balancer. The load balancer is configured with multiple back-end virtual machines that actually run the application, as depicted in Figure 6-6.

FIGURE 6-6   Load balancing

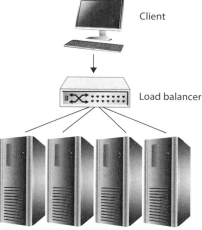

The load balancer keeps track of how busy back-end servers are and also which back-end servers are no longer responding; client requests are routed by the load balancer to the least-busy responsive back-end server. You can configure horizontal autoscaling to add and remove virtual machines, providing the benefit of better application performance and increased resiliency against failure of a single server. You can base autoscaling on metrics such as number of received requests, CPU utilization, and so on.

Watch Autoscaling with a load balancer is considered horizontal scaling because VM nodes are added or removed.	Vertical scaling is related to increasing or decreasing individual VM resources, such as the number of vCPUs or the amount of RAM.

EXERCISE 6-1

Create a Microsoft Azure Virtual Network

In this exercise, you will create a virtual network and subnet in the Microsoft Azure cloud. This exercise depends on having first completed Exercise 1-1.

1. Using a web browser, sign in to https://portal.azure.com.
2. At the top of the navigation pane on the left, click the Create a Resource button.
3. In the Search field, type **virtual network**, select Virtual Network from the results, and click Create.
4. Configure the virtual network with the following settings (accept the default values for all other settings), as shown in Figure 6-7:
   - Name: **VNet90**
   - Address space: **10.3.0.0/16**
   - Resource group: (**New**) **ResGroup90**
   - Subnet name: **Subnet1**
   - Address range: **10.3.1.0/24**
5. Click Create.

FIGURE 6-7   Microsoft Azure VNet creation

EXERCISE 6-2

Configure a Microsoft Azure ExpressRoute Circuit

In this exercise, you will configure a dedicated link between an on-premises network to Azure through ExpressRoute. This exercise depends on having completed Exercise 1-1.

1. In the Azure portal, click Create a Resource in the upper left.
2. In the Search bar, type **expressroute**, select ExpressRoute from the list, and click Create.

3. Configure the ExpressRoute circuit with settings similar to the following example for my location, as shown in Figure 6-8:
   - Name: **HQ_Circuit1**
   - Provider: **Bell Canada**
   - Peering Location: **Toronto**
   - Bandwidth: **100Mbps**
   - Resource group: **(New) ResGroup91**
4. To complete the process in a production environment, you would contact the service provider to provision the circuit and link it to a virtual network through a virtual network gateway.

FIGURE 6-8 Microsoft Azure ExpressRoute circuit creation

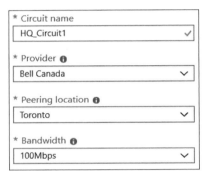

INSIDE THE EXAM

Cloud Networking

Knowing *when* to use a specific cloud network configuration is the key to answering questions correctly on the CompTIA Cloud Essentials+ CLO-002 exam. Remember that some organizational requirements could be met by using a combination of cloud network solutions, such as a VPN to allow secure connections to the cloud to run a cloud-based, load-balanced application.

CERTIFICATION SUMMARY

This chapter discussed how to connect an on-premises network to a public cloud service provider over the Internet or using a dedicated network circuit. You also learned about providing secure connections to a public CSP through VPNs. Depending on your company's needs, you can configure a site-to-site VPN linking your on-premises network to the cloud, or you can enable individual remote users to connect to the cloud through a client-to-site VPN connection.

You also learned about cloud virtual networks such as Microsoft Azure Virtual Networks and Amazon Web Services Virtual Private Clouds and how subnets in the cloud use an IP address range within the network range.

This chapter also described how many of the traditional network protocols, such as SSH, RDP, and DNS, that are used on premises are also used in a cloud computing environment for the same purposes.

The chapter wrapped up by explaining how load balancers can be implemented to provide quick and efficient access to cloud-hosted applications. Client requests to the app are directed to the load balancer, which then routes the requests to the least-busy responsive back-end server. The load-balanced solution can also be autoscaled to adjust the number of back-end virtual machines serving the application.

 TWO-MINUTE DRILL

Cloud Network Components

- ❑ Cloud customers can connect to public CSPs over the Internet or through a private dedicated network circuit.
- ❑ Redundant Internet cloud connections should be used in case one connection fails.
- ❑ Dedicated network circuits provide predictable bandwidth on a private network link.
- ❑ Microsoft Azure dedicated network links are called ExpressRoute circuits.
- ❑ Amazon Web Services dedicated network links are called Direct Connect dedicated connections.
- ❑ VPNs create an encrypted tunnel between two endpoints over an untrusted network.
- ❑ Branch office networks can be connected using a site-to-site VPN. If one branch office has VPN connectivity to the cloud, other branch offices could be configured to also have cloud access through the VPN.
- ❑ On-premises networks can be securely connected to the public cloud via a site-to-site VPN.

❑ Site-to-site VPNs require an on-premises VPN appliance with a public IP address.

❑ Individual user devices can be securely connected to the public cloud using a client-to-site VPN.

❑ Client-to-site VPNs do not require an on-premises VPN appliance.

❑ Software-defined networking (SDN) spares cloud customers from needing detailed network hardware configuration knowledge when configuring cloud network components.

❑ Cloud virtual networks contain subnets and are configured with a specific IP address space.

❑ Microsoft Azure cloud-based virtual networks are called VNets.

❑ Amazon Web Services cloud-based virtual networks are called VPCs.

Network Protocols

❑ Traditional on-premises network protocols are also used in the cloud.

❑ SSH uses TCP port 22 for network device, Unix, and Linux remote management.

❑ RDP uses port TCP 3389 for Windows host remote management.

❑ Cloud services are primarily accessible over HTTP (TCP port 80) and HTTPS (TCP port 443).

❑ LDAP uses TCP port 389 when connecting to a network configuration database.

❑ SNMP uses UDP port 161 when monitoring network devices.

❑ DNS uses UDP port 53 for client requests.

❑ DNS uses TCP port 53 for server-to-server communication.

Cloud Load Balancing

❑ Client connectivity to an application goes through a load balancer.

❑ Load-balanced applications perform better and are resilient to server failures.

❑ Load balancers can serve internal or public-facing applications.

❑ Load balancing uses back-end server pools consisting of VMs running the same application.

❑ App requests are routed to the least-busy back-end server.

❑ App requests are not routed to unresponsive back-end servers.

SELF TEST

The following questions will help you measure your understanding of the material presented in this chapter. As indicated, some questions may have more than one correct answer, so be sure to read all the answer choices carefully.

Cloud Network Components

1. Which term refers to configuring cloud networking without directly having to configure underlying network hardware?
   A. Load balancing
   B. Software-defined networking
   C. Cloud-based routing
   D. Cloud-based virtualization

2. Your company uses a dedicated network circuit for public cloud connectivity. You need to ensure that on-premises–to–public cloud connections are not exposed to other Internet users. What should you do?
   A. Configure a site-to-site VPN
   B. Nothing
   C. Configure a client-to-site VPN
   D. Enable HTTPS

3. What must be configured within a cloud-based network to allow cloud resources to communicate on the network?
   A. Public IP address
   B. VPN
   C. Load balancer
   D. Subnet

4. Which type of IP addressing notation uses a slash followed by the number of subnet mask bits?
   A. SDN
   B. CIDR
   C. VPN
   D. QoS

5. Which word is the most closely related to using a VPN?

   A. Performance

   B. Encryption

   C. Anonymous

   D. Updates

6. Which type of VPN links two networks together over the Internet?

   A. Point-to-site

   B. Branch-to-branch

   C. Client-to-site

   D. Site-to-site

7. Which common VPN type links a single device to a private network over the Internet?

   A. Point-to-site

   B. Branch-to-branch

   C. Client-to-site

   D. Site-to-site

Network Protocols

8. You need to configure your on-premises perimeter firewall to allow outbound Linux remote management. Which port should you open?

   A. TCP 80

   B. UDP 161

   C. TCP 22

   D. TCP 3389

9. Your Microsoft Azure virtual machine has been deployed into an Azure VNet that uses default DNS settings. You are unable to connect to www.site.com from within the VM. What is the most likely problem?

   A. The VNet is configured with custom DNS servers.

   B. Outbound TCP port 22 traffic is blocked.

   C. www.site.com is down.

   D. Azure virtual machines do not support Internet name resolution.

10. You are configuring your on-premises perimeter firewall to allow outbound Windows server remote management. Which port should you open?
   A. 3389
   B. 443
   C. 445
   D. 389

Cloud Load Balancing

11. Which of the following words are most closely related to load balancing? (Choose two.)
   A. Security
   B. Performance
   C. Archiving
   D. Resiliency

12. Which cloud feature automatically adds or removes virtual machines based on how busy an application is?
   A. Load balancing
   B. Elasticity
   C. Autoscaling
   D. Monitoring

13. Which term describes adding virtual machines to support a busy application?
   A. Scaling in horizontally
   B. Scaling out horizontally
   C. Scaling down vertically
   D. Scaling up horizontally

14. After a load balancer is put in place, users report that they can no longer access a web application. What is the most likely cause of the problem?
   A. The load balancer DNS name is not resolving to the website name.
   B. The website DNS name is not resolving to the load balancer.
   C. TCP port 3389 is blocked in the cloud.
   D. TCP port 389 is blocked in the cloud.

15. What normally occurs when a load balancer back-end server is unresponsive?
   A. The load balancer deletes and re-creates the failed server.
   B. The load balancer uses vertical scaling to add servers.
   C. The load balancer does not route client requests to the unresponsive server.
   D. The load balancer prevents client connections to the app.

SELF TEST ANSWERS

Cloud Network Components

1. ☑ **B.** Software-defined networking (SDN) hides the underlying complexities of network device configuration from the cloud user.
   ☒ **A, C,** and **D** are incorrect. Load balancing distributes incoming client app requests among a pool of back-end servers supporting the app. Cloud-based routing is used to direct network traffic flow. Cloud-based virtualization allows VMs to run on CSP equipment.

2. ☑ **B.** Nothing needs to be done; dedicated network circuits are completely separate from Internet connections.
   ☒ **A, C,** and **D** are incorrect. None of the options are correct because nothing needs to be done.

3. ☑ **D.** A subnet is created within a cloud-based virtual network to allow cloud resources to communicate on the network. The subnet IP address range must fall within the cloud-based virtual network address space.
   ☒ **A, B,** and **C** are incorrect. A public IP address is used to provide connectivity to cloud resources over the Internet. VPNs provide encrypted tunnels between two endpoints over an untrusted network such as the Internet. Load balancing distributes incoming client app requests among a pool of back-end servers supporting the app.

4. ☑ **B.** Classless Inter-Domain Routing (CIDR) notation uses an IP network address prefix followed by a slash and the number of bits in the subnet mask.
   ☒ **A, C,** and **D** are incorrect. Software-defined networking (SDN) hides the underlying complexities of network device configuration from the cloud user. VPNs provide encrypted tunnels between two endpoints over an untrusted network such as the Internet. Quality of service (QoS) provides a reasonable guaranteed level of network throughput with minimal packet loss for time-sensitive applications such as Voice over IP (VoIP).

5. ☑ **B.** Virtual private networks (VPNs) create an encrypted tunnel between two endpoints for the secure transmission of data.
☒ **A, C,** and **D** are incorrect. The terms performance, anonymous, and updates are not closely related to VPNs.

6. ☑ **D.** Site-to-site VPNs can be used to connect different networks together over the Internet.
☒ **A, B,** and **C** are incorrect. Point-to-site (P2S) VPN links allow individual client connectivity to a remote network, such as Microsoft Azure client-to-site VPN configurations. Branch-to-branch is not a common VPN term.

7. ☑ **C.** Client-to-site VPNs link individual devices to a VPN endpoint through an encrypted tunnel.
☒ **A, B,** and **D** are incorrect. Point-to-site (P2S) VPN links allow individual client connectivity to a remote network, such as Microsoft Azure client-to-site VPN configurations. Branch-to-branch is not a common VPN term. Site-to-site VPNs can be used to connect different networks together over the Internet.

Network Protocols

8. ☑ **C.** Remote management of Linux hosts is normally performed using Secure Shell (SSH) over TCP port 22.
☒ **A, B,** and **D** are incorrect. TCP port 80 is used by HTTP, UDP port 161 is used by SNMP, and TCP port 339 is used for Windows host remote management using RDP.

9. ☑ **C.** The most likely culprit of the listed items is that www.site.com is down.
☒ **A, B,** and **D** are incorrect. Custom DNS server references are not part of Azure VNet default settings. Connecting to a website uses TCP port 80 or 443, not TCP port 22, which is used for SSH. Azure virtual machines can resolve Internet names if the configuration allows it.

10. ☑ **A.** Windows host remote management occurs over TCP port 3389.
☒ **B, C,** and **D** are incorrect. HTTPS uses TCP port 443, the Server Message Block (SMB) file-sharing protocol uses TCP port 445, and LDAP uses TCP port 389.

Cloud Load Balancing

11. ☑ **B and D.** Load balancing distributes client app requests to a pool of back-end servers to improve application performance and resiliency against server failures.
☒ **A and C** are incorrect. Security and archiving are not closely related to load balancing.

12. ☑ **C.** Autoscaling (also called horizontal scaling) can be configured to add or remove virtual machines when application utilization is above or below configured thresholds.
☒ **A, B,** and **D** are incorrect. Load balancing distributes client app requests to a pool of back-end servers to improve application performance and resiliency against server failures. Elasticity is a cloud computing characteristic that defines the rapid provisioning and deprovisioning of cloud resources. Monitoring is a passive activity that is not related to adding or removing VMs for busy applications.

13. ☑ **B.** Scaling out horizontally means adding virtual machines in response to how busy an application is.

    ☒ **A, C,** and **D** are incorrect. Scaling in means removing virtual machines, not adding VMs. Vertical scaling is related to individual VM resources such as vCPUs and RAM. Scaling up is vertical, not horizontal.

14. ☑ **B.** The DNS name used for web app connectivity most likely points to a now-defunct server IP address. The name must resolve to the load balancer's IP address.

    ☒ **A, C,** and **D** are incorrect. DNS names must, in the end, resolve to an IP address to be resolved correctly. Port 3389 is used for RDP and port 389 is used for LDAP; neither of these is used to access a web application.

15. ☑ **C.** Unresponsive back-end servers no longer receive client requests through the load balancer.

    ☒ **A, B,** and **D** are incorrect. Unresponsive back-end servers are not re-created by a load balancer. Adding servers is horizontal, not vertical, scaling. Just because one back-end server is unresponsive, it does not mean other servers cannot still fulfill client app requests.

Chapter 7

Cloud Compute Infrastructure

V irtual machines are the workhorses of cloud computing. In this chapter you will learn about cloud-based compute resources such as virtual machines. Clusters (collections of virtual machine nodes) also fall under the umbrella of cloud compute services.

We will start with a discussion of how cloud virtualization is possible through hypervisors in cloud service provider data centers, followed by a brief overview of how to plan virtual machine sizing to accommodate VM workloads.

Next, we'll identify specific virtual machine components, such as operating system images, virtual network interfaces, autoscaling, and custom routes. We will also cover remote management of both Linux and Windows cloud VMs in the context of IP addressing and jump boxes.

Finally, we will discuss when and how clusters of parallel processing nodes should be used.

CERTIFICATION OBJECTIVE 7.01

Virtualization in the Cloud

As you will recall from Chapter 1, hypervisors are the physical servers that host guests. Cloud service provider data centers contain vast numbers of Type 1 hypervisors such as VMware ESXi, Microsoft Hyper-V, or the Linux-based Kernel Virtual Machine (KVM). Type 1 hypervisors are also called *bare metal* hypervisors because they run directly on the physical hardware and do not depend on an existing operating system. Type 2 hypervisors run as an application within an existing operating system.

Cloud compute resources—such as virtual machines—run on these hypervisors. Planning cloud virtual machine deployment and usage depends on the workload that will be running in virtual machines.

 on the Job

With both on-premises and cloud computing environments, you will read literature and hear technicians use the term *hypervisor* to refer to the physical server. Technically, the hypervisor is the operating system software; the physical server could be used for non-hypervisor purposes.

Some cloud service providers offer other types of virtualization such as virtual desktop infrastructure (VDI) solutions, which serve up user desktops from a centralized virtualization server; users can connect remotely to access their cloud-stored desktop and applications.

Virtual Machine Sizing

Running a small website with a small number of users on a virtual machine won't require nearly as much horsepower as running complex data analyses on large datasets. The virtual

FIGURE 7-1   Selecting the Amazon Web Services virtual machine instance type

Currently selected: t2.micro (Variable ECUs, 1 vCPUs, 2.5 GHz, Intel Xeon Family, 1 GiB memory, EBS only)

	Family	Type	vCPUs ⓘ	Memory (GiB)	Instance Storage (GB) ⓘ
☐	General purpose	t2.nano	1	0.5	EBS only
☒	General purpose	t2.micro [Free tier eligible]	1	1	EBS only
☐	General purpose	t2.small	1	2	EBS only
☐	General purpose	t2.medium	2	4	EBS only

machine size, sometimes called the *instance type*, determines virtual machine horsepower. Common VM sizing constituents include

- Number of vCPUs
- Amount of RAM
- Number of supported data disks
- Disk IOPS throughput measurement
- Number of supported network interfaces
- Network performance

You might choose a specialized virtual machine sizing that addresses specific needs such as a graphics-intensive application. Just bear in mind that more VM compute power and speed mean higher cost. Another consideration is that some VM sizes might be available only in some geographical regions, depending on the CSP.

Virtual machine sizing not only should be addressed during planning and deploying but should also be monitored over time to ensure the best fit (one size does *not* fit all!). You can change virtual machine sizing, as shown in Figure 7-1, even after the VM already exists, though the VM might require a restart to pick up the new setting.

exam
ⓦatch

While some exam questions might refer to *virtual machine* sizing, you could see questions refer to *instance* sizing.	Both in the exam and the real world with cloud computing, *virtual machine* and *instance* are synonymous.

on the job **You should configure alerts so that you are notified when virtual machines are overly busy or idle to optimize the sizing and, by extension, related costs.**

CERTIFICATION OBJECTIVE 7.02

Cloud Virtual Machine Components

Much like a physical computer consists of many components working together, virtual machines in the cloud also consist of many virtual components. The workload that you plan to run in the virtual machine dictates which virtual components you should use and how you should configure them, as described in this section.

Operating System Selection

Cloud virtual machines use an *operating system image*. In addition to containing the operating system (OS), the image might have specific OS settings, as well as additional software such as a MySQL database server and support for the Python programming language.

As your cloud use increases, you will most likely find yourself creating custom images that will be used with future cloud VM deployments. Figure 7-2 shows how you can select an OS image during deployment in Microsoft Azure.

Connecting to cloud-based Windows virtual machines for management purposes is done differently than for cloud-based Linux virtual machines. Windows and Linux authentication options also differ, but some cloud-based Windows and Linux configurations, such as VM autoscaling, are not specific to the selected OS.

Remote Management

Whether you deploy a Windows VM or a Linux VM, at some point you may need to manage the OS remotely. If you plan on using an on-premises device to remotely manage cloud VMs, you'll need a way to contact those VMs either directly through a VM public IP address assigned to each VM (not recommended for security exposure reasons) or through a single VM configured with a public IP address (a *jump box*), as depicted in Figure 7-3. After you establish a connection to the jump box, you can connect to the internal private IP addresses of cloud VMs.

Windows remote management using Remote Desktop Protocol (RDP) occurs over TCP port 3389. Linux remote management using Secure Shell (SSH) occurs over TCP port 22. Your on-premises firewall needs to allow this type of outbound traffic, and cloud firewalls also need to allow this traffic to the VMs that will be remotely managed.

FIGURE 7-2 Selecting the Microsoft Azure virtual machine image

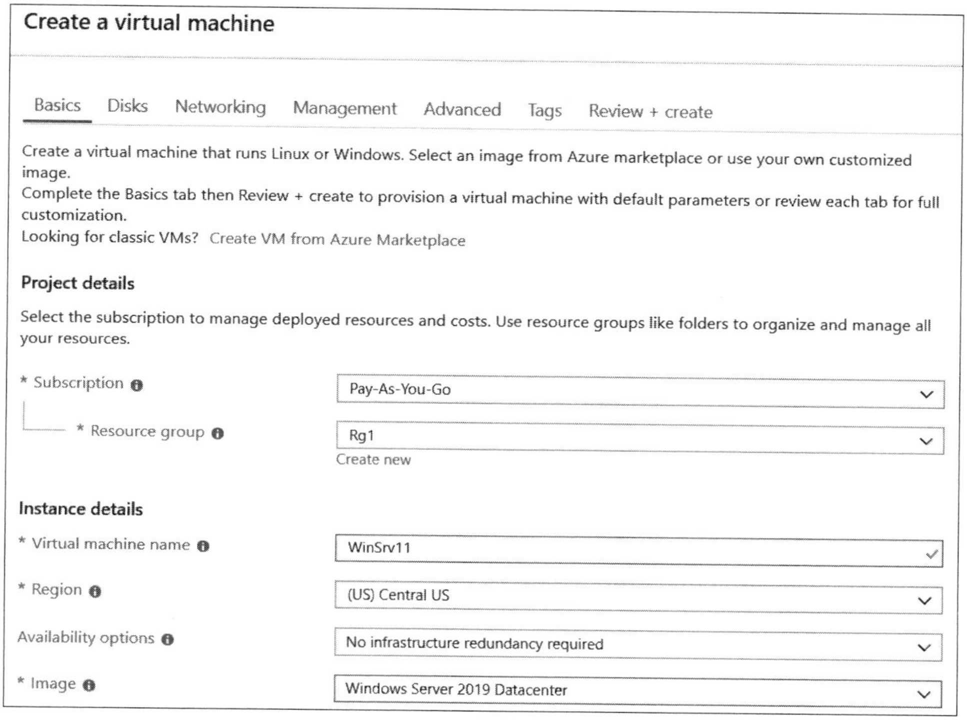

Create a virtual machine

Basics   Disks   Networking   Management   Advanced   Tags   Review + create

Create a virtual machine that runs Linux or Windows. Select an image from Azure marketplace or use your own customized image.
Complete the Basics tab then Review + create to provision a virtual machine with default parameters or review each tab for full customization.
Looking for classic VMs? Create VM from Azure Marketplace

Project details

Select the subscription to manage deployed resources and costs. Use resource groups like folders to organize and manage all your resources.

* Subscription 🛈	Pay-As-You-Go ⌄
└─── * Resource group 🛈	Rg1 ⌄
	Create new

Instance details

* Virtual machine name 🛈	WinSrv11 ✓
* Region 🛈	(US) Central US ⌄
Availability options 🛈	No infrastructure redundancy required ⌄
* Image 🛈	Windows Server 2019 Datacenter ⌄

Linux VM Authentication

Where cloud-based Windows virtual machine authentication is most commonly configured to use usernames and passwords, Linux virtual machines can use one of two authentication methods:

- Username and password
- SSH public key authentication

Authenticating to Linux through a username and password is single-factor authentication (something you know) and not considered as secure as SSH public key authentication. Public key authentication uses a public and private key pair. Both keys are mathematically related. The public key is stored with the Linux host in the cloud, and only the authorized user (or device) has access to the related private key, which should be backed up to a safe location. Depending on the configuration, authentication might only require possession of

FIGURE 7-3 Cloud jump box configuration

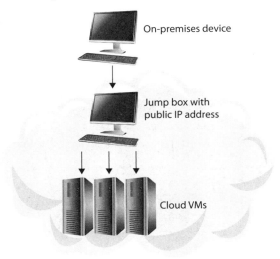

the private key, or it might also require a password and a username. Figure 7-4 shows the SSH public key authentication settings when deploying a Linux VM in Azure.

Virtual Machine Autoscaling

You can deploy sets of VMs together for horizontal scaling. Horizontal scaling comes in two forms:

- **Scaling out** Adding virtual machine nodes
- **Scaling in** Removing virtual machine nodes

FIGURE 7-4 Linux SSH public key configuration in Microsoft Azure

Administrator account	
Authentication type ❶	◯ Password ⦿ SSH public key
* Username ❶	cblackwell ✓
* SSH public key ❶	ssh-rsa AAAAB3NzaC1yc2EAAAABJQAAAQEAuHbjaC38dJQnKY773F2+nzKkg+WdTndU2/vKQz3eYG9y1keC6DXgQtTm+2YXhzkN4bCaY48ex/+S82z1dov+CfVU0RyI38cofxP

FIGURE 7-5 Enabling autoscaling for a Microsoft Azure virtual machine scale set

AUTOSCALE

Autoscale ❶	○ Disabled ⦿ Enabled
* Minimum number of VMs ❶	1
* Maximum number of VMs ❶	10
Scale out	
* CPU threshold (%) ❶	75
* Number of VMs to increase by ❶	1
Scale in	
* CPU threshold (%) ❶	25
* Number of VMs to decrease by ❶	1

When an application is in high demand, virtual machines can be added to handle the workload. When things quiet down, VMs can be removed since they are no longer needed—this also reduces unnecessary cloud costs. Figure 7-5 shows a sample autoscaling configuration.

Virtual Network Interface Cards

To communicate on a cloud virtual network, a virtual machine must be associated with a network interface, which is its own cloud resource, as shown in Figure 7-6. This means you can associate and dissociate network interfaces to and from different VMs over time, as needed.

Each network interface has settings to configure details such as the following, as shown in Figure 7-7:

■ Dynamic or static (unchanging) IP address
■ DNS name resolution
■ Firewall rule settings to control network traffic into and out of the network interface
■ IP forwarding (routing)

FIGURE 7-6   Microsoft Azure network interfaces

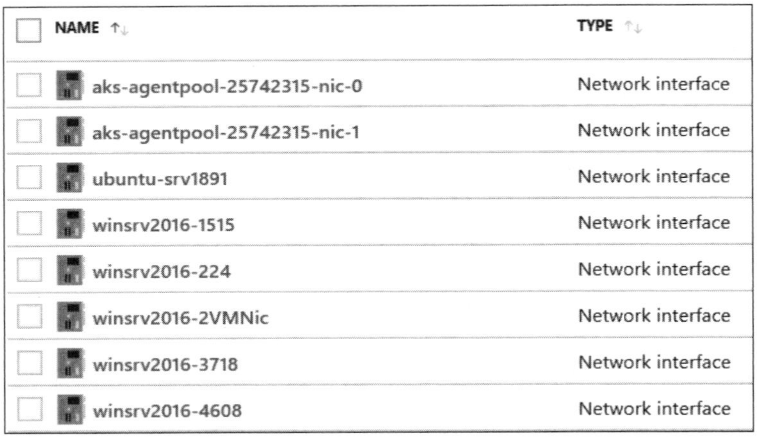

NAME ↑↓	TYPE ↑↓
☐ 🖼 aks-agentpool-25742315-nic-0	Network interface
☐ 🖼 aks-agentpool-25742315-nic-1	Network interface
☐ 🖼 ubuntu-srv1891	Network interface
☐ 🖼 winsrv2016-1515	Network interface
☐ 🖼 winsrv2016-224	Network interface
☐ 🖼 winsrv2016-2VMNic	Network interface
☐ 🖼 winsrv2016-3718	Network interface
☐ 🖼 winsrv2016-4608	Network interface

e x a m

w a t c h   **Think beyond the straight facts presented in this book. You might get exam questions related to multiple network interfaces associated with a single VM—this is a valid configuration and really** **no different than using multiple NICs in a physical machine, such as when it is configured as a routing or firewall appliance. In the same way, a single network interface can have multiple IP configurations.**

FIGURE 7-7   Microsoft Azure virtual network interface settings

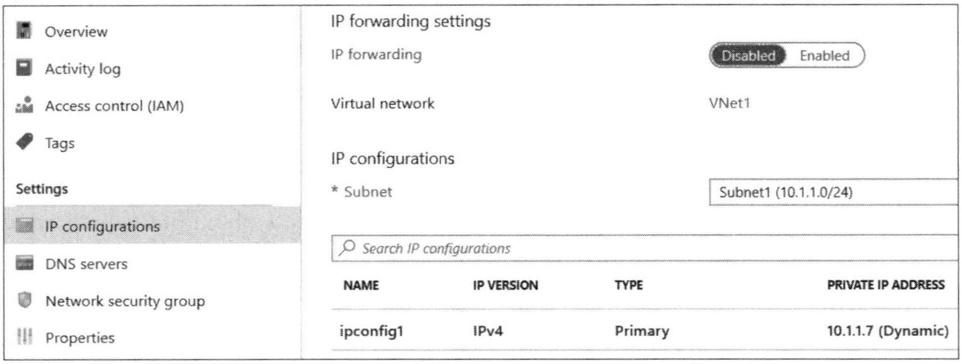

Overview	IP forwarding settings			
Activity log	IP forwarding		(Disabled) Enabled	
Access control (IAM)	Virtual network		VNet1	
Tags				
Settings	IP configurations			
IP configurations	* Subnet		Subnet1 (10.1.1.0/24)	
DNS servers	🔍 Search IP configurations			
Network security group	NAME	IP VERSION	TYPE	PRIVATE IP ADDRESS
Properties	ipconfig1	IPv4	Primary	10.1.1.7 (Dynamic)

FIGURE 7-8   Microsoft Azure custom route

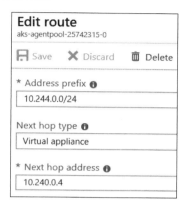

Routing Table Entries

If you need to control network traffic flow, you can configure custom routing table entries. Why would you do this? Normally, you would do so to ensure network traffic is forwarded to a firewall or antimalware appliance of some kind for inspection.

When configuring custom routes, you specify the target network range that must be matched in a network transmission, such as 10.244.0.0/24 in the example shown in Figure 7-8. Any traffic that needs to get to the 10.244.0.0 network will be sent to the next-hop virtual appliance, 10.240.0.4. The emerging pattern is that network settings that were normally configured directly within the OS are no longer configured there; instead, the settings reside in the cloud, and the virtual machine OS consults the cloud network settings.

CERTIFICATION OBJECTIVE 7.03

High-Performance Computing

In a scenario where individual VMs don't have the power or ability to run complex tasks that need to be accomplished, such as in medical research or financial modeling, consider grouping high-performance VMs together. The purpose of *high-performance computing (HPC)* is to speed up complex data analysis of large datasets through a cluster of VM nodes. This is also referred to as *big compute* or *parallel computing*—running tasks in parallel simultaneously across multiple VMs.

FIGURE 7-9   High-performance computing

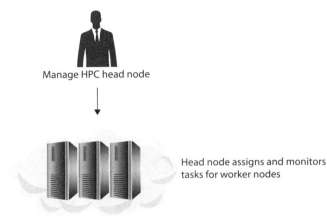

Manage HPC head node

Head node assigns and monitors
tasks for worker nodes

Each HPC VM uses the fastest vCPU configuration, SSD-based storage (as opposed to the older and slower HDD-based storage), large amounts of RAM, and the fastest network throughput. The HPC cluster needs a way to coordinate tasks among the worker nodes. You can get a sense of the HPC layout in Figure 7-9.

HPC clusters can be configured on premises or in the cloud. In the cloud, HPC is a managed service. This means that the complexity of installing and configuring operating system and clustering software to work together is hidden from the cloud customer. Monitoring the performance of cloud-based HPC ensures that complex tasks are processed efficiently with as little cost as possible. An example of monitoring in an AWS cloud environment would be to configure alert notifications through the AWS CloudWatch service. Figure 7-10 shows how an HPC head node can be deployed in Azure by selecting the appropriate OS image.

FIGURE 7-10   Deploying a Microsoft Azure HPC head node

Instance details

* Virtual machine name ❶	HPCCluster1
* Region ❶	(US) Central US
Availability options ❶	No infrastructure redundancy required
* Image ❶	HPC Pack 2016 Head Node on Windows Server 2016
	Browse all public and private images
* Size ❶	**Standard D8s v3** 8 vcpus, 32 GiB memory Change size

EXERCISE 7-1

Deploy a Windows-Based Virtual Machine in the Cloud

In this exercise, you will create a Windows virtual machine in the Microsoft Azure cloud. This exercise depends on having completed Exercise 1-1.

1. Use your web browser to sign in to the Microsoft Azure portal at https://portal .azure.com.
2. At the top of the navigation pane on the left, click Create a Resource.
3. Click the Compute category and select Virtual Machine. This will launch the Create a virtual machine wizard and place you on the Basics screen.
4. Select an existing resource group or create a new one.
5. Use the following values to deploy the Windows virtual machine:
   - Name: **WinSrv1**
   - Image: **Windows Server 2019 Datacenter**
   - Username: **admineast1**
   - Password: *Enter a password that satisfies requirements as per the web page* Note that you will need this password in Exercise 7-2.
   - Public inbound ports: Allow selected ports, RDP (3389)

 on the job

Opening RDP ports directly to the Internet poses a security risk for important VMs, but it serves the purpose of demonstration in this exercise. In the workplace, use a hardened jump box to allow remote access to cloud VMs that are configured with only private IP addresses.

6. Click the Next button at the bottom of the screen repeatedly until you arrive at the Management screen of the wizard. Ensure the Boot Diagnostics option is set to Off.
7. Click Review + Create, then click Create.

EXERCISE 7-2

Remotely Manage a Cloud Windows Virtual Machine

In this exercise, you will connect to an existing Windows virtual machine in the Microsoft Azure cloud. This exercise depends on having completed Exercise 7-1.

1. If you are not already in the Microsoft Azure portal, use your web browser to sign in to it at https://portal.azure.com.

2. In the left-hand navigator, click Virtual Machines.

3. From the list, click WinSrv1.

4. On the Overview page, look to the right side of the screen and copy the IP address of the virtual machine displayed in the Public IP Address field, as shown in Figure 7-11.

5. On your local Windows computer, open the Start menu and launch the Remote Desktop Connection app.

6. Paste the previously copied public IP address into the Computer field.

7. Click Show Options in the lower-left corner and enter **admineast1** into the User Name field, then click Connect.

8. When prompted, enter the password configured for **admineast1**. (This password was established in Exercise 7-1.)

9. If prompted, choose to trust the connection.

10. You are now remotely connected to a Windows VM running in the Microsoft Azure cloud.

11. Move the upper-right corner of the screen and click the X to close the remote desktop connection.

12. In the Azure portal, select WinSrv1. Click the Stop button to prevent unnecessary cloud charges.

FIGURE 7-11   Microsoft Azure virtual machine public IP address

Computer name	: (not available)
Operating system	: Windows
Size	: Standard DS1 v2 (1 vcpus, 3.5 GiB memory)
Ephemeral OS disk	: N/A
Public IP address	: 40.122.43.176
Private IP address	: 172.16.0.4
Virtual network/subnet	: Rg1-vnet/default
DNS name	: Configure

CERTIFICATION SUMMARY

This chapter discussed compute infrastructure in a cloud environment. You learned how hypervisors make operating system virtualization possible and how you should select the appropriate virtual machine sizing based on VM workloads.

You have been exposed to how both Windows and Linux virtual machine images can be deployed and how to manage them over RDP and SSH, respectively, through public IP addresses or a jump box. Cloud-based virtual machines are related to other cloud resources such as virtual network interfaces and custom route tables.

You also learned how autoscaling addresses application performance by scaling out (adding VMs) when the application is busy and scaling in (removing VMs) when demand for the application quiets down.

Finally, you learned how high-performance computing (HPC) can be used to perform large-scale, complex computing tasks across a cluster of VM nodes working together in parallel.

TWO-MINUTE DRILL

Virtualization in the Cloud

❑   Hypervisors run virtual machines.

❑   Virtual desktop infrastructure (VDI) provides user desktops over a network from a central virtualization server.

❑ Virtual machine sizing determines virtual hardware resources such as number of vCPUs, amount of RAM, and disk and network throughput.

❑ The virtual machine "size" is also referred to as "instance type."

❑ Existing virtual machines can be resized to address compute requirements.

❑ Resizing an existing virtual machine requires restarting the VM after resizing.

Cloud Virtual Machine Components

❑ Virtual machines are based on operating system images.

❑ OS images can contain only OS files for Windows or Linux.

❑ OS images can also contain specific OS settings and additional software beyond the OS software.

❑ Cloud customers can create custom images that are used to deploy virtual machines.

❑ Linux virtual machines are remotely managed using SSH over TCP port 22.

❑ Windows virtual machines are remotely managed using RDP over TCP port 3389.

❑ For remote management, each virtual machine can have a public IP address, but this is not recommended for security reasons.

❑ A jump box is a virtual machine with a public IP address through which technicians can then access the private IP addresses of cloud virtual machines.

❑ Windows virtual machines are normally configured to use username and password authentication

❑ Linux SSH public key authentication stores a public key with the virtual machine in the cloud; the related private key is stored on a user device.

❑ Virtual machines can be grouped together for autoscaling purposes to add and remove VMs in response to application requests.

❑ Cloud virtual machines can be associated with one or more virtual network interfaces.

❑ A virtual network interface can have multiple IP configurations using public and private IP addresses.

❑ Custom routes are used to control network traffic flow.

High-Performance Computing

❑ HPC is also referred to as big compute and parallel processing.

❑ HPC uses a cluster of virtual machine nodes working together to process complex jobs.

❑ HPC cluster head nodes receive job instructions and coordinate them among cluster worker nodes.

SELF TEST

The following questions will help you measure your understanding of the material presented in this chapter. As indicated, some questions may have more than one correct answer, so be sure to read all the answer choices carefully.

Virtualization in the Cloud

1. Which term is used to describe the physical host running guests?
- A. Virtualizor
- B. Scale set
- C. Cluster
- D. Hypervisor

2. Which virtualization solution provides user desktops from a centralized virtualization host?
- A. SDN
- B. CDN
- C. VDI
- D. VLAN

3. Which type of hypervisor is also called a bare metal hypervisor?
- A. Type 1
- B. Type 2
- C. Type 3
- D. Type 4

4. Which virtual machine characteristic determines the amount of compute power?
- A. Autoscaling
- B. Load balancer
- C. Sizing
- D. Tagging

Cloud Virtual Machine Components

5. You need to vertically scale a cloud virtual machine to accommodate an increased workload. Which two items should be adjusted?
   A. Public IP address
   B. RAM
   C. vCPU
   D. Load balancer

6. You have deployed a Linux virtual machine named LINUX1 in the cloud. Over time, you realize that LINUX1 does not need the amount of hardware resources that it was originally allocated. What should you do to reduce cloud costs?
   A. Resize LINUX1
   B. Delete and re-create LINUX1 with the correct resources
   C. Add LINUX1 to an autoscaling group
   D. Add LINUX1 to a load balancer back-end server pool

7. After deploying a Windows virtual machine named WINDOWS1 in the cloud, you cannot connect to it over RDP from your on-premises headquarters network. Other office locations can connect to WINDOWS1 over RDP. What is the most likely cause of the problem?
   A. Cloud firewall rules are preventing incoming port 3389 traffic.
   B. Cloud firewall rules are preventing incoming port 389 traffic.
   C. Headquarters network firewall rules are preventing outbound port 3389 traffic.
   D. Headquarters network firewall rules are preventing outbound port 389 traffic.

8. Which statements regarding Linux SSH public key authentication are correct? (Choose two.)
   A. The public key is stored on the connecting device.
   B. The public key is stored in the cloud.
   C. The private key is stored in the cloud.
   D. The private key is stored on the connecting device.

9. You have deployed numerous Linux and Windows virtual machines in the cloud. None of the VMs have a public IP address. You need to be able to manage all VMs from your on-premises network while minimizing exposure to network security threats. Which options should you consider? (Choose two.)
   A. Assign a public IP address to each virtual machine
   B. Deploy a jump box
   C. Configure a virtual machine autoscaling group
   D. Configure a VPN to the cloud

10. You need to configure an existing Linux virtual machine named FIREWALL1 in the cloud so that it can run as a firewall appliance between two virtual network subnets. What should you do? (Choose two.)

   A. Switch the operating system image in FIREWALL1 from Linux to Windows

   B. Resize FIREWALL1 to include more vCPUs

   C. Add a cloud routing table entry

   D. Create a virtual network interface and associate it with FIREWALL1

High-Performance Computing

11. You are the cloud technician for a pharmaceutical research company. Currently, researchers are analyzing vast datasets on premises, but the analysis results are taking too long to generate. What should you propose to speed up analysis results while minimizing IT costs?

   A. CSP

   B. CDN

   C. HPC

   D. SDN

12. Which word is the most closely related to HPC in the cloud?

   A. Security

   B. Clustering

   C. NoSQL

   D. Template

13. You plan on configuring a cloud HPC cluster to analyze terabytes of climate modeling data. What is the first thing you should do?

   A. Deploy an HPC cluster

   B. Deploy a load balancer

   C. Move data into the cloud

   D. Configure virtual machine autoscaling

14. Which type of virtual disk configuration should HPC nodes use?

   A. SDN

   B. IOPS

   C. HDD

   D. SSD

15. You are using an Amazon Web Services (AWS) HPC cluster to analyze medical data. Which AWS option should you configure to monitor HPC cluster performance?
    A. Direct Connect
    B. ExpressRoute
    C. CloudWatch
    D. CDN

SELF TEST ANSWERS

Virtualization in the Cloud

1. ☑ **D.** A hypervisor runs software designed to host guests.
   ☒ **A, B,** and **C** are incorrect. Virtualizor is not a valid term. A scale set groups VMs together for autoscaling purposes. A cluster is a group of VM nodes working together for a single purpose, such as for application high availability or running complex computations.

2. ☑ **C.** Virtual desktop infrastructure (VDI) uses a centralized server to host multiple user desktop environments.
   ☒ **A, B,** and **D** are incorrect. Software-defined networking (SDN) provides a layer between user interfaces that configures underlying network devices, thus hiding those complexities from the cloud user. A content delivery network (CDN) caches content geographically near users that will request that content. A virtual local area network (VLAN) is a logical subdivision of a physical network to reduce network congestion or provide network isolation and security for critical IT systems.

3. ☑ **A.** Type 1 hypervisors run directly on hardware ("bare metal") to support the running of multiple guests.
   ☒ **B, C,** and **D** are incorrect. Type 2 hypervisors run as an application within an existing operating system. Type 3 and 4 hypervisors are invalid types.

4. ☑ **C.** Virtual machine sizing determines the virtual machine compute power.
   ☒ **A, B,** and **D** are incorrect. Autoscaling adds or removes virtual machines in response to how busy an application is. Load balancing takes incoming client app requests and directs them to the least-busy back-end server. Tagging adds metadata to cloud resources to facilitate searching, filtering, and cost management.

Cloud Virtual Machine Components

5. ☑ **B** and **C.** Increasing the amount of memory, or RAM, and the number of virtual CPUs (vCPUs) is referred to as "scaling up"—this is vertical scaling.

☒ **A** and **D** are incorrect. IP addressing and load balancing are not directly related to VM vertical scaling.

6. ☑ **A.** Resizing a virtual machine either increases or decreases its compute power. Decreasing it reduces cloud costs.

☒ **B, C,** and **D** are incorrect. Resizing a VM is a more efficient method of adjusting the required compute power than deleting and re-creating the VM. Autoscaling and load balancing are not directly related to compute power hardware resources.

7. ☑ **C.** Because other offices can successfully connect using RDP, the firewall rules at the headquarters location must be blocking port 3389 RDP traffic.

☒ **A, B,** and **D** are incorrect. Cloud firewall rules are not the problem; other offices can successfully connect using RDP. RDP uses port 3389, not 389.

8. ☑ **B** and **D.** Secure Shell (SSH) public key authentication in the cloud stores public keys with the virtual machine in the cloud. The related private key is stored on the user device.

☒ **A** and **C** are incorrect. Public keys are not stored on the connecting device. Private keys are not stored in the cloud.

9. ☑ **B** and **D.** A jump box provides the public connectivity point for remotely managing cloud virtual machines without exposing each VM directly to the Internet. Configuring a VPN to the cloud uses a single public connectivity point through which VM remote management can be securely conducted.

☒ **A** and **C** are incorrect. Virtual machines should not be directly exposed to the Internet, when possible. Autoscaling does not address remote management or security exposure issues.

10. ☑ **C** and **D.** Custom network routes control network traffic flow, such as to a firewall appliance, which normally has at least two virtual network interfaces.

☒ **A** and **B** are incorrect. Switching the operating system image and resizing the virtual machine will not enable a firewall appliance.

High-Performance Computing

11. ☑ **C.** High-performance computing uses groups of virtual machine nodes to run complex tasks for large datasets.

☒ **A, B,** and **D** are incorrect. A cloud service provider (CSP), content delivery network (CDN), or software-defined networking (SDN) does not provide the means to analyze large datasets.

12. ☑ **B.** High-performance computing (HPC) uses a cluster of virtual machines to process complex tasks in parallel.

☒ **A, C,** and **D** are incorrect. Security, NoSQL, and templates are not as closely related to HPC as the term "cluster" is.

13. ☑ **C.** Before an HPC cluster can process vast datasets in the cloud, the data must first be made available in the cloud.

☒ **A, B,** and **D** are incorrect. Deploying the HPC cluster should occur after the relevant data is in the cloud. HPC clusters do not use load balancers. HPC clusters do autoscale as required, but VM autoscaling is configured after moving the target data into the cloud.

14. ☑ **D.** Solid-state drives (SSDs) provide the best disk performance.

☒ **A, B,** and **C** are incorrect. Software-defined networking (SDN) is not related to disk performance. Input/output operations per second (IOPS) is not a cloud disk configuration; instead, IOPS increases when SSD is selected. Hard disk drives (HDDs) are slower than SSDs.

15. ☑ **C.** The AWS CloudWatch service is used for cloud resource monitoring.

☒ **A, B,** and **D** are incorrect. Direct Connect is the AWS dedicated private network circuit solution; ExpressRoute is Microsoft Azure's solution. A content delivery network (CDN) caches content near users geographically.

Chapter 8

Applications and Big Data in the Cloud

T his chapter explores how software runs in a cloud computing environment. Creating new cloud applications or migrating existing applications to the cloud allows organizations to leverage the enormity of cloud compute, storage, and network resources to support applications and data analysis.

We start by discussing the use of a service-oriented architecture in the cloud to create modular software components. Microservices are a key part of this architecture.

Next, we focus on blockchain technology and how organizations can leverage the cloud for private blockchain use. We will also explore the merits of using application containers compared to running apps within virtual machines.

Finally, we identify what big data refers to, along with how cloud services enable these vast datasets to be stored efficiently in databases and analyzed via clusters.

CERTIFICATION OBJECTIVE 8.01

Service-Oriented Architecture

In the cloud computing world, a service is a computer program hosted in the cloud as a stand-alone cloud function or application programming interface (API), which is a collection of functions.

Cloud services can be used within a cloud virtual machine, within an application container, or even called by on-premises software components. Existing cloud provider services can be leveraged, or custom cloud services can be created. Services provide a specific function, such as updating website content automatically as origin data changes (this is called a content management system, or CMS), or checking the latest stock quotes and analyzing trading trends using cloud analytic services.

Service-oriented architecture (SOA) is a framework that strives to organize distributed software components into services that can interact with each other over a network, whether each service is a part of the same or a different application. The services can reside both on-premises and in the cloud.

Modern cloud software development practices include the creation of microservices that allow interconnectivity from other software components.

Microservices can be written in any programming language, including popular choices such as Java, C++, C#, and F#.

Microservices

Years ago, software developers would build and test an entire application as a single unit, which included the user interface and data processing code, otherwise called a *monolithic* application. Today, software developers decentralize the process and build and test microservices. A *microservice* is an example of service-oriented architecture; it is a small program with a specific function that may also have the ability to send or receive messages to other software components. An application can consist of many microservices, all working together. Think "divide and conquer," where a large app is broken down into smaller functional components. Microservices can speed up software development and updates since smaller specialized app fragments can be focused on instead of a single larger app.

Each microservice performs a specific function. For example, one microservice might be responsible for validating user input on a web form, while another might be responsible for printing the web form. A microservice can make API calls to existing cloud provider APIs, such as calling a cloud storage API. Applications that use only cloud API calls are referred to as *cloud-native applications*.

Loose coupling is a computer programming microservices approach whereby one microservice can pass a message to another microservice through a message queue. In the cloud, software developers can deploy message queues as a type of cloud storage. The benefit is that the receiving microservice does not have to be running when the sending microservice passes the message, because the message can be read at any time from the message queue.

Testing software is a crucial quality assurance (QA) activity. Each microservice can be tested independently from other microservices. This means that testing goals can be very focused on the functionality of each particular microservice. This can speed up testing while other app microservices continue functioning.

Microservice Scaling

Each microservice can also be scaled separately to meet demand. Traditional app scaling uses a load balancer that accepts client requests for an app. The load balancer then routes those requests to the least-busy, most-responsive back-end server. This means each back-end server (virtual machine) has a full copy of the entire application.

With microservices, scaling to meet demand is set per microservice as needed. For example, a shopping website might scale "searching" or "shopping cart checkout" separately from the "print invoice" microservice. This uses underlying compute resources more efficiently, directing compute power where it is most needed.

Microservice Intercommunication

So how do microservices pass messages to one another? As previously stated, microservice messages can be dropped into and read from message queues. But what type of transport does this use over the network?

Hypertext Transfer Protocol (HTTP) is one common network communication protocol used for exchanging messages (usually through a message queue) between microservices. Microservices, for example, can make cloud API calls, such as to process messages in a queue, over HTTP. Ideally, Hypertext Transfer Protocol Secure (HTTPS) is used to encrypt the traffic. HTTPS requires services to be configured with a PKI certificate. The keys in the

PKI certificate are used for encryption and decryption of network transmissions. Where HTTP/S is the transport mechanism, Representational State Transfer (REST) is a method of connecting to resource Uniform Resource Identifiers (URIs) and examining the return codes and values.

on the job **A URI identifies a resource, but it does not specify how to access it over a network as a Uniform Resource Locator (URL) does. URLs specify a protocol, or access method, such as http://, https://, ftp://, and so on. A URL is a type of URI that specifies how to get to the resource.**

Like RESTful communication, Simple Object Access Protocol (SOAP) is also used to exchange messages between microservices, but it is a bit different because it is a standardized protocol. SOAP is not always implemented over HTTP as REST overwhelmingly is; SOAP is often implemented using other network protocols such as Simple Mail Transfer Protocol (SMTP) or File Transfer Protocol (FTP). The SOAP message exchange format is usually Extensible Markup Language (XML) as opposed to the REST norm of JavaScript Object Notation (JSON).

on the job **Technically, REST does not *have* to use HTTP, but it normally does since using other protocols such as Transmission Control Protocol (TCP) would require you to end up making HTTP calls anyway. Software developers know that REST normally uses HTTP, and SOAP is a bit more spread out in terms of the underlying network protocols normally used.**

Content Management Systems

Working with web applications that use a service-oriented architecture, whether on premises or in the cloud, means managing the content served up by those web apps, which can also be a website. A website consists of web pages displayed in a client web browser app. Web apps do not have to use a web browser; for example, consider the Dropbox mobile phone app, which is used to connect to cloud data over the Web. *Content management* encompasses the creation, securing, modification, and deletion of data.

A *content management system (CMS)* facilitates the management of web app content by hiding the underlying creation and management complexities from content managers. As an example, imagine that a small business owner who does not have IT knowledge wants to create a business website. Using a CMS allows this nontechnical user to create a functional website without having to write a single line of code. At the enterprise level, CMS solutions can also handle document management functionality such as versioning and document check-in and checkout. WordPress and Drupal are examples of common CMS solutions.

CERTIFICATION OBJECTIVE 8.02

Blockchain

After the financial crisis of 2008, many people had a reason to distrust governments and the global banking and financial system. This financial meltdown led to the creation of Bitcoin, the first successful implementation of blockchain technology , by the mysterious identity "Satoshi Nakamoto." Blockchain technology uses a combination of cryptography and collaboration among millions of computers to establish a trusted, decentralized public transaction ledger that efficiently and permanently records transactions between parties in a way that is verifiable yet anonymous (with no reliance on banks, governments, or contract managers of any type). Because a blockchain does not depend on an external entity, it is referred to as an *autonomous* environment. Organizations can deploy private blockchains in the cloud for enterprise (and not public) use. Digital assets of many types can be included in a blockchain, such as this small sample:

- Music
- Literature
- Financial transactions
- Smart contracts

A *smart contract* is a contract added to the blockchain using the *Ethereum* platform. Imagine that instead of hiring a manager, an inventor adds technical and contractual details about an invention to the blockchain (this is a smart contract). Payments that result from the smart contract are paid almost immediately and directly to the owner of that intellectual property.

The blockchain is a chronological, verified public ledger of transactions stored across millions of computers (decentralized) around the globe. Every ten minutes, the newest

FIGURE 8-1 Real-time view of blockchain transactions

Bitcoin $8,108.06 BTC	Latest blocks				View more blocks
	Height	Hash	Mined	Miner	Size
Blocks	597696	0..a6a743cc60281bc4a3edc12226d954cc3aa22e...	4 minutes	ViaBTC	1,293,865 bytes
Transactions	597695	0..550e0840fcc046ae01d0449b3d2505a9e18b2f...	11 minutes	Unknown	1,246,494 bytes
Average Fee	597694	0..38d9253d6babe893dad185fdc57ebefc61ee24e...	12 minutes	F2Pool	1,402,449 bytes
Average Value	597693	0..7602674d5041762f3d026722e94b9080a5f2a9...	24 minutes	BTC.com	1,357,460 bytes
Difficulty	597692	0..116d1df3208d61693d3eb38b3980db4c766d0d...	42 minutes	Unknown	1,257,072 bytes
Hashrate	597691	0..7f75d0123c498e344dcd74948b1d9c1bfc4aad6...	42 minutes	Unknown	1,198,402 bytes
Mempool	597690	0..2a7d6433aea624d789e72b2ce908af809f7eac1...	47 minutes	SlushPool	1,393,025 bytes
Price	597689	0..4aae2e967536b7a1ab40335a105985251cb14e...	52 minutes	Unknown	1,321,795 bytes
Tx per day	597688	0..10a653d313e0b5c5f915cf925945e195082e375...	2 hours	BTC.TOP	1,172,035 bytes
Unconfirmed	597687	0..e6427d9aacb3f5ab7c0a8d7ed81109c0f19fb0c7...	2 hours	Unknown	1,232,597 bytes
Ethereum $172.35 ETH	597686	0..eb5128b1032dbebe4f71f68e4b3914b747b03ea...	2 hours	SlushPool	2,093,771 bytes
Bitcoin Cash $218.89 BCH	597685	0..146eecad2f5adfc3ab505da3dbd752aaca67cc5...	2 hours	BTC.com	2,133,210 bytes

set of blockchain transactions (conducted in the last ten minutes) is added to the existing blockchain, but only after *miners* (discussed shortly) verify the block. A block is a collection of transactions. Even though the ledger transactions are public and stored many times over, the identities of parties involved in transactions are not disclosed. Figure 8-1 shows how the blockchain.com block explorer service website can be used to view Bitcoin cryptocurrency blocks.

A set of transactions, or a *block*, is posted across millions of computers worldwide after it has been verified by blockchain nodes. Once the block is added to the chain, it cannot be modified; in other words, it is *immutable*. Cryptocurrencies are digital assets that rely on blockchain technology. Bitcoin is only one example of a cryptocurrency. Blockchain transactions include details such as

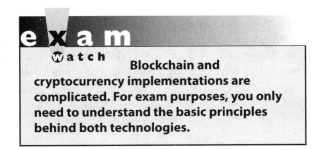

■ A date and time stamp

■ The current block's unique hash value

■ The previous block's unique hash value

■ The actual data added to the blockchain (financial transaction details, smart contract details, etc.)

exam

watch **Blockchain and cryptocurrency implementations are complicated. For exam purposes, you only need to understand the basic principles behind both technologies.**

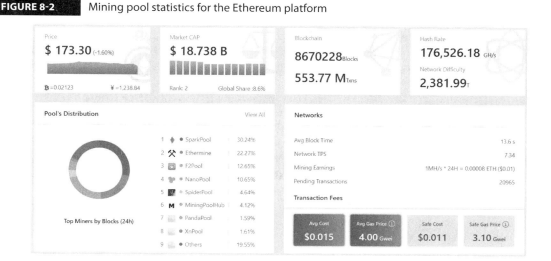

FIGURE 8-2 Mining pool statistics for the Ethereum platform

Cryptocurrency Miners

Consensus among blockchain nodes is required to prove the validity of blocks before they are added to the blockchain. This is in opposition to using traditional banking to send payments, where the bank is the sole trusted entity. Blockchain fees are normally much lower than bank fees.

Miner nodes are computers, or groups of computers, with enormous compute power that compete with one another to validate the authenticity of blockchain transactions. In return, miners are paid a fee, often in Bitcoins, by the parties involved in the transaction. Over the last few years, this fee payment has incentivized malicious users to compromise powerful computer systems to use them as miners, which consumes large amounts of electricity due to the computational power required. Figure 8-2 shows an example of mining pool statistics.

Cryptocurrency Implementations

By far, Bitcoin is the best-known cryptocurrency. There are many others, including Monero, Litecoin, DASH, and NEO, to name just a few.

Cryptocurrencies like Bitcoin are interesting in that, unlike physical currency such as the U.S. dollar (USD) or Swiss franc (CHf), which can be printed as much as deemed appropriate by monetary policy, Bitcoin has a cap of 21 million. This means there will never be more than 21 million Bitcoins available, although Bitcoins can be divided into much smaller units, just as a USD can be broken down into smaller denominations of coins.

The lack of government control with cryptocurrency is also interesting in that it can reduce corruption and questionable practices, since cryptocurrency transactions rely on blockchain technology, and blockchain transactions are transparent; they exist in a digital public transaction ledger. In most countries, however, cryptocurrency gains are taxable. In the United States, the Internal Revenue Service (IRS) has been cracking down on tax cheats who do not report income derived through the use of cryptocurrencies; in Canada, the Canada Revenue Agency (CRA) is now doing the same thing (see Figure 8-3), as are many other governments around the world.

You might be wondering, what does this have to do with the cloud? Organizations can implement their own variations of blockchain technology for use within an enterprise. Cloud service provider blockchain solutions can use blockchain technology to enable organizations to digitize business processes, such as working with smart contracts. Using blockchain with cryptocurrencies is not a cloud service provider solution; blockchain must be decentralized and not owned or managed by a single organization. Software developers can also leverage cloud computing to create and test blockchain and cryptocurrency solutions.

FIGURE 8-3   Canada Revenue Agency cryptocurrency web page

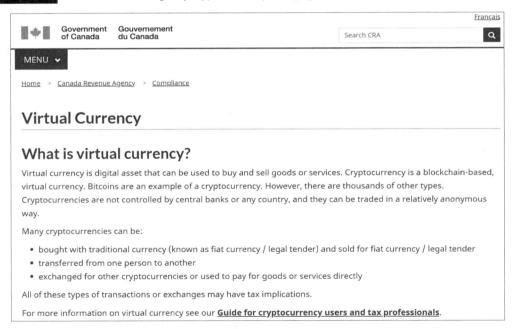

Application Containers

An *application container* provides logical isolation for application files and dependencies from the host system running the container. Containers are based on images. Using application containerization is an alternative to having to install and run application software directly within an operating system. Software developers love application containers because they can focus on the app (and not the OS), app containers can be easily moved to a different container host, and app containers start up much quicker than virtual machines because they use the underlying host OS that is already running.

Docker is the most common software that allows the management and execution of application containers, although other solutions exist, such as the Linux-based LXD container manager solution. Hosting containers in the cloud falls under the Platform as a Service (PaaS) cloud service model. Docker can run within a Unix, Linux, or Windows operating system, including within a cloud virtual machine, and has its own command-line environment. As you can see in Figure 8-4, you can deploy cloud-based virtual machines that already have Docker installed and ready to go.

Container Images

A *container image* consists of files required to run an application or microservice. Unlike a virtual machine, a container image doesn't contain operating system (OS) files. Instead, images rely on the underlying host operating system.

FIGURE 8-4   Deploying a Docker virtual machine in Microsoft Azure

A Linux container image, therefore, will run only on a Linux machine. The way many implementations get around this is to use a single lightweight virtual machine. Docker for Windows, for example, can use an Alpine Linux virtual machine that is only approximately 5MB in size. This allows Linux-based container images to run on a Windows host.

Containers

A *container* is a run-time instance of a container image. This feeds perfectly into microservices; each microservice can be deployed into its own container, which allows portability to different hosts and the ability to update, test, and load-balance specific containers.

Microsoft Azure supports the creation and management of an Azure Container Registry cloud resource. This serves as a private repository of images used by an organization. (Based on that description, you'd think it would be called "Azure *Image* Registry.") AWS offers its own version, called Amazon Elastic Container Registry (ECR).

Because containers rely on the underlying OS (they don't contain any OS files), and the OS is already running on the host, containers start up very quickly compared to spinning up a virtual machine. Containers can also be connected to and managed over the network, such as to manage files in the container, or scripts in the container image that will execute when the container is launched.

CERTIFICATION OBJECTIVE 8.04

Big Data Analytics

Thanks to the widespread use of the Internet by a wide array of devices, the amount of Internet data generated on a daily basis is staggering. Just try to absorb the fact that up to 4 million hours of new YouTube content is uploaded every day! This figure is an approximation; only Google really knows what the exact number is since it owns YouTube.

Now try to imagine manually sifting through vast datasets trying to identify patterns, trends, and relationships—good luck! Thanks to big data analytics in the cloud, it's quick and inexpensive to spin up a cluster, feed it large datasets, and analyze the results to gain insights that otherwise would not be available.

Big data analytics solutions use *clusters*, or collections of virtual machine nodes working together, to analyze large amounts of data. That data is typically stored in NoSQL databases, which are designed to store large amounts of unstructured data, or data that differs greatly from row to row. Unstructured data is the result of many potential different data sources, including any type of database, social media feeds, stock quotes, network security logs, IoT device statistics, and so on. These sources can produce vast amounts of data that do not all follow the same storage format. Compare this to SQL databases, which use a rigid structure for storing data that requires each row to store the same type of data. When this type of solution is a managed service, cloud customers are spared from having to manually configure virtual machines, clusters, and databases. Figure 8-5 shows the initial Getting Started page for the Amazon Athena big data analytics solution.

To optimize cluster performance, you need to determine what "normal" performance of the database and cluster is so that you have a *baseline*, essentially a benchmark, of acceptable database and cluster performance. You can then monitor the cluster performance to determine if you need to increase (or decrease) the amount of compute power or storage space needed to analyze your data.

You can even leverage a hybrid solution where you use both on-premises and cloud-based NoSQL databases and clusters to analyze data. In some cases, for performance reasons, you might need to convert an on-premises virtual machine so that it runs directly on physical hardware, known as a *virtual to physical (V2P)* conversion.

FIGURE 8-5   Deploying the Amazon Athena big data analytics solution

Internet of Things

Contributing to the vast amounts of data being generated daily on the Internet, Internet of Things (IoT) devices have now become commonplace. An IoT device is simply a device that can communicate over the Internet. Examples include

- Baby monitors
- Smart cars (GPS location, vehicle speed statistics)
- Medical devices to monitor patients' health remotely
- Home and industrial environmental controls
- Video surveillance equipment

Cloud service providers offer IoT solutions in the form of centralized IoT data repositories. You can register IoT devices with a cloud repository so that data streamed from the devices over the Internet is available in one location. Streamed data could include video feeds, audio, medical patient vital statistics, and so on. This collected IoT data could then be fed into a cloud data analysis solution to find patterns and perform modeling.

The security angle on this is the fact that many IoT devices ship with default settings that present security problems, such as embedded web interfaces with credentials that cannot be changed. In some cases, vendors do not provide any IoT device updates at all, even when security vulnerabilities are discovered! Bear this in mind when you consider collecting in the cloud IoT data that potentially has been tampered with. One solution is to only use IoT devices that adhere to strict security standards, or have developers write code that analyzes incoming IoT data.

Machine Learning

Artificial intelligence (AI) is a broad concept. AI solutions strive to mimic intelligent human behavior through the use of technology. Machine learning (ML) takes this a few steps further by empowering technicians to "teach" software to make decisions and predictions based on big data. Examples of ML include the ability to learn from past experiences, derive meaning from vast amounts of data to identify future trends, and comprehend speech patterns.

ML tools enable you to create training models to "teach" software how to make decisions that align with human requirements. Microsoft Azure Machine Learning Studio is a GUI tool that lets you drag and drop data source and data analysis components onto a design canvas to identify items such as

- Most likely income bracket related to immigration, marital status, race, and industry
- Financial credit risks
- Medial patients at high risk of heart disease
- Likelihood of abnormal weather events

EXERCISE 8-1

Create a Microsoft Azure Queue

In this exercise, you will create a Microsoft Azure message queue, which first requires a storage account. This exercise depends on having completed Exercise 1-1.

1. Use your web browser to sign in to the Microsoft Azure portal at https://portal .azure.com.
2. At the top of the navigation pane on the left, click Create a Resource.
3. In the Search field, type **storage account** and then click Storage Account in the drop-down list.
4. On the Storage Account screen, click the Create button.
5. Configure the storage account with the following settings (accept the default values for all other settings):
   - Resource group: Create a new one named **ResGroup2**
   - Storage account name: **storacct1290**
6. Click Review + Create, then click Create.
7. When the deployment is complete, click the Go to Resource button to view the storage account properties.
8. In the storage account properties navigation bar, scroll down and click Queues.
9. In the right panel, click the +Queue button.
10. Name the queue **queue1** and click the OK button. You will see the newly created queue, as shown in Figure 8-6.

11. In the storage account properties navigation bar, scroll up and notice the Shared Access Signature and Access Keys options. Software developers can build solutions that use either an access key (either key provides access to the entire storage account) or a more granular shared access signature (can provide access to only queues for a limited period of time) to read and write queued items.

FIGURE 8-6   A Microsoft Azure queue

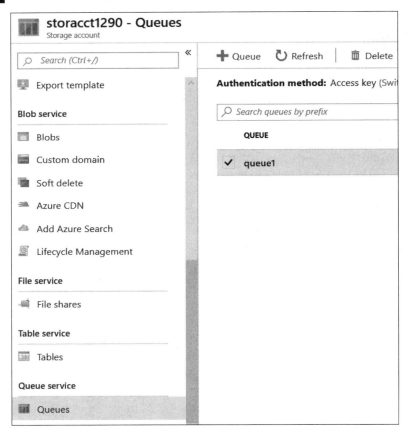

EXERCISE 8-2

Create a Microsoft Azure Container Registry

In this exercise, you will create a Microsoft Azure container registry. This exercise depends on having completed Exercise 1-1.

1. Use your web browser to sign in to the Microsoft Azure portal at https://portal.azure.com.
2. At the top of the navigation pane on the left, click Create a Resource.
3. In the Search field, type **container registry** and then click Container Registry in the drop-down list.
4. On the Container Registry screen, click the Create button.
5. Select an existing resource group or create a new one.
6. Use the following values to deploy the Windows virtual machine. Accept all other default values:
   - Name: **ACR1290**
   - Resource Group: **ResGroup2**
7. Click the Create button.
8. In the upper right of the screen, click the notification icon (shown in Figure 8-7) and click the Go to Resource button.

FIGURE 8-7   Microsoft Azure portal notification area

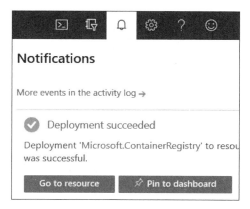

9. In the container registry navigation panel, scroll down to Access Keys. Enabling the admin user option would allow Docker container administrators to push custom images into the cloud-based repository given the login server, username, and password (either one) values. These values are visible when viewing the container registry access keys.

INSIDE THE EXAM

Big Data

The CompTIA Cloud Essentials+ CLO-002 exam could present you with questions related to integrating a variety of data sources for use by big data analytics clusters running in the cloud. If a data source exists on premises, then network quality of service (QoS) might be required to ensure the timely transfer of data into the cloud for analysis. For example, HTTPS traffic from a specific on-premises host can be prioritized to be sent to cloud software components before standard user-generated web browser HTTP traffic. This is especially true if the on-premises data source is constantly updated, such as with on-premises IoT device statistics.

CERTIFICATION SUMMARY

This chapter exposed you to the notion of a service-oriented architecture (SOA), in which a service is a small computer program. Next, the focus shifted to microservices, which provide a modular software development approach in the cloud; each microservice has a specific function and can be updated, tested, and scaled independently of other microservices. A modular software approach lends itself to loose coupling, whereby one microservice can pass messages to a second microservice through a message queue. This means microservices that communicate with one another do not have to be up and running at the same time.

You also learned that a content management system (CMS) allows a person to create and manage website content without having to know the technical details of working with websites or writing code. CMS can also be automated to retrieve source data changes and update website content.

Next, you saw how blockchain provides a trusted, decentralized public ledger of transactions that is stored across millions of computers. The blockchain is updated every ten minutes with new transactions for which a consensus has been reached by blockchain nodes (miners) that the new transactions are valid. A blockchain *block* contains date and time stamp information, financial details about transactions, the unique hash for the current block, and the unique hash of the previous block in the chain. *Cryptocurrency* refers to digital assets that use blockchain technology, such as Bitcoin. Cloud customers can deploy custom blockchain technologies in the cloud for private enterprise use.

You then learned that application containers are run-time instances of images that provide a logical boundary for application files and settings. Each microservice can be deployed into its own container. Containers start very quickly because they rely on the underlying host OS and, unlike a virtual machine, do not have to start up an entire operating system—it's already running!

Finally, you learned that machine learning (ML) is an implementation of artificial intelligence (AI) that can process vast amounts of data (big data) and make intelligent predictions or decisions, such as whether a person presents a credit risk or whether a particular stock might do well in the next quarter.

 # TWO-MINUTE DRILL

Service-Oriented Architecture

- ❑ Services are small computer programs.
- ❑ Microservices are a modular approach to software development.
- ❑ Each microservice provides a very specific function and can be written in any language.
- ❑ Applications can consist of many microservices working together.
- ❑ Loose coupling means a target microservice does not have to be running at the same time that a source microservice sends a message; instead, the target can read the message from a message queue.
- ❑ Microservices can be updated, tested, and scaled independently of one another.
- ❑ Messages are often passed over the network between microservices using HTTP with message handling through REST or SOAP.
- ❑ A content management system (CMS) allows nontechnical users to create and manage website content without writing code.

Blockchain

❏ A blockchain is a publicly transparent digital ledger of transactions (a collection of blocks) that cannot be modified.

❏ Each block (list of transactions) contains details such as date and time stamps, financial values, the current block's unique hash, and the previous block's unique hash.

❏ A blockchain is decentralized, meaning it is stored across many computers.

❏ A smart contract is added to the blockchain and can automate the execution of contract details, such as payments to intellectual property owners.

❏ The blockchain is chronological and updated every ten minutes.

❏ Blockchain updates occur only after a consensus has been reached among blockchain nodes about the validity of the blocks.

❏ Cryptocurrency refers to digital assets consisting of any commodity that has value, such as Bitcoins, intellectual property, or contracts.

❏ Cryptocurrency miners are computers or groups of computers with a large amount of compute power that are used to validate blockchain transactions.

❏ Cryptocurrency is not controlled by governments or financial institutions.

Application Containers

❏ Images contain application files and settings.

❏ Images do not contain operating system files.

❏ Images are contained in either private or public repositories where new images can be uploaded and existing images can be downloaded, depending on permissions.

❏ Images are portable, meaning they can easily be moved to other hosts running application containerization software such as Docker.

❏ Containers are run-time instances of images.

❏ Containers start up very quickly because they use the host operating system that is already running.

❏ Microservices are often created to run in their own containers.

❏ Most cloud service providers can host image repositories.

Big Data Analytics

❏ Big data refers to vast datasets that can come from a variety of different sources, including Internet of Things (IoT) devices.

❏ IoT refers to devices that communicate over the Internet, such as home environmental controls or smart car data such as GPS location or car speed statistics.

❏ Most cloud service providers offer an IoT repository where registered IoT devices can send their data for further processing.

❏ NoSQL databases are designed to store massive amounts of unstructured data.

❏ Big data analytics uses clusters of virtual machines working together to analyze large amounts of data.

❏ Virtual to physical (V2P) refers to converting a VM to an OS configuration that runs on physical hardware. This is sometimes necessary when all of the compute power of a physical host must be allocated to a single task.

❏ Artificial intelligence (AI) refers to software behaving in a manner similar to human beings.

❏ Machine learning (ML) takes AI further by allowing technicians to "teach" software to make decisions and predictions based on big data.

SELF TEST

The following questions will help you measure your understanding of the material presented in this chapter. As indicated, some questions may have more than one correct answer, so be sure to read all the answer choices carefully.

Service-Oriented Architecture

1. Which of the following terms is most closely associated with the term "microservice"?
   A. Encryption
   B. Machine learning
   C. Modular
   D. Blockchain

2. You have developed a microservice that can pass messages to other microservices even if they are not running. Which term best encompasses this configuration?
   A. Loose coupling
   B. Monolithic
   C. Machine learning
   D. Blockchain

3. Which of the following benefits is most likely to be derived from the use of microservices in application development?

   A. Encryption using HTTPS

   B. Facilitated cloud service provider exit strategy

   C. Ability to add to a blockchain

   D. Ability to test one component while others remain running

4. Which of the following identifies a network resource, but not how to access the resource?

   A. URI

   B. REST

   C. SOAP

   D. URL

Blockchain

5. Which blockchain characteristic prevents the modification of past transactions?

   A. Hashing

   B. Encryption

   C. Immutability

   D. Decentralization

6. Which piece of data uniquely identifies a blockchain block?

   A. Block size

   B. Miner node name

   C. Date and time stamp

   D. Hash

7. How often is a blockchain on the Internet updated?

   A. Every minute

   B. Every five minutes

   C. Every ten minutes

   D. Every hour

Application Containers

8. Which of the following is designed to run application containers?

   A. CMS

   B. Docker

   C. Blockchain

   D. Machine learning

   9. How are container images and containers related?
      A. The terms are synonymous.
      B. Images are run-time instances of containers.
      C. Containers are run-time instances of images.
      D. Images contain operating system files, whereas containers do not.

  10. Why do application containers start very quickly?
      A. They use SSD storage.
      B. They contain a small optimized version of the operating system.
      C. They use the underlying host operating system.
      D. They are cached in memory.

Big Data Analytics

  11. Which type of storage is designed for big data?
      A. SQL
      B. NoSQL
      C. Message queue
      D. Image registry

  12. When working with big data analytics clusters, what is required before determining whether performance is acceptable or not?
      A. Metric alerts
      B. Image registry
      C. Baseline
      D. Message queue

  13. Your company has vast amounts of medical research data that needs to be analyzed to predict future health patterns. Which cloud solution should you implement?
      A. Machine learning
      B. Artificial intelligence
      C. Blockchain
      D. Internet of Things

  14. Which of the following terms is the most closely associated with machine learning?
      A. Blockchain
      B. Application container
      C. Image registry
      D. Training model

15. Which of the following are benefits derived from the use of machine learning? (Choose two.)
- A. Establishing baselines
- B. Predicting outcomes
- C. Deploying VMs
- D. Recognizing patterns

SELF TEST ANSWERS

Service-Oriented Architecture

1. ☑ **C.** Microservices are a module-based approach to software development, where each microservice performs a specific function. An application can consist of many microservices.
☒ **A, B,** and **D** are incorrect. Encryption scrambles data so that only authorized users with the correct key can decrypt it. Machine learning means training machines to analyzes large datasets to make informed decisions and to identify patterns to predict future trends. On the Internet, a blockchain is a decentralized, verified public ledger of transactions that cannot be modified.

2. ☑ **A.** Loose coupling refers to using microservices that can exchange messages even if they are not running simultaneously, by using message queues.
☒ **B, C,** and **D** are incorrect. Monolithic apps are those that unify all app functionality instead of dividing the app into functionally specific components, or microservices. Machine learning analyzes large datasets to make informed decisions and to identify patterns to predict future trends. A blockchain is a decentralized, verified public ledger of transactions that cannot be modified.

3. ☑ **D.** Applications can consist of multiple microservices, which are modular software components that can each be tested independently of others.
☒ **A, B,** and **C** are incorrect. Encryption using HTTPS secures HTTP-based network communications but is not directly related to microservices. CSP exit strategies are used to plan to cease the use of a specific CSP. Microservices are not necessarily related to adding blockchain transactions.

4. ☑ **A.** A Uniform Resource Identifier (URI) specifies a network resource, but not exactly how to access it, such as using HTTP, HTTPS, or FTP, as does a URL.

☒ **B, C,** and **D** are incorrect. Representational State Transfer (REST) is a style of extracting data from a network resource such as a web service. Simple Object Access Protocol (SOAP) is a standardized protocol used to extract data over a network using XML as the data format.

Blockchain

5. ☑ **C.** When something is immutable, it cannot be modified. Past blockchain transactions are immutable; they cannot be tampered with.
    ☒ **A, B,** and **D** are incorrect. Hashing generates a unique value that can be used to determine if modifications have taken place, but it does not prevent modification. Encryption scrambles data so that only authorized parties with the correct key can decrypt the data. Decentralization means that a blockchain is spread across many computers; this does not prevent the modification of past transactions.

6. ☑ **D.** A hash results from feeding data into a one-way hashing algorithm. It uniquely represents the blockchain block.
    ☒ **A, B,** and **C** are incorrect. A blockchain transaction is not uniquely identified by the block size, miner node name, or date and time stamp.

7. ☑ **C.** New blockchain transactions are added once every ten minutes.
    ☒ **A, B,** and **D** are incorrect. These do not represent the blockchain update interval.

Application Containers

8. ☑ **B.** Docker is software running on a Windows-based or Linux-based host that can run and manage application images and containers.
    ☒ **A, C,** and **D** are incorrect. A content management system (CMS) enables a person to create and manage website content without requiring detailed technical knowledge or coding skills. A blockchain is a decentralized, verified public ledger of transactions that cannot be modified. Machine learning analyzes large datasets to make informed decisions and to identify patterns to predict future trends.

9. ☑ **C.** Application containers are launched from application images. A container is a run-time instance of an image.
    ☒ **A, B,** and **D** are incorrect. Application images contain app files and settings; when the image is running, it is called a container. Neither images nor containers contain operating system files.

10. ☑ **C.** Application containers start quickly because they use the host operating system that is already running.
    ☒ **A, B,** and **D** are incorrect. Solid-state drive (SSD) storage is not the reason application containers start quickly. Application containers do not contain an operating system, nor are they cached in memory.

Big Data Analytics

11. ☑ **B.** NoSQL allows unstructured data storage, which means each row could store completely different types of data.

☒ **A, C,** and **D** are incorrect. SQL databases use a rigid schema, or blueprint, of what is allowed to be stored. Message queues are used to temporarily store messages passed between software components, not big data. Image registries, which can be private or public, store application images.

12. ☑ **C.** A baseline is a measure of normal activity, which helps to identify outliers from that normal performance.

☒ **A, B,** and **D** are incorrect. Metric alerts feed into establishing a baseline, but do not by themselves help determine if performance is acceptable or not. Image registries, which can be private or public, store application images, but are not related to performance. Message queues are used to temporarily store messages passed between software components.

13. ☑ **A.** Machine learning (ML) analyzes large datasets and can be "trained" to make informed decisions and to identify patterns to predict future trends.

☒ **B, C,** and **D** are incorrect. Artificial intelligence (AI) is a broad term that relates to software mimicking human behavior. ML is an implementation of AI. A blockchain is a decentralized, verified public ledger of transactions that cannot be modified. Internet of Things (IoT) refers to devices that can communicate over the Internet.

14. ☑ **D.** Machine learning analyzes large datasets and can be "trained" to make informed decisions and to identify patterns to predict future trends.

☒ **A, B,** and **C** are incorrect. A blockchain is a decentralized, verified public ledger of transactions that cannot be modified. Application containers contain application files and settings. Image registries, which can be private or public, store application images, but are not related to performance.

15. ☑ **B** and **D.** Machine learning (ML) analyzes datasets and can be "trained" to make decisions or future predictions, as well as to identify patterns.

☒ **A** and **C** are incorrect. Baselines and deployment are not directly related to machine learning.

Chapter 9

Cloud DevOps

T his chapter focuses on the marriage of cloud software development and the IT operational tasks involved to efficiently deploy the initial software as well as updates.

First, we will discuss the role of APIs and data exchange formats in cloud DevOps. Next, we will focus on software testing, including the use of sandboxing to conduct tests securely and the use of various software testing types to ensure a high quality of software.

Next, we will focus on the continuous integration and delivery of software solutions in an automated fashion, which depends on code repositories and automation triggers such as code builds and tests that result from code check-ins. Finally, we will examine the relevance of cloud orchestration and how it differs, yet depends on, cloud automation.

CERTIFICATION OBJECTIVE 9.01

Software Development in the Cloud

DevOps is an IT term that combines the words development and operations to describe the intersection of developing software solutions and continuously deploying related updates efficiently and securely. You'll even come across the term *DevSecOps* to emphasize the importance of security at all phases of development, deployment, and ongoing management.

Software developers use cloud-based services such as databases, centralized code repositories, and code pipelines that automate code builds, testing, and deployment. These types of cloud services fall under the Platform as a Service (PaaS) cloud service model and are sometimes called *serverless* because they are always supported by an underlying virtual machine server; they are also considered *managed services* because the developer need not be concerned with deploying and managing the virtual machine supporting the service.

Using the cloud to develop and host software services involves calling upon or creating application programming interfaces (APIs) and determining how data will be exchanged between software components, as discussed next.

Application Programming Interfaces

Think of an API as a collection of related functions that can be called upon by, or hooked into, other software components. If you were writing code back in the 1990s, you probably called on Win32 APIs to perform a wide variety of tasks in the Windows operating system. These days, you can build your own APIs in the cloud or you can use existing cloud APIs for programmatic access to cloud resources. You can also call existing APIs from within your own custom software solutions; this is referred to as *API* integration. Common API message exchange mechanisms include SOAP and REST, as discussed in Chapter 8.

Using Existing Cloud APIs

APIs are available for devices, for operating systems, for applications, and (normally) for each type of cloud service offering. For example, the Elastic Cloud Compute (EC2) API supports programmatic access to VM instances in the Amazon Web Services (AWS) cloud. If you're into developing health and fitness apps, there is even an API for Fitbit fitness activity monitoring devices.

Most cloud service providers offer software development kits (SDKs) to developers. SDKs consist of tools used for developing software in a variety of programming languages, such as the AWS SDK for the C++ programming language, a link to which is shown in Figure 9-1.

To access an existing API, you only need the API documentation. API documentation will let you know the following:

- How to authenticate to the API
- The names of API functions
- Parameters that need to be passed to the functions, including their data types
- API return values, including their data types

FIGURE 9-1 Amazon Web Services programming options

Creating Custom APIs

You can use the cloud to create and host your own custom APIs. What will the APIs do? Anything! The sky is the limit. You might create a hotel and airline reservation API that is triggered when employees in your organization are scheduled to travel for work. Or you might create an API that ingests data gathered by a drone for analysis and then uses a cloud push notification service to send results to smartphones as an SMS text message. You can even integrate existing API function calls within your own APIs.

APIs can be hosted in the cloud through an API *gateway*, an intermediary between clients making API calls and the actual API itself. Yet another option is to host APIs within application containers, which lends itself nicely to module development because each application container hosts one or more related APIs that can be tested and scaled independently of other containers.

Data Exchange Formats

Developing cloud-based software solutions typically involves ingesting, processing, and outputting data. Software components process and transmit this data among one another and among storage media in a variety of different ways, normally over the HTTP/S or SMTP protocols using the XML or JSON formats.

Extensible Markup Language

XML is a standard information exchange format that uses tags to describe data. Using XML tags to describe data looks like this:

```
<Customer>
    <Fname>John</Fname>
    <Lname>Smith</Lname>
    <Email>jsmith@fakeacme.com</Email>
</Customer>
```

JavaScript Object Notation

Referred to as JSON, this is just a different way of expressing data, such as when software components communicate over a network. You can see an example of JSON output from the Microsoft Azure CLI `az vm list` command in Figure 9-2, which lists virtual machine details. JSON syntax uses key–value pairs and looks like this example:

```
{"fname": "John"},
{"lname": "Smith"}
```

```
b3287290-66b8-4bb7-8df8-d1aa50c2@Azure:~$ az vm list
[
  {
    "additionalCapabilities": null,
    "availabilitySet": null,
    "billingProfile": null,
    "diagnosticsProfile": {
      "bootDiagnostics": {
        "enabled": true,
        "storageUri": "https://az400terra.blob.core.windows.net/"
      }
```

FIGURE 9-2   Virtual machine listing using the Microsoft Azure CLI

e x a m

ⓦatch   **XML and JSON do not replace the option of using message queues to store messages between software components. Recall from Chapter 8 that using message** queues allows for the *loose coupling* of **software components. This means software components do not have to be running at the same time to exchange messages.**

CERTIFICATION OBJECTIVE 9.02

Software Testing

An important aspect of DevOps is ensuring the highest level of quality for deployed IT services, otherwise referred to as *quality assurance*. Properly testing software initially and after any changes are made is crucial to ensuring its success. You can employ a number of techniques when it comes to testing.

Sandboxing

Children love playing in sandboxes. IT technicians love having a controlled testing environment (a sandbox). In the cloud, this can be achieved in a number of ways, as you'll see in this section.

The key is to keep testing environments separated from production environments while mimicking the production environment as closely as possible. This includes mimicking not only the infrastructure but also the type of data that the IT system will consume. Depending on your organization, using a copy of production data might be acceptable for sandbox testing, but using live production data is never acceptable.

Virtual Network Isolation

When you define a virtual network in the cloud, you can configure it such that limited or no network traffic can enter or leave that virtual network. You can do so by configuring incoming and outgoing firewall rules and by modifying routing table entries to prevent traffic from being routed into or out of a given network. Figure 9-3 shows how a Microsoft Azure storage account can be configured to limit access from other Azure networks.

Virtual Machines

Virtual machines can also be used as a sandboxing solution. Testing software and various configurations often can occur within a single virtual machine, but sometimes the testing may need to occur across multiple VMs, such as testing a multitiered web app that uses both a web front end deployed on a publicly accessible network and a back-end database on a private network.

Be wary of VMs with more than one network interface card (NIC). You want to avoid a situation where one NIC is correctly connected to a private testing network and the other is connected to a production network.

Application Containers

Even more granular than VMs, containers can execute application code. As discussed in Chapter 8, apps can consist of multiple containers. While each container can present a sandboxed solution (app component isolation), what about running more than one container?

FIGURE 9-3   Microsoft Azure Storage account network access settings

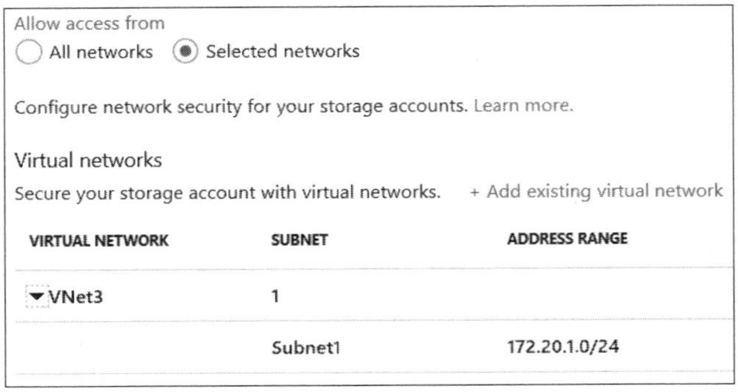

Allow access from
◯ All networks ◉ Selected networks

Configure network security for your storage accounts. Learn more.

Virtual networks
Secure your storage account with virtual networks.   + Add existing virtual network

VIRTUAL NETWORK	SUBNET	ADDRESS RANGE
▼ VNet3	1	
	Subnet1	172.20.1.0/24

TABLE 9-1	Common Testing Types	

Testing Type	Description
Functional	Ensures that the IT solution meets design requirements and is acceptable to users.
Unit	Testing occurs for a single-function application unit (a microservice), such as an application container.
Regression	After a change has been made to software, tests whether existing application components have been adversely affected by the change.
Load	Simulates above-average workloads to determine if application response is acceptable.
Fuzz	Unanticipated random data is fed to an application to ensure the app does not crash or disclose sensitive data.

If the containers are running on a single host, then VM and network isolation settings can prevent connectivity to a production network. If the containers are spread among multiple VMs on the same network, network isolation solves the problem. If the containers are spread among VMs on different networks, then consider relocating the VMs to a single network, or use VPN connectivity or firewall rules to control inter-VM traffic.

Testing Types

After establishing a sandbox testing environment, you need to determine the appropriate type of testing to use for your specific needs. The nature of the software (commercial or custom), the dispersion among hosts, and the networks are only a few factors that influence the decision of which type of testing to conduct. Table 9-1 summarizes common types of tests.

CERTIFICATION OBJECTIVE 9.03

Continuous Integration and Delivery

Commonly referred to as CI/CD, this crucial aspect of DevOps is about ensuring the automated and timely delivery of software solutions over the Internet. Cloud service providers offer many managed services that facilitate code creation, sandbox testing, and the automated delivery of updated software. Updates that focus on specific critical issues are called *patches*. Applying updates and patches falls under the umbrella of configuration management, which strives to ensure software security, stability, and optimal performance.

Amazon Web Services code repositories

Code Repositories

As the name implies, a *code repository* is a central storage location for programming code. You can implement a code repository on premises, but you can also quickly and easily provision one in the cloud, as shown in Figure 9-4. There are also plenty of public code repositories available, such as GitHub, Bitbucket, and SourceForge.

Developers are granted permissions to create new code or modify existing code and check it into the code repository. When changes to code are required, the developer checks out the code, which prevents other developers from modifying it. A microservices approach to software development (introduced in Chapter 8) allows code modules with specific functionality to be separate from other code modules. This provides many efficiencies in scenarios where developers are checking code in and out for a large app that consists of many microservices. The use of microservices allows simultaneous code changes for different microservices, which ultimately speeds up code changes, testing, and deployment. In the cloud, developers are spared from having to manually install and configure servers to support code repositories.

How CI/CD Works

Cloud computing offers economies of scale (many customers, less cost for each customer, etc.) and quick resource provisioning. Add to that automation, and cloud DevOps teams are easily able to achieve CI/CD. Here is how that normally plays out:

1. Developers provision a cloud-based code repository. This could even be linked to a public code repository such as GitHub.
2. Developers create code or modify existing code and check it into the repository. Modifying existing code means checking it out, which prevents modifications from other software developers.
3. Checking in code triggers a new code build.

4. A new code build triggers a variety of automated tests.

5. Upon successful testing, the changed solution is packaged and deployed. Deployment could occur through push notifications or simply publishing updates on a website for consumers to download and apply.

AWS CodeCommit, CodeBuild, CodePipeline, and CodeDeploy are some examples of cloud solutions that provide CI/CD. First of all, these are all managed cloud solutions, so their initial provisioning is quick and easy. Second, each allows for a cloud-based code repository with automated builds, testing, and package deployment.

CERTIFICATION OBJECTIVE 9.04

Cloud Resource Deployment

Cloud resources such as VMs, databases, storage accounts, and web apps can be deployed manually. In some cases, this is the best solution, but in other cases, time can be saved by automating the deployment of cloud resources, which is especially useful when deploying sandbox testing environments over and over.

Cloud Automation

Cloud automation can reduce human error and speed up the creation, modification, and deletion of cloud resources. Consider the following methods of achieving cloud automation:

- Using command-line tools that support iterative loops
- Creating scripts that use command-line tools
- Deploying cloud resources using cloud resource templates, which often are in XML or JSON file formats, also referred to as infrastructure as code (IaC)
- Executing cloud-based batch jobs either on a schedule or by specific triggering events, such as the reception of a specific HTTP request or the presence of a new message in a message queue.

The following Microsoft Azure CLI example uses a JSON template file to deploy a test virtual machine into the ResGroup1 resource group. The template file contains all of the details, such as the name of the VM, the number of virtual disks, and so on.

```
az group deployment create --resource-group ResGroup1 --template-file
D:\Templates\DevTestVM.json
```

on the **Job**

A Microsoft Azure resource group organizes related cloud resources so that they can be managed as a unit. For example, you can organize in a single resource group web application components such as the web server, storage account, load balancer, and back-end database.

Cloud Orchestration

Cloud automation and *cloud orchestration* sometimes are used interchangeably, but they are not the same thing. The preceding section discussed cloud automation; cloud orchestration works on a larger scale. Think of cloud automation as a single musician in an orchestra, whereas cloud orchestration is analogous to the conductor bringing all of the musicians together at the same time to achieve a result not possible with only a single musician.

While cloud automation could be used to deploy a VM without human intervention, cloud orchestration could be used to deploy an entire web application, including VMs, cloud storage, a load balancer, a back-end database, cloud-based user accounts and e-mail boxes, firewall rules, and so on—you get the picture. Organizing individual automation tasks to work with other automation tasks is orchestration, which can also require some tasks to complete before others.

Cloud runbooks are part of a cloud orchestration solution. A *runbook* organizes multiple automation tasks together in a workflow. Runbooks typically can run entirely without human intervention, but some might require values at run time. Runbooks can also be triggered by specific cloud events, such as a VM's CPU time rising above 90 percent for an extended period of time.

on the **Job**

Orchestration is not exclusive to the cloud. On-premises tools such as Microsoft System Center Orchestrator use the concept of runbooks that organize multiple automation tasks into a single workflow.

EXERCISE 9-1

Deploy Cloud Virtual Machines Using Templates

In this exercise, you will deploy a Microsoft Azure virtual machine using a template. This exercise depends on having completed Exercise 1-1.

1. Use your web browser to sign in to the Microsoft Azure portal at https://portal .azure.com.

2. At the top of the navigation pane on the left, click Create a Resource.

3. In the Search field, type **template**, choose Template Deployment (deploy using custom templates), and then click Create.

4. On the Custom Deployment page, under Common Templates, select the Create a Linux Virtual Machine link.

5. On the Deploy a Simple Ubuntu Linux VM page, configure the VM with the following settings (you can accept the default values for all other settings):

   ■ Resource group: Create a new one named **ResGroup4**

   ■ Admin username: **testuser**

   ■ Authentication type: **password**

   ■ Admin Password Or Key: **Pa$$w0rdABC123**

   ■ DNS Label Prefix: **ubuntuserver**

6. Scroll down and check the *I agree to the terms and conditions stated above* option, then click the Purchase button. Creating a VM normally requires many more details. Depending on the template used, you may have to provide little to no information at all.

7. In the left-hand navigator, choose Virtual Machines. Notice the new virtual machine named MyUbuntuVM with a status of Creating.

INSIDE THE EXAM

Templates

Cloud resource creation and management are often automated using templates. The CompTIA Cloud Essentials+ CLO-002 exam may present questions with possible answers that imply automation with templates is done only at the command line. This is not true. Templates can also be used in cloud GUI tools for single-use scenarios.

CERTIFICATION SUMMARY

In this chapter, you were exposed to cloud DevOps; essentially, the methodology combining software development and its efficient and automated delivery using cloud solutions such as code repositories. Next, we discussed how developers can call upon existing APIs or create and host APIs in the cloud. APIs normally exchange data over HTTP/S or SMTP using XML or JSON formats.

You also learned about sandboxing to isolate development and testing from the production environment. Sandboxing is possible at the network, virtual machine, and container levels. We covered software testing types such as load testing, which simulates above-average workloads, and regression testing, which ensures existing application functionality is not adversely affected by code changes.

Next, you learned how CI/CD ensures the automated and timely delivery of software solutions. Developers create and work with code through centralized code repositories. Code that is checked out cannot be modified by other developers.

Finally, you learned about a variety of cloud automation techniques, including command-line tools and templates. You also learned that cloud orchestration brings together multiple automation tasks in a single workflow.

TWO-MINUTE DRILL

Software Development in the Cloud

❑ DevOps combines software development and IT operations to deliver high-quality solutions as efficiently as possible.

❑ The use of software development solutions in the cloud falls under the PaaS cloud service model.

❑ Application programming interfaces (APIs) are collections of functions for a hardware device or a software solution.

❑ Software developers can call upon APIs to execute hardware or software functions defined in the API.

❑ Software developers can create and host APIs in the cloud.

❑ Software components communicate over common protocols such as HTTP/S and SMTP.

❑ Extensible Markup Language (XML) is a common data exchange format that uses tags to describe data.

❑ JavaScript Object Notation (JSON) uses key–value pairs to define data.

Software Testing

❑ Sandboxing is used in the IT world to isolate development and testing environments from production environments.

❏ There are various sandboxing solutions, such as network isolation, VMs with limited network connectivity, and application containers.

❏ Functional testing is used to ensure that IT solutions meet design requirements.

❏ Unit testing applies to a specific code function, or microservice.

❏ Regression testing ensures that software changes have not adversely affected other, unrelated areas of that software.

❏ Load testing simulates above-average workloads to determine if application response is acceptable.

❏ Fuzz testing feeds unexpected data to an application. Behavior is observed in order to improve application stability and prevent the disclosure of sensitive information.

Continuous Integration and Delivery

❏ Continuous integration and continuous delivery (CI/CD) is the DevOps practice of delivering efficient and high-quality IT solutions in a timely and automated fashion.

❏ Code repositories are centralized collections of software code.

❏ Developers can check out code from a repository when updates are required. Checked-out code cannot be modified by other developers.

❏ CI/CD can use triggers such as code check-in to automate code builds, testing, packaging, and deployment.

Cloud Resource Deployment

❏ Cloud automation can be achieved through cloud-based command-line tools, scripts, templates, and batch jobs.

❏ Infrastructure as code (IaC) comes in the form of cloud automation templates, which normally use the JavaScript Object Notation (JSON) file format.

❏ Cloud automation can use triggers such as the receipt of an HTTP message or the presence of a message in a message queue.

❏ Cloud orchestration brings cloud automation tasks together in a single workflow.

❏ Runbooks are often used with cloud orchestration to execute a series of automation tasks.

SELF TEST

The following questions will help you measure your understanding of the material presented in this chapter. As indicated, some questions may have more than one correct answer, so be sure to read all the answer choices carefully.

Software Development in the Cloud

1. Software developers in your organization have begun creating, testing, and deploying code for custom software applications in the cloud without manually deploying cloud resources. To which type of cloud computing model does this example best apply?
    A. PaaS
    B. IaaS
    C. SaaS
    D. STaaS

2. You are using the cloud to develop a microservice. Your solution must have the ability to scale and be tested independently of other microservices. What should you use for your microservices?
    A. Metal as a Service
    B. Virtual machine
    C. Container
    D. Code repository

3. Which of the following represents a standard data exchange format over a network?
    A. PDF
    B. PKI
    C. XML
    D. HTML

4. You are planning the creation of a custom line of business software that will be hosted in the cloud. You plan on using the Java programming language to code the solution. Using which of the following will most greatly facilitate this endeavor?
    A. API
    B. XML
    C. SDK
    D. PKI

Software Testing

5. Which type of software testing applies an above-average workload to an application?
   A. Vulnerability
   B. Penetration
   C. Load
   D. Compliance

6. You have configured automated cloud-based code builds and testing. One configured test ensures that new code changes have not adversely affected other code modules. What type of testing is this?
   A. Fuzz
   B. Vulnerability
   C. Regression
   D. Penetration

7. A custom application consists of multiple microservices. You need to test code changes made to one microservice. Which of the following presents the fastest and most efficient sandboxing solution?
   A. VMs
   B. APIs
   C. Containers
   D. Fuzzing

Continuous Integration and Delivery

8. Which term describes a central location where developers create, modify, check in, check out, and test software solutions?
   A. API
   B. CI/CD
   C. DevOps
   D. Code repository

9. What benefit is derived when software developers check out code from a repository?
   A. Other developers cannot modify the checked-out code.
   B. Other developers can modify the checked-out code.
   C. Automated testing against the checked-out code begins.
   D. Automated deployment of the checked-out code begins.

10. Which actions are common examples of automatically triggered tasks that execute when developers check code into a code repository? (Choose two.)
    A. Virtual machine deployment
    B. Code building
    C. Testing
    D. Template creation

Cloud Resource Deployment

11. Which of the following terms is the most closely related to infrastructure as code?
    A. CI/CD
    B. Template
    C. Code repository
    D. Container

12. How does cloud orchestration differ from cloud automation?
    A. It doesn't; the terms are synonymous.
    B. Only cloud automation coordinates a collection of tasks.
    C. Only cloud orchestration coordinates a collection of tasks.
    D. Cloud automation uses command-line tools, whereas cloud orchestration uses GUI tools.

13. Which of the following is the most common cloud resource template file format?
    A. JSON
    B. CSV
    C. TXT
    D. HTML

14. Which of the following items is most commonly considered a cloud orchestration component as opposed to a cloud automation component?
    A. Script
    B. Cloud resource template
    C. Runbook
    D. Code repository

15. Which term is described as organizing multiple automation tasks into a single workflow?
    A. Script
    B. Cloud resource template
    C. Runbook
    D. Orchestration

SELF TEST ANSWERS

Software Development in the Cloud

1. ☑   **A.** Platform as a Service (PaaS) is a cloud service model that hides the underlying resource provisioning from the cloud customer. PaaS is often used by software developers.
    ☒   **B, C,** and **D** are incorrect. Infrastructure as a Service (IaaS) is a cloud service model that allows cloud customers to deploy infrastructure components, such as storage, networks, and virtual machines, in the cloud. Software as a Service (SaaS) refers to a software solution available over a network, such as web e-mail service provided over the Internet by a cloud service provider. Storage as a Service (STaaS) is a specific subset of IaaS focused on cloud storage, such as for cloud backup and archive storage.

2. ☑   **C.** Application containers consist of the files necessary to run an app, along with settings and app tools. Each app container can be scaled and tested independently.
    ☒   **A, B,** and **D** are incorrect. Metal as a Service (MaaS) provides cloud customers with a dedicated hypervisor to run virtual machines. Using virtual machines to host a single microservice is less efficient than using an application container. Code repositories are not required when developing microservices.

3. ☑   **C.** Extensible Markup Language (XML) is a file type that uses tags to describe data rather than defining the formatting of data. XML is a common data format used to exchange data between dissimilar systems.
    ☒   **A, B,** and **D** are incorrect. Portable Document Format (PDF) is a standard document file format. Public Key Infrastructure (PKI) is a hierarchy of digital security certificates. Hypertext Markup Language (HTML) is a file type that uses tags to define data formatting.

4. ☑   **C.** A software development kit (SDK) provides developer tools for a specific software platform, such as Java. SDKs are composed of many APIs.
    ☒   **A, B,** and **D** are incorrect. An application programming interface (API) is a collection of related functions that can be called upon, or hooked into, by other software components. SDKs contain many APIs. Extensible Markup Language (XML) is a file type that uses tags to describe data rather than defining the formatting of data. XML is a common data format used to exchange data between dissimilar systems. Public Key Infrastructure (PKI) is a hierarchy of digital security certificates.

Software Testing

5. ☑ **C.** Load testing applies an above-average workload to an application in order to determine application security and stability.

   ☒ **A, B,** and **D** are incorrect. Vulnerability testing identifies security weaknesses. Penetration testing identifies and attempts to exploit discovered weaknesses. Compliance testing is used to ensure compliance with standards, laws, or regulations.

6. ☑ **C.** Regression testing ensures that changes have not adversely affected other components or functionality not related to the change.

   ☒ **A, B,** and **D** are incorrect. Fuzz testing provides random and unanticipated data to an application. Application behavior is then observed to determine its security and stability. Vulnerability testing identifies security weaknesses. Penetration testing identifies and attempts to exploit discovered weaknesses.

7. ☑ **C.** Application containers consist of application files and settings. Each microservice comprising a larger application can run within its own container. This allows container code updates, testing, and scaling independently of other containers.

   ☒ **A, B,** and **D** are incorrect. Virtual machines (VMs) are slower to start and stop than application containers because they contain an entire operating system. An application programming interface (API) is a collection of related functions that can be called upon, or hooked into, by other software components. Fuzz testing provides random and unanticipated data to an application.

Continuous Integration and Delivery

8. ☑ **D.** A code repository is a central location where developers create, modify, check in, check out, and test software solutions. Code can be checked out so that it cannot be modified by other developers until it is checked back in. Private code repositories can be configured, or public repositories can be used.

   ☒ **A, B,** and **C** are incorrect. An application programming interface (API) is a collection of related functions that can be called upon, or hooked into, by other software components. Continuous integration and continuous delivery (CI/CD) ensures the timely delivery of software solutions, ideally in an automated fashion, over the Internet. Development and operations (DevOps) is a term that refers to developing software solutions and continuously deploying related updates efficiently and securely.

9. ☑ **A.** Checking out code from a code repository prevents other software developers from modifying that checked-out code.

   ☒ **B, C,** and **D** are incorrect. The listed statements regarding checked-out code are not correct.

10. ☑ **B** and **C.** Automation can be configured with some code repositories, such as automatically building and testing code when it is checked in.

    ☒ **A** and **D** are incorrect. Virtual machine deployment and template creation are not common examples of code repository check-in actions.

Cloud Resource Deployment

11. ☑ **B.** Infrastructure as code refers to using syntax statements to create and manage cloud resources, such as through template files.

    ☒ **A, C,** and **D** are incorrect. Continuous integration and continuous delivery (CI/CD) ensures the timely delivery of software solutions, ideally in an automated fashion over the Internet. A code repository is a centralized storage location for programming code. Application containers consist of application files and settings. Containers are isolated and portable and can be moved to different hosts.

12. ☑ **C.** Cloud orchestration involves coordinating multiple related automation tasks.

    ☒ **A, B,** and **D** are incorrect. Cloud automation and cloud orchestration are not the same. Orchestration coordinates multiple automation tasks. Orchestration is not exclusive to GUI tools.

13. ☑ **A.** The JavaScript Object Notation (JSON) format is a commonly used file syntax for cloud resource templates.

    ☒ **B, C,** and **D** are incorrect. Comma-separated value (CSV) is a text file format that uses commas as a delimiter to separate values. TXT is a standard text file format. Hypertext Markup Language (HTML) is a file format that uses tags to format the display of content.

14. ☑ **C.** A runbook is a cloud orchestration component used to run a series of tasks.

    ☒ **A, B,** and **D** are incorrect. While scripts, templates, and code repositories are related to cloud orchestration, runbooks are the most closely related.

15. ☑ **D.** Cloud orchestration involves coordinating multiple related automation tasks.

    ☒ **A, B,** and **C** are incorrect. Scripts, templates, and runbooks are related to cloud orchestration, but orchestration itself coordinates multiple automation tasks.

Part IV

Securing the Cloud

Chapter 10
Security and the Cloud

T he three pillars upon which all IT security solutions are built are confidentiality, integrity, and availability, collectively referred to as the CIA security triad or simply CIA. Organizational roles such as the chief information officer (CIO) and chief information security officer (CISO) will have great interest in how CIA can be assured for any proposed cloud computing solution, so you need to be prepared to address their security concerns.

Every IT security solution is designed to reinforce one or more of the CIA security pillars. This is done through security controls. Security controls get implemented to address security weaknesses, such as protecting data at rest through encryption. This chapter focuses first on how methods such as encryption can ensure the confidentiality of cloud-based assets. Next, you will see how hashing and digital signatures can provide assurance of data integrity and authenticity.

Then, you will learn how IT systems and data availability are important aspects of cloud security. Finally, this chapter examines how cloud identities are used for authentication to systems and then authorized to use cloud resources.

CERTIFICATION OBJECTIVE 10.01

Confidentiality

One common method of securing IT systems and data on premises and in the cloud is by issuing Public Key Infrastructure (PKI) certificates to users, devices, and software components. These certificates contain public and private key pairs that can be stored in files or in smartcards. Public keys can be made publicly available to all, but private keys must be stored securely and made available only to the owner. Figure 10-1 shows the creation of a PKI certificate in a Microsoft Azure key vault. Common examples of PKI certificate usage include the following:

- File and disk volume encryption
- Network transmission encryption
- Client VPN authentication

Confidentiality is essentially about securing sensitive data, ensuring that only authorized entities have access to that data. Security standards such as PCI DSS (applicable to customer credit card data, as discussed in Chapter 4) have confidentiality requirements, ensured through measures such as encryption and the use of security protocols, as discussed next.

Encryption

Encryption has been used for millennia to protect sensitive data. In the digital age, the original data, or *plain text*, is fed into an encryption algorithm along with an encryption key. The resultant data is encrypted and is referred to as *ciphertext*. Think of encryption algorithms as complex mathematical formulas, with the keys being mathematical shortcuts to the solution. Only the possessor of the appropriate decryption key can decrypt data—in other words, revert ciphertext back into the original plain text.

FIGURE 10-1 Creating a PKI certificate in a Microsoft Azure key vault

Encryption key size is measured in binary bits (0s and 1s). With proper implementation, the more bits a key has, the harder it is to crack. Figure 10-2 shows the creation of an RSA 2048-bit key in Microsoft Azure. This key could be used, among other possibilities, to encrypt VM disk volumes. Depending on the implementation, symmetric, asymmetric, or both of these key types can be used.

FIGURE 10-2 Creating an encryption key within a Microsoft Azure key vault

Encrypting data stored in the cloud does not necessarily require a PKI certificate. A sole encryption key, provided by **the cloud provider or cloud customer, can be used instead. Most public cloud providers have cloud storage encryption enabled by default.**

Symmetric Encryption

Symmetric encryption uses a single key, also called a *secret key*, for encryption and decryption. The problem with this, especially on a large scale such as over the Internet with many users, is securely transmitting the symmetric key. Using a pre-shared key (PSK) to secure a Wi-Fi network is an example of symmetric key usage. You can also use symmetric keys to encrypt data stored in the cloud or to encrypt mobile device storage. RC4, Blowfish, and Advanced Encryption Standard (AES) are examples of symmetric encryption algorithms.

Secured web server connection using symmetric and asymmetric cryptography

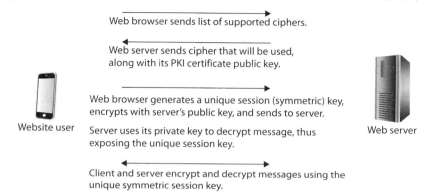

Asymmetric Encryption

Asymmetric encryption uses two mathematically related keys—a public key and a private key. These public/private key pairs are issued to devices, users, or software components for security purposes such as the encryption of files, disk volumes, or network transmissions. RSA, ECC, and ElGamal are examples of asymmetric encryption algorithms.

Encrypting network transmissions requires having the recipient's public key. The recipient then decrypts the transmission with the related private key, as shown in Figure 10-3.

1. Web browser sends list of supported ciphers.
2. Web server sends cipher that will be used, along with its PKI certificate public key.
3. Web browser generates a unique session (symmetric) key, encrypts with server's public key, and sends to server.
   Server uses its private key to decrypt message, thus exposing the unique session key.
4. Client and server encrypt and decrypt messages using the unique symmetric session key.

Transport Layer Security

Securing access to web applications is normally done by configuring Hypertext Transfer Protocol Secure (HTTPS). As an example, a web server can be configured to use a PKI certificate containing encryption and decryption keys. Then, clients and servers are configured to use a network security protocol such as Transport Layer Security (TLS), which supersedes the deprecated Secure Sockets Layer (SSL). SSL HTTPS bindings

FIGURE 10-4   TLS settings for a Microsoft Azure web application

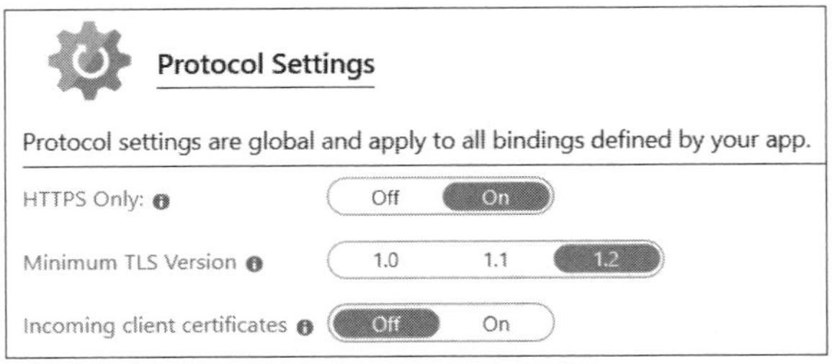

should not be used due to SSL's many security vulnerabilities.

Using TLS instead of SSL is one way to harden web applications. SSL and TLS are configured on the client side by configuring web browser settings, and on the server side by configuring web server protocol settings, as shown in Figure 10-4. HTTP clients normally connect to HTTP servers on port 80, whereas HTTPS connections normally use port 443.

e x a m

ⓦ a t c h   **Questions asking for the "best" solution are prevalent on the CLO-002 exam. Using TLS is always better than using SSL to secure network communications.**

on the ⓙ o b   **The secure use of cloud computing by U.S. government agencies is governed by the Federal Risk and Authorization Management Program (FedRAMP). One requirement is the use of TLS version 1.1 or higher, but using the latest version of TLS (version 1.3) where possible is the most secure option.**

CERTIFICATION OBJECTIVE 10.02

Data Integrity and Message Authentication

Cryptographic algorithms and keys can be used to ensure the integrity of data—that the data has not been tampered with—which is crucial when considering evidence admissibility in a court of law. Authentication can also be used to ensure that a network transmission came from who it says it came from, in order to prevent network impersonation attacks. The next sections demonstrate how hashing relates to data integrity and how message authentication works.

FIGURE 10-5   File hash generation using Microsoft PowerShell

```
PS D:\SampleFiles> Get-FileHash .\CustomerDatabase.accdb

Algorithm        Hash
---------        ----
SHA256           881EA0ABA2C0202AB224C13CAE80A6747916D5F6D7DECFEB7CD24CB5F5F2BB64
```

Hashing

Hashing feeds data such as file system objects or network transmissions into a one-way cryptographic algorithm, which results in a unique value called a *hash* or a *message digest*. Generating a hash in the future will result in the exact same hash value if the data has not been modified in any way, so this ensures data validity. If the data has changed, even through data corruption, then the newly generated hash will not match the original hash.

Common hashing algorithms include MD5 and the newer SHA-256. Figure 10-5 shows file hash generation using the Microsoft PowerShell Get-FileHash cmdlet. You can use encrypting and hashing within a cloud VM even if the cloud service provider does not explicitly offer this service.

Hashing can be used to track file modifications and is used extensively with digital forensic evidence gathering to ensure that digital evidence is not tampered with.

Digital Signatures

Digital signatures are used extensively when there is a need to prove that data has not been modified and that it has come from who (or what) it purports to come from. Basically, digital signatures are all about trust.

As mentioned earlier in this chapter, both public and private keys can be stored within a PKI certificate. In addition to being used for decryption, private keys are used to create digital signatures. Only the mathematically related public key can be used to verify the signature. Digital signatures are often used in cloud SaaS apps such as e-mail or document management solutions.

CERTIFICATION OBJECTIVE 10.03

Availability

You might wonder how availability is related to security. Consider a denial of service (DoS) attack that renders an IT system unavailable to legitimate users, such as by flooding a network with useless traffic. If the malicious attacker employs multiple hosts to execute the attack, it is known as a distributed denial of service (DDoS) attack. Potentially important IT services on the network would then be unreachable. Therefore, business-critical IT systems and data must be configured and protected to be highly available, which could include using intrusion prevention systems (IPSs) to detect and then block suspicious traffic. Service level agreements (SLAs) for cloud services provide details regarding expected service uptime and availability (as discussed in Chapter 2).

High availability can be achieved in many ways, including the following:

- Hardware redundancy (power, network, disk)
- Network connectivity redundancy (multiple Internet connections to the cloud)
- Application reachability (load balancing and clustering)
- VM reachability (replicating to a secondary geographical region, also called *geo-redundancy*)
- Frequent data backups (to ensure sufficient data recovery)

CERTIFICATION OBJECTIVE 10.04

Identity and Access Management

Users, devices, and software are all considered *security principles*, which means they can be assigned permissions to access resources based on their identity, also known as *identity and access management (IAM)*. Examples include

- Cloud user accounts granted permissions to access cloud applications
- Cloud-hosted web applications granted permissions to access a back-end database
- Registered devices granted permissions to connect to the network

Figure 10-6 shows an example of cloud user accounts in Microsoft Azure Active Directory.

Identity providers store security principal credentials. The following sections describe how single sign-on and multifactor authentication relate to security principles.

FIGURE 10-6 Microsoft Azure Active Directory user account listing

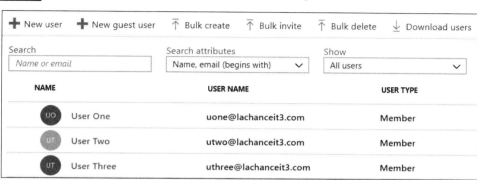

Identity Providers

Security principles are created and managed by identity providers (IPs). Examples of IPs include on-premises Microsoft Active Directory Domain Services installations and cloud-based Microsoft Azure Active Directory, Google Cloud Directory, and Amazon Web Services Directory Service.

On-premises and cloud-based IPs can be synchronized so that users can use their existing on-premises credentials to access on-premises and cloud-based applications. Cloud-based applications can also be configured to use Internet-based IPs; using a centralized IP is referred to as *identity federation.* This is beneficial because multiple copies of user identities are not required when accessing applications across many different providers, including between organizations.

Single Sign-On

As the name suggests, *single sign-on (SSO)* is an IAM feature that can be enabled so that users don't have to enter their credentials each time they access an application. SSO is configured at two levels: the identity provider and the application. Applications are configured to trust IPs. Another great thing about many SSO implementations is that the IP issues a digital security token signed with its private key that represents a successfully authenticated user. This means the actual user credentials are not sent around to each app. Instead, apps can verify the digitally signed token using the IP's public key.

Multifactor Authentication

An IAM system typically requires users to authenticate their identity by presenting proof from one or more of the following categories of authentication factors:

- **Something you know** The most common method of authenticating users is by requiring them to enter a username and password.
- **Something you are** This is synonymous with biometric authentication, which comes in the form of fingerprint scanning, retinal scans, voice recognition, and other methods of measuring unique physical characteristics.
- **Something you do** Gesture-based authentication uses unique movements to authenticate users.
- **Something you have** This category requires the possession of an authentication item, such as a smartcard or a hardware keyfob device that displays a unique numeric code for authentication.

An IAM system that relies on only one of these categories uses *single-factor authentication*. For example, although a username and a password are two separate items that a user must present to be authenticated, both items fall under the "something you know" category and thus constitute a single factor. A system that combines categories of authentication factors provides multifactor authentication (MFA). For example, requiring cloud user authentication by username and password along with a PIN sent to a smartphone device constitutes MFA. Figure 10-7 shows how selected users can have MFA enabled.

FIGURE 10-7 MFA configuration for Microsoft Azure Active Directory users

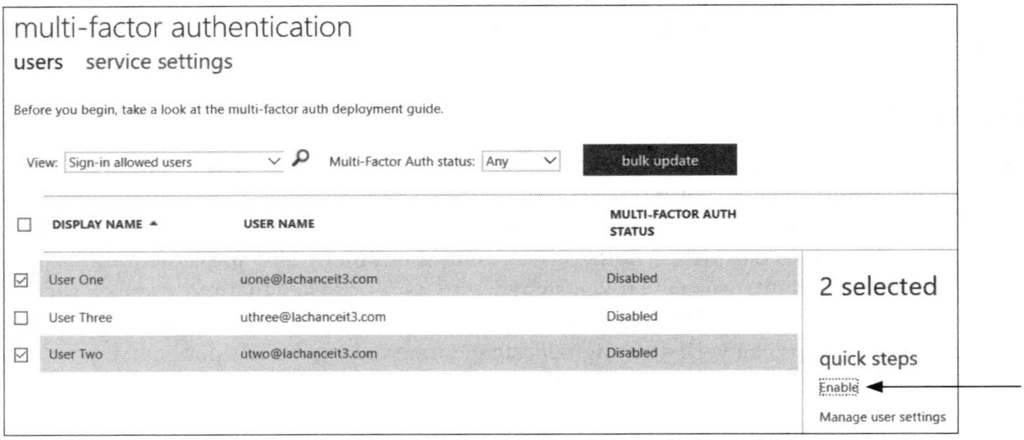

Successful authentication doesn't mean that the user has unlimited access to cloud resources. An authenticated user can access only the cloud resources he or she is authorized to access. Cloud technicians can add labels (tags) to cloud resources to categorize items (for example) as public, private, or sensitive. Tags can be applied either manually or through cloud policies that automatically add default tags. Policies can apply to all cloud resources or a subset of resources. Permissions can then be applied based on resource labeling; for example, only specific groups might have read and write permissions to any resource labeled as confidential, whereas everybody might have read access to resources labeled as public.

EXERCISE 10-1

Check Virtual Machine Disk Encryption Compliance

In this exercise, you will use Microsoft Azure Policies to identify virtual machines using unencrypted virtual disks. This exercise depends on having completed Exercise 1-1.

1. Use your web browser to sign in to the Microsoft Azure portal at https://portal .azure.com.
2. At the top of the navigation pane on the left, click Create a Resource.
3. In the Search field, type **policy** and then click Policy in the drop-down list.
4. In the left-hand navigator, click Assignments.
5. Click the Assign Policy button at the top center of the screen.
6. On the Assign Policy page, under the Basics section, click the button to the right of the Policy Definition field.
7. In the Search field, type **encrypt**.
8. From the results list, choose the Disk Encryption Should Be Applied on Virtual Machines policy definition, then click the Select button. Notice the default scope is set at the subscription level, as shown in Figure 10-8; this means all virtual machines in the subscription will be checked for disk encryption.
9. Click the Review + Create button, then click the Create button. You may have to wait 15 to 30 minutes before seeing compliance results.
10. After 15 to 30 minutes, in the left-hand navigation pane, click Compliance, then click the Disk Encryption Should Be Applied on Virtual Machines policy assignment.

| FIGURE 10-8 | Creating a Microsoft Azure policy assignment |

Assign policy

Basics   Parameters   Remediation   Review + create

Scope
* Scope (Learn more about setting the scope)

Pay-As-You-Go

Exclusions

Optionally select resources to exempt from the policy assignment

Basics
* Policy definition

Disk encryption should be applied on virtual machines

* Assignment name ❶

Disk encryption should be applied on virtual machines

Description

Policy enforcement

Enabled   Disabled

Assigned by

Review + create   Cancel   Previous   Next

11. Virtual machines without disk encryption will be listed as shown in Figure 10-9. You can use the Microsoft PowerShell Set-AzVMDiskEncryptionExtension cmdlet to encrypt VM disks using an encryption key previously defined in a Microsoft Azure key vault.

FIGURE 10-9   Viewing Microsoft Azure virtual machine disk encryption compliance

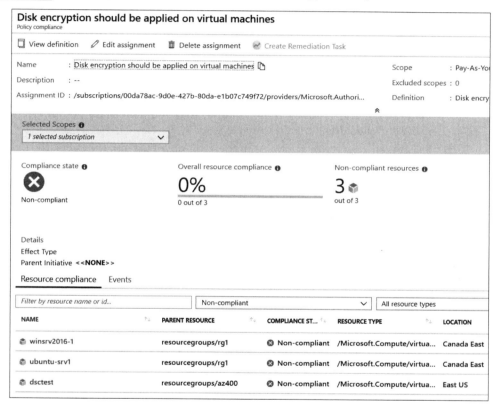

EXERCISE 10-2

Create a Microsoft Azure Active Directory Tenant

In this exercise, you will create a Microsoft Azure Active Directory tenant. This exercise depends on having completed Exercise 1-1.

1. Sign in to the Microsoft Azure portal at https://portal.azure.com.
2. At the top of the navigation pane on the left, click Create a Resource.
3. In the Search field, type **active directory** and then click Azure Active Directory in the results list. Click the Create button.
4. On the Create Directory page, specify an organization name, including six random numbers as the suffix to make the name unique. For example, specify **FakeCorp356378** (change these numbers to random ones) for both the organization name and the initial domain name.
5. Select your country or region from the drop-down list and then click the Create button.
6. After a few moments, click the link labeled Click Here to Manage Your New Directory, as shown in Figure 10-10.
7. In the left-hand navigator, click Users, then click the +New User button.

FIGURE 10-10 Creating a new Microsoft Azure Active Directory tenant

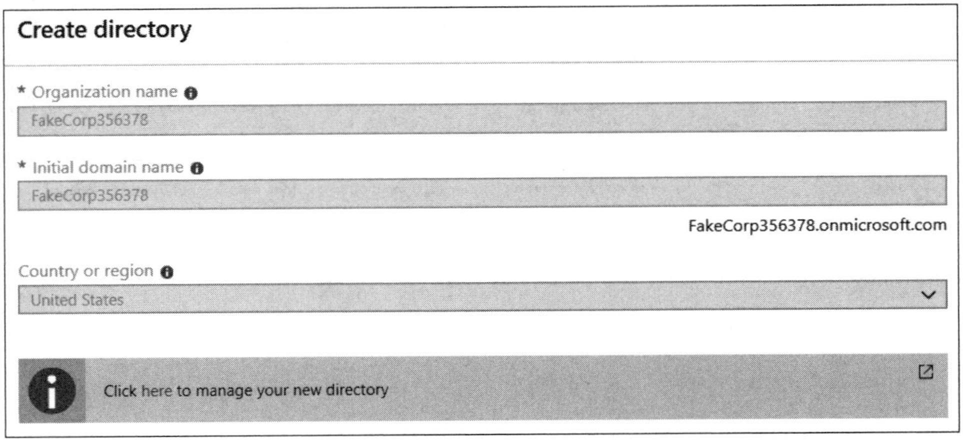

8. Specify a username of **uone**. Notice that the DNS name of your tenant forms part of the overall username, which looks like an e-mail address.

9. For the name, specify **User One** (**User** for the first name, **One** for the last name).

10. In the Password section, specify an initial password of **Pa$$w0rdABC123**.

11. Click the Create button.

12. In the Users view, click the More button (in the upper right of the screen, as shown in Figure 10-11), then click Multi-Factor Authentication.

13. In the new web browser window, check the check box to the left of User One, then click Enable on the far right.

14. Click the Enable Multi-Factor Auth button, then click the Close button. Notice the Multi-Factor Auth Status column for User One now displays Enabled. When User One next logs in, he or she will need to specify additional information (such as a phone number) to allow MFA logins.

FIGURE 10-11   The More button options

INSIDE THE EXAM

Security Controls

The CompTIA Cloud Essentials+ CLO-002 exam will most likely present many scenario-based questions that ask you to choose the "best" or "most appropriate" security control. All listed answer choices might be technically correct, so be sure to choose the best solution for each scenario. For example, encryption is most likely the best security control for a scenario that requires providing data confidentiality for credit card user data.

CERTIFICATION SUMMARY

In this chapter, you learned about the CIA security triad (confidentiality, integrity, and availability). You learned that security controls are put in place to address security weaknesses and that cloud security controls are very similar to on-premises IT security controls. Familiar solutions such as encryption can be applied in the cloud to provide confidentiality for digital assets. Encryption can be applied to data stored in the cloud using symmetric encryption keys and can be applied to network communications using security protocols such as TLS, which uses both symmetric and asymmetric cryptography.

You also learned how integrity checking through hashing and digital signatures is used to ensure data validity and to provide assurances of who sent a network transmission. Availability was discussed in the context of ensuring continuous access to IT systems and data in the cloud, such as replicating cloud-hosted virtual machines to secondary geographic regions.

This chapter also covered how identity providers can be centralized and trusted by third parties (aka identity federation). You learned how multifactor authentication enhances sign-in security, and finally, you learned how single sign-on removes the need for users to re-authenticate (after initial authentication) to each additional app they want to access.

 TWO-MINUTE DRILL

Confidentiality

❑ Confidentiality protects sensitive data from unauthorized users.

❑ PKI certificates can be used to implement confidentiality and can be issued to users, devices, and software.

❑ PKI certificates contain public–private key pairs.

❑ Data confidentiality security controls can apply to data storage and network communications.

❑ Data encryption feeds data into an encryption algorithm along with an encryption key.

❑ More bits in an encryption key generally means better encryption strength.

❑ Unencrypted data is referred to as plain text, and encrypted data is referred to as ciphertext.

❑ Symmetric encryption uses the same key for encryption and decryption.

❑ Asymmetric encryption uses a public key for encryption and a mathematically related private key for decryption.

❑ RC4, Blowfish, and AES are examples of symmetric encryption algorithms.

❑ RSA, ECC, and ElGamal are examples of asymmetric encryption algorithms.

❑ Transport Layer Security (TLS) is a network security protocol that supersedes SSL.

❑ TLS requires a server-side PKI certificate to support HTTPS connections over port 443.

Data Integrity and Message Authentication

❑ Integrity security controls are used to ensure that data has not been modified by unauthorized users.

❑ Hashing applies an algorithm to data that results in a unique value called a hash or message digest. Hash generation determines data validity; if a current hash of a file matches a past hash of the same file, the file has not been modified.

❑ MD5 and SHA-256 are examples of hashing algorithms.

❑ Digital signing is used to ensure that a message came from the user or device it says it came from.

❑ Private keys are used to create digital signatures; public keys are used to verify digital signatures.

Availability

❑ Availability security controls ensure that IT services and data are continuously accessible.

❑ Cloud service level agreements (SLAs) include details about service availability.

❑ Network attacks such as DoS and DDoS attempt to render systems unavailable for legitimate use.

❑ IT system and data availability can be achieved through data backups, replication, and redundancy.

Identity and Access Management

❑ Identity and access management begins with security principles (users, devices, software).

❑ Security principles are stored with identity providers.

❑ Centralized identity providers trusted by third parties define identity federation.

❑ Identity providers can use their private key to digitally sign authentication tokens, which are verified by apps using the related public key.

❑ Single sign-on (SSO) removes the need for repeated user authentication for apps after initial authentication.

❑ Multifactor authentication (MFA) combines authentication categories such as "something you know" and "something you have."

❑ Data labeling can be used to further control (authorize) access to sensitive data.

SELF TEST

The following questions will help you measure your understanding of the material presented in this chapter. As indicated, some questions may have more than one correct answer, so be sure to read all the answer choices carefully.

Confidentiality

1. Which of the following is the most closely related to data confidentiality?
   A. Hashing
   B. Digital signature
   C. Encryption
   D. Authentication

2. You need to secure a cloud-hosted web application using HTTPS. What is required to accomplish this?
   A. PKI certificate
   B. SSL certificate
   C. TLS certificate
   D. IPSec certificate

3. You have decided to use your own key to encrypt and decrypt data stored in the cloud. Which type of encryption is this?
   A. PKI
   B. Symmetric
   C. Asymmetric
   D. TLS

Data Integrity and Message Authentication

4. Hashing is an example of providing data:
   A. Integrity
   B. Availability
   C. Confidentiality
   D. Authentication

5. You have generated file hashes for files stored in the cloud. How does this provide integrity?
   A. It creates a digital signature.
   B. Future hashes are compared with older hashes; if they match, the data has been modified.
   C. It encrypts files stored in the cloud.
   D. Current hashes are compared with older hashes; if they match, the data has not been modified.

6. You are configuring a cloud-hosted web application in a federated identity environment. What is required for the web application to trust digitally signed security tokens from the identity provider?
   A. Identity provider private key
   B. Web app private key
   C. Web app public key
   D. Identity provider public key

7. How do digital signatures and hashing differ, if at all?
   A. They are the same thing.
   B. Unlike digital signatures, hashing proves message sender authenticity.
   C. Unlike hashing, digital signatures prove message sender authenticity.
   D. Hashing encrypts, while digital signatures do not.

Availability

8. Which of the following is the most closely related to data availability?
   A. Encryption
   B. Backups
   C. Digital signatures
   D. Authentication

9. A malicious attacker uses a compromised host to attack a web server virtual machine, causing it to crash. Which type of attack is this?
   A. Ransomware
   B. Directory traversal
   C. DoS
   D. DDoS

10. A malicious attacker uses a network of compromised hosts to attack a web server virtual machine, causing it to crash. Which type of attack is this?

    A. Ransomware

    B. Directory traversal

    C. DoS

    D. DDoS

Identity and Access Management

11. What do web apps use to establish trust from identity providers?

    A. Encrypted identity provider tokens

    B. Encrypted web app tokens

    C. Digitally signed web app tokens

    D. Digitally signed identity provider tokens

12. Which of the following best describes identity federation?

    A. Exporting user accounts from one directory service to other directory services

    B. Copying user accounts from one directory to other directories

    C. Configuring applications to trust a central identity provider

    D. Disburdening users from having to enter credentials for each app they access

13. Which of the following best describes SSO?

    A. Exporting user accounts from one directory service to other directory services

    B. Copying user accounts from one directory to other directories

    C. Configuring applications to trust a central identity provider

    D. Disburdening users from having to enter credentials for each app they access

14. Which of the following are examples of multifactor authentication? (Choose two.)

    A. Username and password

    B. Username, password, and authentication server IP address

    C. Username, password, and PIN sent to a phone

    D. Username, password, and smartcard

15. Your organization requires cloud resources in the Eastern U.S. region to be labeled with a default Project ID and Project Manager. The solution must be implemented with the least possible amount of administrative effort. What should you configure?

    A. Template

    B. Custom API

    C. Role-based access control

    D. Resource tagging policy

SELF TEST ANSWERS

Confidentiality

1. ☑ **C.** Encryption is a form of confidentiality.
☒ **A, B,** and **D** are incorrect. Hashing ensures that data has not been tampered with or corrupted. Digital signatures are used to verify message authenticity. Authentication is the proving of one's identity.

2. ☑ **A.** A PKI certificate is required before enabling an HTTPS binding for a web application.
☒ **B, C,** and **D** are incorrect. PKI certificates can be used with SSL, TLS, or IPSec, which are all network security protocols; however, technically, they are not types of certificates.

3. ☑ **B.** A symmetric key is one that is used for both encryption and decryption.
☒ **A, C,** and **D** are incorrect. Public Key Infrastructure (PKI) is a hierarchy of digital security certificates, not an encryption type. Asymmetric encryption uses two keys; a public key for encryption and a private key for decryption. Transport Layer Security (TLS) is a network security protocol that supersedes Secure Sockets Layer (SSL).

Data Integrity and Message Authentication

4. ☑ **A.** Hashing is used to detect modifications made to data.
☒ **B, C,** and **D** are incorrect. Availability ensures that IT systems and data are continuously accessible. Confidentiality protects sensitive data from unauthorized users. Authentication is the proving of one's identity.

5. ☑ **D.** File hashes are unique values. If the file is modified in any way, when a hash is generated again, a different unique value will result.
☒ **A, B,** and **C** are incorrect. Hashes do not create digital signatures. Hashing does not encrypt files.

6. ☑ **D.** The identity provider public key can be used to verify security tokens digitally signed by the identity provider's private key.
☒ **A, B,** and **C** are incorrect. The identity provider private key is used to create digital signatures. Web app keys are not involved in this scenario.

7. ☑ **C.** Digital signatures use the sender's public key to authenticate the message, which was signed using the sender's private key.
☒ **A, B,** and **D** are incorrect. Hashing and digital signatures are not the same thing. Hashing is used to detect data modifications, and digital signatures are used to authenticate messages. Neither hashing nor digital signatures encrypt data.

Availability

8. ☑ **B.** Data backups are related to availability.
☒ **A, C,** and **D** are incorrect. Encryption is a form of confidentiality that protects sensitive data from unauthorized users. Digital signatures are used to ensure message authenticity. Authentication is the proving of one's identity.

9. ☑ **C.** A denial of service (DoS) attack involves an attacker using (normally) a single attacking system to render a victim system unusable for legitimate users.
☒ **A, B,** and **D** are incorrect. Ransomware is malware that encrypts files and demands a ransom payment to potentially receive decryption keys. Directory traversal is a type of web server attack that traverses the web server file system hierarchy. A distributed DoS (DDoS) attack consists of an attacker using multiple compromised hosts to attack a victim network or host, such as flooding a network with useless traffic.

10. ☑ **D.** A distributed denial of service (DDoS) attack consists of an attacker using multiple compromised hosts to attack a victim network or host, such as flooding a network with useless traffic.
☒ **A, B,** and **C** are incorrect. Ransomware is malware that encrypts files and demands a ransom payment to potentially receive decryption keys. Directory traversal is a type of web server attack that traverses the web server file system hierarchy. A denial of service (DoS) attack involves an attacker using (normally) a single attacking system to render a victim system unusable for legitimate users.

Identity and Access Management

11. ☑ **D.** Identity providers digitally sign tokens upon successful user authentication. Apps are configured to trust the signature of the identity provider.
☒ **A, B,** and **C** are incorrect. Encryption is not used to establish trust from identity providers. Web apps do not generate security tokens; identity providers do.

12. ☑ **C.** Identity federation uses a central identity provider that is trusted by third parties.
☒ **A, B,** and **D** are incorrect. Exporting, importing, and copying user accounts between directory services does not centralize identities, which is a core concept of identity federation. Disburdening users from having to enter credentials for each app they access is the purpose of single sign-on (SSO).

13. ☑ **D.** Single sign-on (SSO) relieves users from having to enter credentials for every app they access.
☒ **A, B,** and **C** are incorrect. Exporting, importing, and copying user accounts between directory services does not centralize identities, which is a core concept of identity federation. Identity federation uses a central identity provider that is trusted by third parties.

14. ☑ **C** and **D.** Multifactor authentication combines two or more authentication categories such as "something you know" (username, password) and "something you have" (PIN from phone or a smartcard).

☒ **A** and **B** are incorrect. Username, password, and server IP address all fall under the category of "something you know."

15. ☑ **D.** Cloud policies can apply default tags to a subset of cloud resources, including within a region, if none are specified upon resource creation.

☒ **A, B,** and **C** are incorrect. While a template can apply tags to cloud resources, policies are more automated since nothing must be invoked; templates must be invoked in some manner. A custom application programming interface (API) is a collection of programming functions, and while an API could be used for tagging, it requires more effort than configuring a cloud policy. Role-based access control is not related to automated resource tagging.

Chapter 11

Managing Cloud Risk

In this chapter, you'll be exposed to the reality that the use of cloud computing always introduces risk—as does the use of on-premises IT solutions. The two main questions to be answered when an organization is considering cloud computing are

- What is the organization's risk appetite?
- What can the organization do to eliminate or reduce the impact of realized threats?

We will start by discussing risk management approaches that are designed to gauge the amount of risk related to engaging a cloud service and the corresponding threats to assets. Next, we'll address how to protect assets from threats by ensuring security controls are effective.

We'll finish the chapter by examining how to test infrastructure and applications for weaknesses with fuzz and vulnerability testing and how to test the exploitability of discovered weaknesses through penetration testing.

CERTIFICATION OBJECTIVE 11.01

Risk Management

Any worthwhile business endeavor involves *risk*, defined generally as the possibility of loss. Without risk, there is no possibility of gain. The key is how to manage that risk, from cloud adoption to cloud usage. An organization that is looking to adopt cloud computing can either assess cloud solutions in house or engage the professional services of an IT consulting firm to create a Request for Proposal (RFP) that outlines how the organization can use cloud services to meet business requirements.

While the cloud shares common risks with on-premises IT systems, it also introduces new risks, such as the dependency on the cloud service provider for IT system and data availability and the dependency on the Internet service provider (ISP) for the network connection to the cloud. Reducing the impact of negative incidents is accomplished through a properly implemented risk management framework.

Risk Assessments

Assessing risk involves determining which assets the organization has, ranking those assets by value to the organization, and then determining the risk related to those assets. For example, storing sensitive data (asset) in the cloud presents risks, such as cloud service provider personnel accessing that data or malicious users attacking the CSP because it is a large target, and those risks must be addressed. Risk assessments include the following activities:

1. Identify assets by creating an asset inventory (discussed a bit later in the chapter).
2. Assign asset ownership.
3. Classify (label) asset relevance or sensitivity.
4. Sort assets by value to the organization.
5. Identify asset threats and their likelihood of occurrence and compile them in a risk register.
6. Prioritize threats.
7. Examine the efficacy of existing security controls.
8. Implement adequate security controls.
9. Periodically reevaluate security control efficacy.

Identifying assets and threats is not a one-time activity; this is an ongoing process. Because IT threats change constantly, a crucial component of risk management is to periodically review how assets are used, along with related threats and security controls.

Risk Treatments

After identifying assets and related threats, an organization can implement measures to respond to risk concerns. Table 11-1 summarizes common cloud-related risk treatments and examples.

TABLE 11-1   Common Risk Treatments

Risk Treatment	Meaning	Example
Risk acceptance	Acknowledging the risk associated with a given action and continuing with the activity without implementing any risk mitigation	Knowing a public CSP potentially could go out of business but choosing not to prepare a cloud exit strategy
Risk transfer	Outsourcing risk to a third party	The use of cloud computing (shared responsibility) where the cloud provider guarantees cloud service uptime in an SLA or acquiring cyber insurance to cover security incident costs
Risk avoidance	Choosing to not engage in a risky activity	Using proven third-party software components when developing applications in the cloud instead of creating custom components
Risk mitigation	Applying effective security controls to eliminate or reduce the impact of negative incidents	Replicating cloud backups to alternative geographic regions to increase data availability

CERTIFICATION OBJECTIVE 11.02

Assets and Threats

Managing risk related to cloud computing begins with identifying assets and related threats. Threats are then prioritized, which allows a focus on the most prevalent security issues. These days you will often hear media reports of security breaches of sensitive data achieved through malicious attacks, including malicious encryption of data files through ransomware. These breaches are normally not directed against CSPs, but rather cloud users connected to cloud services.

Asset Inventory

Every organization has assets that are valuable to the organization. Assets must be discovered and organized in an *asset inventory* before they can be secured. Asset inventories can also prove useful when assessing which existing IT systems are safe candidates for cloud computing. Examples of digital assets include the following:

- Payroll records
- Credit card transactions
- Patient medical records
- Intellectual property (IP), including music, inventions, and designs
- Medical research data

Most cloud service providers offer automated methods of discovering and classifying data in the cloud and even on premises. Figure 11-1 shows cloud discovery of data assets

FIGURE 11-1   Microsoft Azure data discovery labels and information types

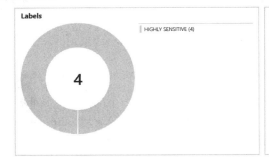

organized by information type. *Classification* means identifying data such as credit card numbers, street addresses, or social insurance numbers as being sensitive.

Asset inventory also includes computing devices such as smartphones and laptops. Most enterprises will have a configuration and change management solution in place that provides an inventory of computing resources.

Some assets, such as customer data, have more value than others, such as the database server housing customer data. Assets must be organized by value in order to determine where time and money should be spent securing assets. Asset ownership must also be determined to focus responsibility for securing that asset (and possibly paying for securing the asset). For example, if the Research and Development (R & D) department begins developing a new custom line of business app in the cloud, the secure use of cloud services for this purpose is the responsibility of the R & D department.

e x a m

ⓦ a t c h   **Tagging cloud resources with metadata is another method of identifying cloud resources that present value to the organization. This is useful when it comes to sorting cloud assets by relevance.**

Threat Prioritization

After an organization identifies and classifies its assets, it must identify related threats. For example, if you determine that customer details related to purchases through a cloud-hosted e-commerce website are valuable assets, then you need to identify related threats, such as data theft, if the data is not encrypted.

Threat prioritization requires compiling and maintaining a *risk register*—a centrally organized list of assets and threat likelihood. Threat likelihood can also be based on past incidents. An organization's periodic evaluation of assets and threats must also include updating the risk register. Table 11-2 shows a simplified example of a risk register.

TABLE 11-2   Sample Risk Register

Asset	Risk	Risk Rating Value	Mitigation
Employee payroll system	Malware attack	5	Antimalware solution with daily updates and continuous monitoring
Customer profiles	Sensitive data leak	1	Encrypt data at rest using cloud customer–generated keys, secure storage of decryption keys
Storage array equipment	Rogue IT technicians	5	Background checks, correct storage management skills, unique user accounts, storage auditing

CERTIFICATION OBJECTIVE 11.03

Threat Mitigation

After an organization has compiled an asset inventory and a corresponding risk register of related threats, it can select and deploy security controls that mitigate those threats. Remember that security controls should be monitored continuously where possible to ensure their effectiveness. Direction for how security controls address security weaknesses can vary from one organization to another. Each organization has its own set of security policies that addresses this issue. While security controls can reduce threat impact, disaster recovery plans are still needed to address realized threats.

Organizations must also ensure that IT technicians adhere to standard operating procedures (SOPs), which ensure the consistent management of cloud resources such as users, VMs, or storage accounts. SOPs can even be department-specific. For example, cloud technicians might have to ensure that finance department data replicated in the cloud resides within national boundaries. This can also be automated in the cloud through policies that can limit administrative capabilities.

Security Policies

Organizational security policies are often influenced by laws and regulations such as the European Union's General Data Protection Regulation (GDPR), as well as by industry security standards such as the Payment Card Industry Data Security Standard (PCI DSS).

Access and control policies define which permissions specific users, devices, or software components should have to cloud resources such as databases. How resources are accessed over the network is governed by communications policies that could specify that sensitive credit card processing systems must reside on an isolated network that uses a network security protocol such as TLS to encrypt transmissions.

Depending on the organization, operational and security policies might vary by department. For example, in a real estate firm, selling agents might be permitted to access company IT systems remotely through a VPN, but payroll staff might have to be physically present in the office to access payroll systems. Because cloud computing threats are constantly changing, security control review is important, which in turn can also require updates to organizational security policies.

Control Objectives and Security Controls

Many industry security standards, laws, and regulations reference *control objectives*. A control objective provides requirements that must be satisfied by a security control to safeguard an asset.

Table 11-3 provides examples of control objectives and possible mitigation solutions.

TABLE 11-3	Common Control Objectives and Security Control Mitigations
Control Objective	**Mitigation**
Encrypt network connections to websites	Configure the web application with a PKI certificate and enable Transport Layer Security (TLS); do not use Secure Sockets Layer (SSL), deprecated for security reasons
Encrypt remote management sessions for Linux virtual machines	Enable the use of Linux remote management using Secure Shell (SSH), such as through a Microsoft Azure Network Security Group (NSG) (as shown in Figure 11-2)
Protect on-premises databases being migrated to the cloud	Establish a site-to-site virtual private network (VPN) tunnel between the on-premises network and the cloud provider
Allow inbound Remote Desktop Protocol (RDP) traffic from and to specific hosts	Configure cloud firewall rules accordingly
Ensure data availability in the event of a regional outage	Replicate data to other regions
Ensure VM availability in the event of a data center rack problem such as lost power or a failed network switch	Verify original equipment manufacturer (OEM) redundancy features and deploy an availability set consisting of VMs running the same workloads; this spreads VMs across equipment racks, also called *availability zones*

on the **job** **Microsoft Azure NSGs can be associated with VM network interfaces or subnets.**

Disaster Recovery

Disaster recovery (DR) involves planning for inevitable business disruptions. Organizations can take proactive steps to eliminate, or at least reduce the impact of, realized threats to

FIGURE 11-2	Microsoft Azure Network Security Group firewall rules

Linux_FirewallRules - Inbound security rules
Network security group

🔍 Search (Ctrl+/)   ➕ Add   Default rules

- Access control (IAM)
- Tags
- Diagnose and solve problems

Settings
- Inbound security rules

PRIORITY	NAME	PORT	PROTOCOL	SOURCE	DESTINATION	ACTION
100	Allow_Inbound_SSH	22	TCP	Any	Any	Allow
65000	AllowVnetInBound	Any	Any	VirtualNetwork	VirtualNetwork	Allow
65001	AllowAzureLoadBalancerInBound	Any	Any	AzureLoadBalancer	Any	Allow
65500	DenyAllInBound	Any	Any	Any	Any	Deny

assets. An incident response plan (IRP) specifies immediate actions to be taken when a negative incident occurs, such as isolating the security breach and communicating with the organization's information technology security officer about the incident.

A disaster recovery plan (DRP) is more detailed than an IRP and can apply to a specific IT system or asset such as an e-commerce website hosted in the cloud, or it could apply to restoring deleted or corrupted data files.

The DRP provides detailed sequential steps to follow to restore business operations as quickly as possible with minimal disruptions. As discussed in Chapter 5, the recovery time objective (RTO) specifies the maximum allowable downtime, whereas the recovery point objective (RPO) specifies the maximum tolerable amount of data loss. Both RTO and RPO are expressed in units of time.

The mean time to repair (MTTR) is an important availability metric that specifies the average amount of time it takes to recover a service or component after a failure. This differs from the RTO, which is not an average value, but rather a strict maximum downtime value.

Cloud service level agreements (SLAs) differ from one cloud service to another, but one thing all SLAs have in common is a specified amount of guaranteed service uptime. You must consider this in conjunction with your organization's cloud DRPs.

Watch CompTIA expects exam candidates to understand the granular details. While RTO and MTTR may share some similarities, they are not the same thing. Watch exam question wording carefully.

Removing single points of failure is key to IT system and data availability. In the cloud, it's easy to configure scheduled backups of cloud resources such as virtual machines and databases. You can also configure the backup of on-premises IT systems and data to the cloud.

exam

Watch Watch for exam questions related to replication. Depending on the scenario, in order for replication to provide true high availability, data might need to be synchronized to a different geographical region to meet organizational availability requirements.

Continuous Monitoring

We've already established that security controls must be reviewed periodically to ensure their effectiveness, but they must also be continuously monitored. Some cloud providers offer centralized cloud-based monitoring solutions, which are referred to as Monitoring as a Service (MaaS).

Security information and event management (SIEM) tools provide a centralized way to collect, analyze, correlate, and report on suspected security incidents. SIEM solutions can ingest many different types of data, including from databases, cloud management activity logs, identity providers, VMs running any type of workload, and so on. Having this centralized facilitates the configuration of alerts; it provides visibility into all security aspects of the cloud environment. SIEM needs to be configured for the specific environment in which it is running; what one organization considers "suspicious" may be normal to another. One monitoring challenge with cloud computing is the disposable nature of many cloud services. For example, spinning up a virtual machine to support an application workload can take only seconds, especially if the procedure is automated. Any security incidents arising from this new virtual machine can be hard to trace later since the virtual machine can be shut down and deleted as quickly as it was started up. Consider the alert notification shown in Figure 11-3; high CPU utilization in a VM that normally has a low utilization could be indicative of a denial of service (DoS) attack or even a malware infection that uses VMs for Bitcoin mining.

FIGURE 11-3   Microsoft Azure alert configuration

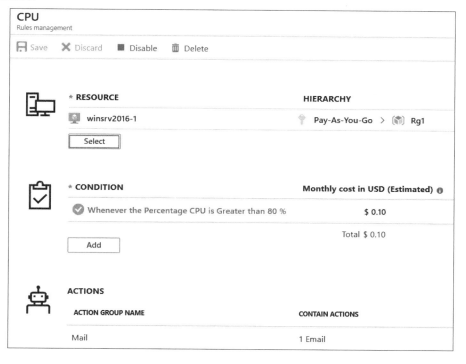

CERTIFICATION OBJECTIVE 11.04

Security Testing and Auditing

Using cloud services typically involves shared security responsibility between the cloud customer and the cloud service provider. For example, deploying an IaaS VM means the CSP is responsible for the underlying infrastructure supporting the VM, but the cloud customer is responsible for managing and hardening the VM OS. In the same way, security testing and auditing apply to cloud customers and CSPs alike. Cloud customers can enable usage auditing for a variety of cloud services, including database usage, VM management, and cloud storage.

Just because a CSP has successfully passed a security audit, that does not mean cloud customer use of the CSP platform is automatically secured. The relationship is analogous to that of an automobile company and its customers. Just because the auto company manufactures vehicles that meet safety standards, that does not mean reckless drivers won't make those same vehicles unsafe to themselves and others.

Ensuring CSP compliance with industry security standards such as PCI DSS or data privacy regulations such as GDPR is important, but it's also important to conduct security assessments, through a variety of methods, to assess the security posture of an organization that is using cloud services. Cloud customers can use in-house or third-party auditors who in turn report their audit findings through prepared audit documents.

Vulnerability Scanning

A *vulnerability* is a weakness. *Hardening* is the process of reducing the attack surface of an IT solution to minimize the number of potential weaknesses. Vulnerability scanning capabilities can be a built-in CSP service or can be deployed as an appliance in the cloud, such as a vulnerability scanning VM. Figure 11-4 shows the automated Security Center recommendations in the Microsoft Azure cloud environment.

Infrastructure such as cloud storage settings, cloud network configurations, and cloud VMs can be passively assessed to determine how secure they are; in other words, to identify weaknesses.

Web applications can be scanned for vulnerabilities by using, for example, fuzz testing tools such as the ZED Attack Proxy. Fuzzing sends random unexpected data ("fuzz") to the application to observe the application's behavior and enhance application stability and security.

FIGURE 11-4   Microsoft Azure Security Center recommendations

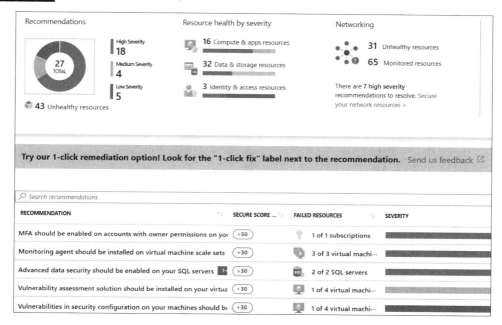

Access control mechanisms can also be assessed to determine if too many permissions have been granted to a resource, a violation of the *principle of least privilege (PoLP)*, which states that only the required permissions to perform a task should be granted.

Penetration Testing

Whereas vulnerability scanning only identifies weaknesses, penetration testing (pen testing) actively attempts to exploit discovered weaknesses. This can result in sensitive data disclosure or the disruption of IT systems. Written approval from the CSP and cloud tenants must be obtained prior to executing penetration tests.

on the job **Most public CSPs allow limited pen tests of some cloud services. Always ensure you are allowed to conduct a pen test prior to executing it.**

EXERCISE 11-1

Secure Data at Rest

In this exercise, you will create an Azure key vault and encryption key that you can use to encrypt data stored in the cloud. This exercise depends on having completed Exercise 1-1 and Exercise 5-1.

1. Use your web browser to sign in to the Microsoft Azure portal at https://portal .azure.com.
2. In the leftmost navigation pane, click Storage Accounts.
3. In the Storage Account view on the right, click the storacct1289 storage account that you created in Exercise 5-1.
4. In the Storage Account navigation pane, ensure Overview is selected. In the right pane, note the Location. The key vault you create will also be deployed to this location.
5. At the top of the leftmost navigation pane, click Create a Resource.
6. In the center pane Search field, type **key vault**. Choose Key Vault from the list and then click the Create button.
7. On the Create Key Vault Basics page, create a new resource group named **ResGroup5**.
8. Name the key vault **KVMHE2020**. Click the Review + Create button.
9. Upon receiving the Validation Passed message at the top of the screen, click the Create button.
10. On the Your Deployment Is Complete page, click the Go to Resource button.
11. In the Key Vault navigation pane, click Keys.
12. Click the +Generate/import button.
13. Name the key **Key2020**, as shown in Figure 11-5.
14. Accept all other defaults and click the Create button.
15. In the leftmost navigation pane, click Storage Accounts.
16. In the Storage Account view on the right, click the storacct1289 storage account created in Exercise 5-1.
17. In the Storage Account navigation pane, click Encryption.
18. Check the Use Your Own Key check box, as shown in Figure 11-6.
19. Under Encryption Key, click the Select from Key Vault radio button.
20. Under Key Vault, click the Select link and choose KVMHE2020.
21. Under Encryption Key, click the Select link and choose Key2020.
22. Click the Save button.

FIGURE 11-5 Creating a Microsoft Azure key vault key

Create a key

Options
Generate ⌄

* Name ⓘ
Key2020 ✓

Key Type ⓘ
RSA   EC

RSA Key Size
2048   3072   4096

Set activation date? ⓘ ☐

Set expiration date? ⓘ ☐

Enabled?   Yes   No

FIGURE 11-6 Configuring a custom key for Microsoft Azure storage account encryption

☑ Use your own key

Encryption key
◯ Enter key URI
◉ Select from Key Vault

* Key Vault
KVMHE2020
Select
* Encryption key
Key2020
Select

INSIDE THE EXAM

Activity Sequence

The CompTIA Cloud Essentials+ CLO-002 exam will most likely present you with plenty of questions related to the order in which activities should be undertaken. For example, you can't create a risk register until you have identified the organization's assets in an asset inventory. In the same way, the risk register must be created before you can determine where the most time and resources should be allocated to protect assets.

CERTIFICATION SUMMARY

In this chapter, you learned about managing risk in a cloud computing environment. A successful risk management implementation starts with identification, ownership assignment, classification, and prioritization of assets that will be exposed to the cloud, which is followed by identification of corresponding threats and their probability of occurring, compiled in a central risk register that is then used to prioritize threats. Next comes evaluation of whether existing security controls are effective for cloud security or need to be supplemented with new controls. Finally, periodic asset and security control reviews are crucial to ensuring continued effective asset protection.

This chapter also introduced you to common risk treatments such as risk acceptance, transfer, avoidance, and mitigation. The adoption of cloud computing is one example of risk transfer, where some of the responsibility for cloud service uptime lies with the cloud service provider.

You learned that control objectives are stated requirements for protecting assets, while security controls are implemented to address those security concerns. An example of a control objective might be to ensure that cloud data is available even in the event of a regional disaster, so replicating it to a secondary region is the security control. Because negative incidents are inevitable over time, disaster recovery planning is important so that the impact of disruptions can be minimized when they occur. In the cloud, disaster recovery can include backing up on-premises data to the cloud.

Next, you learned that SIEM solutions ingest a variety of data sources, such as logs, to identify potential security incidents and issue alerts. Finally, you learned how penetration testing goes beyond vulnerability scanning in the sense that it not only identifies weaknesses but also attempts to exploit those discovered weaknesses.

TWO-MINUTE DRILL

Risk Management

- ❏ An organization that is planning to adopt cloud computing can engage the professional services of IT consulting firms to create a Request for Proposal (RFP) aligning cloud services with business needs.
- ❏ The use of cloud services introduces business dependencies on the CSP and ISP.
- ❏ Risk assessments begin with identifying assets, followed by assigning asset owners, asset labeling and sorting by value, threat identification and prioritization, security control efficacy review, and security control modification or implementation.
- ❏ Security controls require period reviews to ensure they continue to be effective against constantly evolving threats.
- ❏ A risk register is a central list of organizational assets and related threats, with a threat likelihood rating value.
- ❏ Risk acceptance means engaging in an activity and acknowledging related risks while not mitigating those risks.
- ❏ Risk transfer shifts some or all risk to a third party, such as an insurance provider.
- ❏ Risk avoidance means not partaking in an activity due to the unacceptably high level of associated risk.
- ❏ Risk mitigation involves implementing security controls to reduce the impact of realized threats.

Assets and Threats

- ❏ Standard operating procedures (SOPs) provide guidance for the deployment and management of cloud resources under normal circumstances.
- ❏ Cloud policies can limit cloud technician administrative capabilities.
- ❏ Digital asset discovery can be automated or conducted manually, including cloud resource tagging.
- ❏ Threats are related to assets; assets must be identified before threats are identified.
- ❏ A risk register is a centralized list of assets, related threats, and threat likelihood rating values.

Threat Mitigation

- ❏ Security controls are used to mitigate threats.
- ❏ Standard operating procedures (SOPs) ensure the consistent management of cloud resources.
- ❏ Security policies define how an organization uses IT solutions in a secure manner.
- ❏ Access and control policies define which permissions specific users, devices, or software components should have to cloud resources. Communications policies define how resources are securely accessed over the network.
- ❏ Department-specific policies define how a specific business unit executes business processes and uses technology securely.
- ❏ Control objectives are requirements for securing assets, such as "network connections must be encrypted."
- ❏ Security controls reduce the likelihood of realized threats, such as by using PKI certificates to secure network connections over HTTPS.
- ❏ Network security groups (NSGs) contain firewall rule sets that allow or deny network traffic in the cloud.
- ❏ An incident response plan (IRP) specifies immediate actions to be taken when a negative incident occurs.
- ❏ A disaster recovery plan (DRP) is more detailed than an IRP and specifies how a business process, IT system, or data is recovered in the event of a disaster.
- ❏ The recovery time objective (RTO) specifies the maximum allowable downtime; the recovery point objective (RPO) specifies the maximum tolerable amount of data loss.
- ❏ The mean time to repair (MTTR) specifies the average amount of time it takes to recover a service or component after a failure.
- ❏ Security information and event management (SIEM) tools provide a centralized way to collect, analyze, correlate, and report on suspected security incidents.
- ❏ SIEM needs to be configured for the specific environment in which it is running.

Security Testing and Auditing

- ❏ Vulnerability scanning identifies weaknesses.
- ❏ Penetration testing attempts to exploit discovered weaknesses, after receiving permission.
- ❏ Fuzzing submits random unanticipated data to an application in order to observe the application's behavior and enhance application stability and security.

SELF TEST

The following questions will help you measure your understanding of the material presented in this chapter. As indicated, some questions may have more than one correct answer, so be sure to read all the answer choices carefully.

Risk Management

1. What is the first step in a risk assessment?
   A. Threat identification
   B. Threat prioritization
   C. Asset identification
   D. Vulnerability scanning

2. Which type of risk treatment acknowledges the risk associated with an activity and takes no corrective action?
   A. Acceptance
   B. Transfer
   C. Avoidance
   D. Mitigation

3. Which type of risk treatment spreads the risk out to a third party, such as a cloud service provider?
   A. Acceptance
   B. Transfer
   C. Avoidance
   D. Mitigation

4. Your company backs up on-premises files to the cloud to ensure data availability. To which risk treatment is this scenario most closely related?
   A. Acceptance
   B. Transfer
   C. Avoidance
   D. Mitigation

Assets and Threats

5. Which type of documentation provides guidance for normal cloud management activities?

    A. SLA

    B. DRP

    C. SOP

    D. IRP

6. Which risk management activity must take place before threats can be identified?

    A. Vulnerability assessment

    B. Penetration test

    C. Risk register creation

    D. Asset inventory

7. Which cloud activity adds metadata to cloud resources, which can be helpful in organizing cloud assets?

    A. Logging

    B. Tagging

    C. Auditing

    D. Vulnerability scanning

Threat Mitigation

8. You need to address security concerns related to how your organization stores sensitive data. Current data protection measures have been deemed inadequate. What should you consult to list current data protection controls?

    A. Risk register

    B. SIEM

    C. SLA

    D. Audit file

9. Which term is used to describe general security requirements related to asset security?

    A. Security control

    B. Control objective

    C. Risk register

    D. SIEM

10. Which disaster recovery term refers to the average amount of time required to recover a failed component or service?
   A. SLA
   B. DRP
   C. IRP
   D. MTTR

Security Testing and Auditing

11. Users requiring cloud VM administrative access are granted full global access to all types of cloud resources. Which security term is the most closely related to this scenario?
   A. SIEM
   B. Control objective
   C. Vulnerability assessment
   D. Principle of least privilege

12. Which term is used to describe securing an IT solution by reducing the attack surface?
   A. Penetration testing
   B. Hardening
   C. Vulnerability testing
   D. Fuzzing

13. Which type of testing submits random unexpected data to a web application?
   A. Penetration
   B. Fuzz
   C. Vulnerability
   D. Regression

14. Which type of testing only identifies security weaknesses?
   A. Penetration
   B. Fuzz
   C. Vulnerability
   D. Regression

15. Which type of testing actively exploits discovered weaknesses?
   A. Penetration
   B. Fuzz
   C. Vulnerability
   D. Regression

A

SELF TEST ANSWERS

Risk Management

1. ☑ **C.** Assets must be identified before identifying threats or running vulnerability scans.
☒ **A, B,** and **D** are incorrect. Threats relate to assets; assets must be identified first. Vulnerability scans should be conducted periodically after assets and threats have been identified.

2. ☑ **A.** Risk acceptance acknowledges the risk associated with an activity but takes no steps to mitigate the risk, usually because the risk impact is minimal.
☒ **B, C,** and **D** are incorrect. Risk transfer describes shifting some risk to an outside party such as an insurance provider or a cloud service provider. Risk avoidance means not partaking in an activity due to the unacceptably high level of associated risk. Risk mitigation involves applying security controls to eliminate or reduce the impact of realized threats.

3. ☑ **B.** Risk transfer shifts some risk to an outside party such as an insurance provider or a cloud service provider.
☒ **A, C,** and **D** are incorrect. Risk acceptance acknowledges the risk associated with an activity but takes no steps to mitigate the risk, usually because the risk impact is minimal. Risk avoidance means not partaking in an activity due to the unacceptably high level of associated risk. Risk mitigation involves applying security controls to eliminate or reduce the impact of realized threats.

4. ☑ **D.** Risk mitigation involves applying security controls to eliminate or reduce the impact of realized threats.
☒ **A, B,** and **C** are incorrect. Risk acceptance acknowledges the risk associated with an activity while taking no steps to mitigate the risk, usually because the risk impact is minimal. Risk transfer describes shifting some risk to an outside party, such as an insurance provider or a cloud service provider. Risk avoidance means not partaking in an activity due to the unacceptably high level of associated risk. Risk mitigation involves applying security controls to eliminate or reduce the impact of realized threats.

Assets and Threats

5. ☑ **C.** Standard operating procedures (SOPs) provide guidance on how to conduct an activity under normal circumstances, such as deploying cloud resources.
☒ **A, B,** and **D** are incorrect. Service level agreements (SLAs) are contracts between cloud customers and cloud service providers that outline guaranteed cloud service uptime as well as the consequences if uptime is not met. Disaster recovery plans (DRPs) provide details regarding how to quickly recover a failed business process, IT system, or data with as little disruption as possible.

Incident response plans (IRPs) specify immediate actions to take when a negative incident occurs, such as isolating the security breach and communicating with the organization's information technology security officer about the incident.

6. ☑ **D.** Threats are related to assets. An asset inventory must be compiled first.
☒ **A, B,** and **C** are incorrect. Vulnerability assessments identify weaknesses, and penetration tests exploit discovered weaknesses; these are methods of identifying threats, not precursors to identifying threats. A risk register is a centralized list of assets, threats, and controls and thus is created after the asset inventory.

7. ☑ **B.** Tagging adds custom metadata to cloud resources. This can be used to organize resources for the purposes of securing assets.
☒ **A, C,** and **D** are incorrect. Logging, auditing, and vulnerability scanning do not add metadata to cloud resources.

Threat Mitigation

8. ☑ **A.** A risk register is a centralized list of assets, threats, and controls.
☒ **B, C,** and **D** are incorrect. Security information and event management (SIEM) tools provide a centralized way to collect, analyze, correlate, and report on suspected security incidents. A service level agreement (SLA) is a contract between a cloud service provider and customer defining cloud service details such as expected uptime. While audit files could be related to security controls, they do not list data protection controls.

9. ☑ **B.** A control objective provides requirements that must be satisfied by a security control to safeguard an asset.
☒ **A, C,** and **D** are incorrect. Security controls are put in place to protect assets, such as the encryption of cloud-stored data. A risk register is a centralized list of assets, threats, and controls. Security information and event management (SIEM) tools provide a centralized way to collect, analyze, correlate, and report on suspected security incidents.

10. ☑ **D.** The mean time to repair (MTTR) is an important availability metric that specifies the average amount of time it takes to recover a service or component after a failure.
☒ **A, B,** and **C** are incorrect. Service level agreements (SLAs) are contracts between cloud customers and cloud service providers that outline guaranteed cloud service uptime as well as the consequences if uptime is not met. Disaster recovery plans (DRPs) provide details regarding how to quickly recover a failed business process, IT system, or data with as little disruption as possible. Incident response plans (IRPs) specify immediate actions to take when a negative incident occurs, such as isolating the security breach and communicating with the organization's information technology security officer about the incident.

Security Testing and Auditing

11. ☑ **D.** The principle of least privilege states that only the required permissions to perform a task should be granted.

    ☒ **A, B,** and **C** are incorrect. Security information and event management (SIEM) tools provide a centralized way to collect, analyze, correlate, and report on suspected security incidents. A control objective provides requirements that must be satisfied by a security control to safeguard an asset. Vulnerability assessments identify weaknesses but do not attempt to exploit them as penetration tests do.

12. ☑ **B.** Hardening refers to securing an asset, which includes reducing the attack surface.

    ☒ **A, C,** and **D** are incorrect. Vulnerability assessments identify weaknesses but do not attempt to exploit them as penetration tests do. Fuzzing submits random unanticipated data to an application in order to observe the application's behavior and enhance application stability and security.

13. ☑ **B.** Fuzzing submits random unanticipated data to an application in order to observe the application's behavior and enhance application stability and security.

    ☒ **A, C,** and **D** are incorrect. Vulnerability assessments identify weaknesses but do not attempt to exploit them as penetration tests do. Regression testing ensures that one change has not adversely affected other, unrelated areas of an application.

14. ☑ **C.** Vulnerability assessments identify weaknesses but do not attempt to exploit them as penetration tests do.

    ☒ **A, B,** and **D** are incorrect. Penetration tests attempt to exploit discovered vulnerabilities. Fuzzing submits random unanticipated data to an application in order to observe the application's behavior and enhance application stability and security. Regression testing ensures that one change has not adversely affected other, unrelated areas of an application.

15. ☑ **A.** Penetration tests attempt to exploit discovered vulnerabilities.

    ☒ **B, C,** and **D** are incorrect. Fuzzing submits random unanticipated data to an application in order to observe the application's behavior and enhance application stability and security. Vulnerability assessments identify weaknesses but do not attempt to exploit them as penetration tests do. Regression testing ensures that one change has not adversely affected other, unrelated areas of an application.

Part V

Appendix and Glossary

Appendix

About the Online Content

This book comes complete with TotalTester Online customizable practice exam software with 150 practice exam questions and a complete copy of the book in PDF format for online viewing.

System Requirements

The current and previous major versions of the following desktop browsers are recommended and supported: Chrome, Microsoft Edge, Firefox, and Safari. These browsers update frequently, and sometimes an update may cause compatibility issues with the TotalTester Online or other content hosted on the Training Hub. If you run into a problem using one of these browsers, please try using another until the problem is resolved.

Your Total Seminars Training Hub Account

To get access to the online content you will need to create an account on the Total Seminars Training Hub. Registration is free, and you will be able to track all your online content using your account. You may also opt in if you wish to receive marketing information from McGraw-Hill Education or Total Seminars, but this is not required for you to gain access to the online content.

Privacy Notice

McGraw-Hill Education values your privacy. Please be sure to read the Privacy Notice available during registration to see how the information you have provided will be used. You may view our Corporate Customer Privacy Policy by visiting the McGraw-Hill Education Privacy Center. Visit the **mheducation.com** site and click **Privacy** at the bottom of the page.

Single User License Terms and Conditions

Online access to the digital content included with this book is governed by the McGraw-Hill Education License Agreement outlined next. By using this digital content you agree to the terms of that license.

Access   To register and activate your Total Seminars Training Hub account, simply follow these easy steps.

1. Go to this URL: **hub.totalsem.com/mheclaim**
2. To Register and create a new Training Hub account, enter your e-mail address, name, and password. No further personal information (such as credit card number) is required to create an account.

   Note: If you already have a Total Seminars Training Hub account, select Log in **and enter your e-mail and password. Otherwise, follow the remaining steps.**

3. Enter your Product Key: `tf3j-p7gq-mt9j`
4. Click to accept the user license terms.
5. Click **Register and Claim** to create your account. You will be taken to the Training Hub and have access to the content for this book.

Duration of License   Access to your online content through the Total Seminars Training Hub will expire one year from the date the publisher declares the book out of print.

Your purchase of this McGraw-Hill Education product, including its access code, through a retail store is subject to the refund policy of that store.

The Content is a copyrighted work of McGraw-Hill Education, and McGraw-Hill Education reserves all rights in and to the Content. The Work is © 2020 by McGraw-Hill Education, LLC.

Restrictions on Transfer   The user is receiving only a limited right to use the Content for the user's own internal and personal use, dependent on purchase and continued ownership of this book. The user may not reproduce, forward, modify, create derivative works based upon, transmit, distribute, disseminate, sell, publish, or sublicense the Content or in any way commingle the Content with other third-party content without McGraw-Hill Education's consent.

Limited Warranty   The McGraw-Hill Education Content is provided on an "as is" basis. Neither McGraw-Hill Education nor its licensors make any guarantees or warranties of any kind, either express or implied, including, but not limited to, implied warranties of merchantability or fitness for a particular purpose or use as to any McGraw-Hill Education Content or the information therein or any warranties as to the accuracy, completeness, correctness, or results to be obtained from, accessing or using the McGraw-Hill Education Content, or any material referenced in such Content or any information entered into licensee's product by users or other persons and/or any material available on or that can be accessed through the licensee's product (including via any hyperlink or otherwise) or as to non-infringement of third-party rights. Any warranties of any kind, whether express or implied, are disclaimed. Any material or data obtained through use of the McGraw-Hill Education Content is at your own discretion and risk and user understands that it will be solely responsible for any resulting damage to its computer system or loss of data.

Neither McGraw-Hill Education nor its licensors shall be liable to any subscriber or to any user or anyone else for any inaccuracy, delay, interruption in service, error or omission, regardless of cause, or for any damage resulting therefrom.

In no event will McGraw-Hill Education or its licensors be liable for any indirect, special or consequential damages, including but not limited to, lost time, lost money, lost profits or good will, whether in contract, tort, strict liability or otherwise, and whether or not such damages are foreseen or unforeseen with respect to any use of the McGraw-Hill Education Content.

TotalTester Online

TotalTester Online provides you with a simulation of the CompTIA Cloud Essentials+ exam. Exams can be taken in Practice Mode or Exam Mode. Practice Mode provides an assistance window with hints, references to the book, explanations of the correct and incorrect answers, and the option to check your answer as you take the test. Exam Mode provides a simulation of the actual exam. The number of questions, the types of questions, and the time allowed are intended to be an accurate representation of the exam environment. The option to customize your quiz allows you to create custom exams from selected domains or chapters, and you can further customize the number of questions and time allowed.

To take a test, follow the instructions provided in the previous section to register and activate your Total Seminars Training Hub account. When you register you will be taken to the Total Seminars Training Hub. From the Training Hub Home page, select **CompTIA Cloud Essentials+° Certification Study Guide, Second Edition (Exam CLO-002) TotalTester** from the Study drop-down menu at the top of the page, or from the list of Your Topics on the Home page. You can then select the option to customize your quiz and begin testing yourself in Practice Mode or Exam Mode. All exams provide an overall grade and a grade broken down by domain.

Ebook PDF

You can access the complete copy of the book in PDF format through the Total Seminars Training Hub. From the Training Hub Home page, you can either select the Resources tab, or select **CompTIA Cloud Essentials+° Certification Study Guide, Second Edition**

(**Exam CLO-002**) **Resources** from the Study drop-down menu at the top of the page or from the list of Your Topics on the Home page. Locate the book on the right side of the screen.

Technical Support

For questions regarding the TotalTester or operation of the Training Hub, visit **www.totalsem.com** or e-mail **support@totalsem.com**.

For questions regarding book content, visit **www.mheducation.com/customerservice**.

Glossary

access control list (ACL)   A list of permissions to a resource such as a firewall or shared folder.

Anything as a Service (XaaS)   A general term for a cloud-based IT service delivered over a network.

application container   An isolated boundary used to run an application that contains application files and settings, but not operating system files.

application programming interface (API)   A set of related functions that can be called programmatically.

application service provider (ASP)   An organization offering a software application over a network.

artificial intelligence (AI)   Technology that strives to mimic intelligent human behavior.

autoscaling   Adjusting underlying resources automatically to accommodate increases and decreases in demand.

availability   Ensuring that IT systems and data are accessible, often achieved through redundant configurations of disks, servers, network connections, or copies of data.

availability zone   A collection of physical equipment, such as a power source and network switch, which is used to distribute IT services across physical equipment racks to increase availability.

big data   Large datasets that are often fed into big data analytics solutions to identify trends, patterns, and likely future outcomes.

binary large object (blob)   Binary data, such as files stored in the cloud.

blockchain   A decentralized public ledger of transactions that cannot be modified.

bring your own license (BYOL)   A licensing model that allows cloud customers to reuse existing licenses in the cloud to reduce costs.

broad network access   Access to IT services from any device, any time, over any network.

Business Process as a Service (BPaaS)   Cloud-based software solutions serving common business needs such as payroll and e-commerce.

capacity on demand   Ability to automatically increase or decrease cloud storage, data analytics processing, or application performance.

capital expense (CAPEX)   A large up-front investment, such as for IT hardware on premises.

central processing unit (CPU)   The "brain" of a computing device that processes instructions.

chief financial officer (CFO)   An organizational role responsible for an organization's finances.

chief information officer (CIO)   An organizational role responsible for all aspects of how information is managed in an IT environment.

chief information security officer (CISO) An organizational role responsible for ensuring the efficacy of security controls in safeguarding digital information assets.

chief technology officer (CTO) An organizational role responsible for ensuring the secure, effective, and cost-efficient use of technology to support business requirements.

ciphertext The scrambled data that results from feeding plain text into an encryption algorithm with an encryption key. The correct decryption is required to return the ciphertext back into plain text.

cloud orchestration Organizing multiple related cloud automation tasks together into a cohesive workflow.

cloud service provider (CSP) An organization offering IT infrastructure, developer, and software services to cloud customers over a network in accordance with cloud computing characteristics such as metered usage and self-service.

cloud tenant A cloud customer in a multitenant environment. Multitenancy refers to multiple cloud customers using a cloud service provider, with each tenant's configurations and data kept isolated from the other tenants' configurations and data.

Communications as a Service (CaaS) Cloud-based communication solutions such as Voice over IP (VoIP).

community cloud A cloud type that provides solutions for customers with similar requirements, such as for medical or financial institutions.

content delivery network (CDN) A global collection of cloud service provider content caching servers. Clients' requests for content can be fulfilled by the closest caching server, which reduces network latency.

content management system (CMS) A manual or automated method of updating website content that does not require content updaters to understand the underlying technical details for formatting that content.

continuous integration and continuous delivery (CI/CD) A combination of software development and IT management that ensures the automated and timely delivery of software solutions over a network to customers.

customer relationship management (CRM)   Software that facilitates the tracking of interactions with existing and potential future customers for the purposes of customer relationship improvement.

data sovereignty   Controlling the physical location of data to control the jurisdictional rule of law related to sensitive data.

Database as a Service (DBaaS)   Database solutions offered in a cloud computing environment, normally as a managed service, meaning customers are spared from configuring virtual machines and database software.

denial of service (DoS)   A type of malicious attack that renders a service unusable by legitimate users, such as by flooding a server with useless network traffic.

departmental chargeback   Measuring resource consumption, such as the use of cloud computing services, for billing on a per-department basis.

DevOps   The combination of software development practices and IT operations practices. The result is the efficient deployment of software updates in a secure manner.

digital signature   A unique mathematical result stemming from the use of a cryptographic private key to encrypt a message hash. The verification of the signature with the related cryptographic public key means the message is authentic.

disaster recovery plan (DRP)   A document applying to a specific business process or system that is used to recover the service in the event of a failure in as little time and as securely as possible.

Domain Name Service (DNS)   A collection of servers that is most commonly used to resolve friendly names, such as www.mheducation.com, to the corresponding IP address.

elasticity   The dynamic provisioning and deprovisioning of resources to meet demand.

encryption   The application of a key and mathematical algorithm to plain text resulting in ciphertext, or encrypted data. Symmetric encryption uses a single key for encryption and decryption, whereas asymmetric encryption uses a public key to encrypt and uses the mathematically related private key to decrypt.

End User Licensing Agreement (EULA)   A legally binding contract specifying how software can be used by the purchaser.

enterprise resource planning (ERP)   The use of software solutions to manage business processes such as payroll, inventory, and so on.

Extensible Markup Language (XML)   A method of expressing data using tags. XML files are text-based files.

feasibility study   A study that determines whether or not cloud computing can address business needs.

Federal Risk and Authorization Management Program (FedRAMP)   A set of standards regarding the secure use of cloud computing for U.S. federal government agencies, although any organization can view and apply the standards for its own use.

File Transfer Protocol (FTP)   A method of uploading and downloading files between hosts on a network using ports 20 and 21. FTP does not encrypt any network transmissions.

functional testing   A type of test that ensures a solution addresses initial design requirements.

fuzz testing   A type of test that presents unexpected data to an application for ingestion. Observing the application's behavior to fuzz testing can help improve the security and stability of the application.

gap analysis   A study of existing IT solutions and how they meet (or do not meet) business requirements and what needs to be done to address business needs.

General Data Protection Regulation (GDPR)   An act of legislation of the European Union (EU) that is designed to control the collection, storage, processing, and sharing of EU citizens' private data.

hard disk drive (HDD)   Older disk storage technology that uses mechanical motors to spin rigid disk platters for data reading and writing.

hardening   Reducing the attack surface of an app, host, or network by applying updates, changing default configurations, removing unneeded components and user accounts, enabling storage and network encryption, and so on.

hashing   Feeding data into a one-way mathematical algorithm that results in a unique value (the hash, also called a message digest). Unlike encryption, hashing does not require a cryptographic key.

Health Insurance Portability and Accountability Act (HIPAA)   An act of legislation in the United States intended to protect sensitive patient medical information, specifically related to health care.

high-performance computing (HPC)   The use of clusters of physical or virtual machines to analyze large datasets; also called big compute and parallel computing.

horizontal scaling   The manual, scheduled, or automated addition or removal of virtual machines in response to changes in application demand.

hybrid cloud   The combining of different cloud types, such as private and public, or the combination of on-premises IT solutions with cloud solutions.

Hypertext Transfer Protocol (HTTP)   A network transmission standard used to exchange web-based messages between clients, such as web browsers, and servers, such as web servers. Connectivity to HTTP hosts occurs over TCP port 80.

hypervisor   Software running on a physical server that is designed to run multiple virtual machine guests concurrently. Type 1, or bare-metal, hypervisors run as the operating system, whereas Type 2 hypervisors run as an app within an existing standard operating system.

identity and access management (IAM)   The creation, modification, configuration, and ongoing maintenance of user, software, and device identities. Also includes the maintenance of authentication and authorization settings.

identity federation   The use of a central identity provider that is trusted by multiple parties. Reduces the need to create user credentials for each app. An example is using your Facebook credentials to authenticate to multiple unrelated websites.

immutable   Describes data that cannot be modified, such as archived digital data that is flagged as immutable.

Information Technology as a Service (ITaaS)   The provision of IT-related hardware, software, and support services over a network. Usage is tracked and customers are billed accordingly.

Information Technology Infrastructure Library (ITIL)   An IT service framework that strives to provide IT services as efficiently and cost-effectively as possible through IT service phases such as service strategy, service design, service transition, service operation, and continuous improvement of services.

Infrastructure as a Service (IaaS)   The provision of underlying IT services, such as storage, networking, and virtual machines, all delivered over a network with self-services capabilities and metered usage.

input/output operations per second (IOPS)   A unit of measurement used to describe the amount of throughput for disk storage solutions; higher IOPS means better performance but more cost in the cloud.

Internet of Things (IoT) device   Any type of computing device that can be uniquely identified on a network. IoT devices have the ability to communicate over the Internet. Examples include video surveillance systems, home environmental controls, and devices used to track a patient's medical statistics.

Internet service provider (ISP)   An entity that offers Internet connectivity as a commodity.

ISO/IEC 27017:2015   An international standard specifying methods of securing cloud services.

JavaScript Object Notation (JSON)   A text-based data exchange format based on the JavaScript programming language syntax.

jump box   A central connectivity point in the form of a server, often a virtual machine, used as a launch pad for remote management. Administrators first connect to a jump box, which then provides access to a restricted network where manageable hosts reside.

Kernel Virtual Machine (KVM)   A Linux-based virtualization solution used to host multiple virtual machine guests concurrently.

lift and shift   A cloud migration strategy whereby on-premises IT solutions can be moved into the cloud with little to no modification.

Lightweight Directory Access Protocol (LDAP)   A method of accessing a network configuration database over TCP port 389, where the database can contain application configuration settings, user accounts, computer accounts, and so on.

load balancing   A configuration that receives client application requests and routes those requests to the least busy responsive back-end server; improves app availability and performance.

load testing Applies an expected workload to an application to measure application security, stability, and performance.

loose coupling A software and systems development method by which components are not dependent on one another. For example, instead of two software components having to be available on a network at the same time to exchange messages, an intermediary storage queue can be used; the receiving software component can read the message from the queue at any time.

machine learning (ML) An implementation of artificial intelligence that can mimic intelligent human behavior, such as having the ability to learn from past experiences, derive meaning from vast amounts of data to predict future trends, or recognize speech patterns.

managed disk A cloud service provider solution that relieves cloud users from having to manually configure virtual disks used by virtual machines.

managed service A cloud service provider solution that shields the cloud customer from the underlying configuration complexities of a solution, such as a big data analytics cluster.

managed service provider (MSP) *See* managed service.

mean time to repair (MTTR) Represents the average amount of time needed to repair a failed component or service.

media sanitization The thorough removal of data from storage media to ensure that no data remnants exist that can be used to reconstruct deleted data.

Metal as a Service (MaaS) The dedicated use of cloud service provider physical servers by cloud customers.

metered usage A method of charging for cloud services based on resource consumption, such as the amount of cloud storage used, the amount of network traffic into a cloud-hosted website, or the amount of time virtual machines were running during a month.

microservice A modular software component with specific functionality. For example, an app might consist of many microservices, such as one focused on validating user input and another focused on printing. Each microservice can also be updated or scaled independently of others.

Monitoring as a Service (MaaS)   Cloud-based services that provide the capability to monitor a wide variety of devices and software solutions centrally in the cloud.

multifactor authentication (MFA)   The use of multiple authentication factors to enhance sign-in security. For example, requiring a username and password combination (something you know), a smartcard (something you have), and a PIN for the smartcard (also something you know) constitutes MFA.

network intrusion detection system (NIDS)   A hardware or software solution designed to detect suspicious network activity and log, report, or notify of the activity. A NIDS must be tweaked for the specific environment in which it is used for monitoring.

network security group (NSG)   A Microsoft Azure resource that acts as a firewall to allow or deny incoming and outgoing traffic. NSGs can be associated with a cloud subnet or virtual machine network interface.

NIST SP 800-53, Rev. 4   *Security and Privacy Controls for Federal Information Systems and Organizations*, a National Institute of Standards and Technology (NIST) Special Publication (SP) related to U.S. federal government information systems and the security controls used to protect information.

NoSQL   A database that does not use a rigid storage schema like SQL does; it can store many different types of unstructured data on a massive scale; often used for big data storage.

open source   A type of software model where the source code is made freely available to all. Source code modifications are free and must be shared back on the Internet.

operating expense (OPEX)   An ongoing type of expense such as a monthly cloud subscription fee.

original equipment manufacturer (OEM)   The original manufacturer of hardware or software solutions.

pay-as-you-go   A metered usage model where cloud fees are based on monthly usage.

Payment Card Industry Data Security Standard (PCI DSS)   An industry security standard related to the safekeeping of cardholder data for credit cards such as Visa, MasterCard, and American Express.

penetration testing   A type of security testing that attempts to discover and exploit weaknesses. *See also* vulnerability assessment.

personally identifiable information (PII)   Any combination of information that can be traced back to an individual, such as street address, mother's maiden name, and credit card number.

physical to virtual (P2V)   Uses software agents to capture the software configuration of a physical server in order to re-create a virtual machine with the same configuration.

pilot program   A small-scale implementation of a solution whose results are then analyzed to determine if a larger-scale deployment will succeed.

Platform as a Service (PaaS)   A cloud service model whereby the underlying infrastructure such as virtual machines and database software is already configured. PaaS is commonly used by software developers to quickly deploy databases, application containers, and virtual machine clusters for specific data analysis engines.

private cloud   A cloud environment owned, controlled, and used by a single organization.

proof of value (PoV)   In the context of cloud computing, identifying the business value of cloud computing.

protected health information (PHI)   Any combination of medical information that can traced back to an individual. Examples include blood type, prescriptions, health plan payment details, and so on.

public cloud   A self-provisioned and metered IT solution offered to everyone over the Internet. The IT solutions run on cloud service provider equipment. *See* Software as a Service (SaaS), Infrastructure as a Service (IaaS), *and* Platform as a Service (PaaS).

Public Key Infrastructure (PKI)   A hierarchy of digital security certificates that is used to secure storage systems and network communications.

quality of service (QoS)   In a cloud networking context, the ability to prioritize network traffic to ensure that higher-priority or time-sensitive traffic is transmitted before lower-priority traffic.

recovery point objective (RPO)   A disaster recovery term used to convey the maximum tolerable amount of data loss, normally measured in minutes, hours, days, weeks, or months.

recovery time objective (RTO)   A disaster recovery term used to convey the maximum tolerable amount of service downtime.

redundant array of independent disks (RAID)   The grouping of multiple physical disks to enhance data redundancy and/or disk performance.

refactoring   Often referred to as *rip and replace*, redesigning or acquiring a new IT solution that functions correctly in the cloud because an existing on-premises solution will not functional correctly in the cloud.

regression testing   A testing method that test areas of a solution that are unrelated to recent code or configuration change to ensure there are no unanticipated negative impacts of the change.

rehosting   Also referred to as *lift and shift*, a cloud migration strategy that allows the moving of an on-premises IT solution to the cloud with little to no modification.

Remote Desktop Protocol (RDP)   Used to remotely manage Windows hosts over port 3389.

Representational State Transfer (REST)   A programmatic method of connecting to HTTP-based resources and examining the return codes and values.

request for information (RFI)   A formal query to an organization for more information, such as requesting that a cloud service provider furnish specific service level agreement details.

request for proposal (RFP)   A solicitation inviting responses to a stated business need, such as requesting that a cloud service provider outline how its cloud services address business requirements.

reserved instance   An up-front commitment to use cloud compute services (virtual machines) over at least a one-year period. Reserved instances provide significant cost saving compared to using the pay-as-you-go model over the same period of time.

resource tagging   Adds metadata, or additional data labels, to cloud resources, such as flagging specific virtual machines as belonging to Project A.

return on investment (ROI)   A calculation used to determine if an expenditure, such as monthly cloud computing costs, has increased or decreased in value over time.

right-sizing   The optimal matching of a cloud service to demand, such as reducing the amount of RAM for a virtual machine due to smaller memory requirements for a given workload.

rip and replace   *See* refactoring.

risk register   A centralized list of an organization's assets and their related threats and security controls. Each threat can also have a priority or likelihood rating value.

risk treatments (accept, transfer, avoid, mitigate)   A variety of methods of dealing with risk, such as risk acceptance (small risk, so do nothing to mitigate), risk transference to a third party (CSP or insurance provider), risk avoidance (do not engage in the activity at all), and risk mitigation (apply security controls to reduce threat impact).

sandboxing   Isolating IT environments for security or testing purposes, such as creating an isolated cloud virtual network with virtual machines used for testing software configurations.

Sarbanes-Oxley Act (SOX)   U.S. legislation focusing on the truthfulness of reported corporate financial documents and the protection of whistleblowers.

scaling down   Decreasing the underlying compute power (number of CPUs, amount of RAM) for a cloud solution such as a virtual machine; also called *virtual scaling*.

scaling up   Increasing the underlying compute power (number of CPUs, amount of RAM) for a cloud solution such as a virtual machine; also called *vertical scaling*.

Secure Shell (SSH)   An encrypted command line–based method of remotely managing network devices and Linux hosts.

Secure Sockets Layer (SSL)   A network security protocol that uses keys in a PKI certificate to secure traffic such as HTTP or SMTP. Superseded by Transport Layer Security (TLS).

security information and event management (SIEM)   A centralized system that can ingest vast amounts of log and network traffic data for the purpose of correlating events over time to detect security issues.

self-service   In the context of cloud computing, the ability of the cloud customer to provision or deprovision cloud resources on demand.

service level agreement (SLA)   A contractual document between a service provider and a customer that provides service details, such as the designated level of guaranteed uptime.

service-oriented architecture (SOA)   A framework that strives to organize distributed software components into software services that can interact with one another over a network.

Simple Mail Transfer Protocol (SMTP)   Used to transfer e-mail messages between mail servers; uses port 25.

Simple Network Management Protocol (SNMP)   Used to remotely configure and monitor network hosts and devices.

Simple Object Access Protocol (SOAP)   Protocol used by software components to exchange messages over a network.

single sign-on (SSO)   Authentication solution that uses digital security tokens after initial user authentication to allow the user continuing access to apps without having to provide user credentials for each app.

Software as a Service (SaaS)   Cloud-hosted software applications accessed over a network.

software-defined networking (SDN)   A software layer between user interfaces and underlying network devices. Users are spared from needing device-specific technical knowledge when configuring cloud-based network resources.

solid state drive (SSD)   Storage media that does not contain moving parts. Generally provides better performance than HDD. *See also* hard disk drive (HDD).

spot instance   A type of cloud virtual machine deployment that uses extra available compute capacity at a price discount, but the virtual machine capacity is not guaranteed and is therefore not suitable for mission-critical workloads.

storage area network (SAN) A network dedicated to the transmission of only storage-related traffic. Servers using SAN storage see storage devices as if they were local to the host.

Structured Query Language (SQL) A programming language used to construct database queries against relational database systems.

total cost of ownership (TCO) A method of identifying costs associated with using a product or service, including ongoing management and maintenance costs over time.

Transport Layer Security (TLS) A network security protocol that uses keys in a PKI certificate to secure traffic such as HTTP or SMTP. TLS supersedes SSL.

unit testing A testing technique applied to a subset of software code.

vendor lock-in A dependency on a specific vendor's systems and data formats that makes switching to another vendor difficult.

vertical scaling *See* scaling up *and* scaling down.

virtual desktop infrastructure (VDI) Users remotely access their computing desktop environment and applications from a central server.

virtual hard disk (VHD) A type of virtual disk file used by virtual machines.

virtual private network (VPN) An encrypted network tunnel between two endpoints over an untrusted network such as the Internet.

virtual to physical (V2P) The conversion of a virtual machine's configuration to run on a physical server.

virtual to virtual (V2V) The conversion of one type of virtual machine to another type, such as from Microsoft Hyper-V to VMware.

vulnerability assessment A type of security test that identifies weaknesses but does not attempt to exploit them. *See also* penetration testing.

INDEX

E

R

RAID (Redundant Array of Independent Disks), 87
RAID levels, 87
RAM (random access memory), 5, 86, 87, 134
random access memory (RAM), 5, 86, 87, 134
RC4 encryption, 194
RDP (Remote Desktop Protocol), 112, 128
recovery point objective (RPO), 90, 222
recovery time objective (RTO), 90, 222
Redundant Array of Independent Disks. *See* RAID
refactoring, 53
regulations. *See* laws/regulations
regulatory compliance, 66–67, 75
rehosting migrations, 53
Remote Desktop Protocol (RDP), 112, 128
replication, 90
Representational State Transfer. *See* REST
request for information (RFI), 29
Request for Proposal (RFP), 216
reserved instances, 31
resource groups, 178
resource tagging, 30
REST (Representational State Transfer), 89, 148
REST API, 6
return on investment (ROI), 27
RFI (request for information), 29
RFP (Request for Proposal), 216
rip and replace migration strategy, 55
risk, 215–236
  acceptance of, 217
  assessing, 216–217
  avoiding, 217
  cloud computing and, 68, 215–236
  considerations, 68
  defined, 216

FedRAMP, 69–70, 196
  managing, 216–217
  transferring, 217
risk mitigation, 52, 217
risk register, 219, 228
risk treatments, 217
ROI (return on investment), 27
routing table entries, 133
RPO (recovery point objective), 90, 222
RSA key, 193
RTO (recovery time objective), 90, 222
runbooks, 178

S

SaaS (Software as a Service), 10
sandboxing, 173–175
SANs (storage area networks), 87
Sarbanes-Oxley (SOX) Act, 71
scalability, 5–6
scaling, 114, 130–131, 147
scrubbing data, 72
SDKs (software development kits), 171
SDN (software-defined networking), 106, 110
secret key, 194
Secure Shell (SSH), 112, 128
Secure Sockets Layer (SSL), 195–196
security, 191–213. *See also* security controls
  auditing, 224–228
  authentication. *See* authentication
  availability and, 197–198
  CIA triad, 191–192
  confidentiality, 192–196
  data integrity, 196–197
  digital signatures, 197
  DoS/DDoS attacks, 197–198
  encryption. *See* encryption